Applied Anthropology

Applied Anthropology

AN INTRODUCTION

Third Edition

JOHN VAN WILLIGEN

BERGIN & GARVEY
Westport, Connecticut • London

Library of Congress Cataloging-in-Publication Data

Van Willigen, John.
    Applied anthropology : an introduction / John van Willigen.—3rd ed.
        p.   cm.
    Includes bibliographical references and index.
    ISBN 0–89789–832–X (alk. paper)—ISBN 0–89789–833–8 (pbk. : alk. paper)
    1. Applied anthropology.   I. Title.
  GN397.5.V36   2002
  307.1'4—dc21   2001043793

British Library Cataloguing in Publication Data is available.

Library of Congress Catalog Card Number: 2001043793
ISBN: 0–89789–832–X
        0–89789–833–8 (pbk.)

First published in 2002

Bergin & Garvey, 88 Post Road West, Westport, CT 06881
An imprint of Greenwood Publishing Group, Inc.
www.greenwood.com

Printed in the United States of America

The paper used in this book complies with the
Permanent Paper Standard issued by the National
Information Standards Organization (Z39.48–1984).

10 9 8 7 6 5 4 3 2 1

To Jacqueline, Anne, Juliana, and Elizabeth

Contents

Preface

SOLVING PROBLEMS ANTHROPOLOGICALLY

Ever since anthropology has existed as a research discipline, it has had a practical aspect, in which men and women trained in anthropology used their skills and knowledge to solve practical problems. Historically this aspect of anthropology has been called applied anthropology. As the number of anthropologists who applied their knowledge and skills to activities other than basic research and teaching increased, so did the number of different terms for practical activities. Besides applied anthropology, many other terms are used for the different forms of practice. These include public anthropology, practicing anthropology, action anthropology, research and development anthropology, and advocacy anthropology. All these terms carry meanings appropriate to the specific circumstances that are considered in this book. It is important to recognize that "names" matter and that the use of the term applied anthropology is in some contexts contentious. The meanings associated with applied anthropology will be discussed in a later chapter. Here I use applied anthropology as a general label for the entire array of situations and approaches for putting anthropology to use. In doing this we must recognize that some will disagree with this usage.

The view of applied anthropology expressed here has both research and intervention aspects. It provides anthropologists with a number of effective action strategies that can be used to assist communities in reaching their goals within the context of self-determination. Applied and practicing anthropologists can draw upon experiences from the past as effective guides for work in both intervention and research; thus, knowledge of history is very useful. Activities done by anthropologists in both the past and present provide choices for problem solving. The foundation of most of the techniques presented here is the ideology of self-determination by communities and individuals. The research techniques presented also have at their base the idea of systematically identifying local viewpoints and needs as these relate to development efforts or program functioning.

SHARING A TRADITION OF PRACTICE

While this book is intended to teach the reader how to put anthropology to use, reading it is not the best way to learn this skill. The way to learn it is to do it, especially—when possible—under the supervision of a qualified applied anthropologist. Basically, it is too much of an art to convey efficiently through books, term papers, and other more traditional assignments—one needs direct experience. So, why read this book? The answer is simple enough: many applied anthropologists work in isolation, operating in agencies or firms which hire few other anthropologists. They spend time tracking over the same ground and solving many of the same problems in ways which may seem to them unique. This book attempts to describe applied anthropology in its breadth and to build a shared tradition of practice as much as teaching some techniques of application. It is useful to grasp the breadth of activity found in anthropological practice because it helps us see the power of the ideas produced within the discipline. That discovery will enhance our own ability to be effective users of anthropological knowledge. Further, the knowledge presented in this book will help link the experiences associated with contemporary practices to those of the past.

The basic point is a simple one: there are many kinds of anthropological practice, and knowledge of these different ways of practice is useful for the applied or practicing anthropologist. Not all useful practices are represented in this book.

ORIENTATION OF THE TEXT

Before we go on to consider the content of the book, it is useful to say something about its orientation. While this text presents approaches that are useful in many different settings and political traditions, it will be immediately clear that the tradition of application drawn upon and presented is that of anthropologists from the United States of America. There are, however, other national traditions which also present useful experiences for us to consider. For example, contemporary Canadian applied anthropology has undergone rapid development (Price 1987), and application has been at the core of Mexican anthropology since the 1917 revolution. Certainly, one could consider other regional traditions as well.

The value orientation of the applied anthropology described in this book is consistent with the political culture within which it developed; that is, it is pragmatic and democratic. It is pragmatic in that it stresses practices which work to achieve people's goals. It is democratic in that all the approaches, whether they are for research or intervention, have at their core the commitment to discover and communicate the community's perspective. A function of the democratic orientation is a consistent regard for interests of the local community. You will see these attributes manifested continually throughout the text. You may find it useful to regard these features as a kind of bias.

Depending on the circumstances, the approaches can be both radical and conservative. In some cases, these different kinds of applied anthropology can be used to slow and redirect change which political authorities are advocating. In other cases, the practices discussed here can be used to transform communities into more powerful organizations, giving control where none existed previously. It is important for you, the reader, to realize these features are at the core of all the approaches to using anthropology discussed here. It is not about getting people to change against their will; it is about helping people express their will. Yet the framework for action which we discuss here is practical; it has to do with the job market, and it has to do with politics, power, and will.

Although most of the technique chapters have to do with change-producing strategies, this book is also about cultural persistence. You will notice that even in the more explicit change-producing approaches, there is a strenuous commitment to identifying the community perspective in the development process. None of the approaches involve unilateral imposition of development goals from outside the community. The basic task is to foster acceleration of the adaptation process. Sometimes expressed simply as "getting more" for the community, the process involves creating a better adaptation for the people of the community. Adaptation questions are ultimately survival questions. Therefore, we should recognize that community-defined development aided by the applied anthropologist is basically a culture-conserving activity.

IS IT ANTHROPOLOGY?

This book does not ask the question, "Is this anthropology?" The question itself is viewed as basically destructive from both intellectual and action perspectives in that it generally limits competition and protects vested intellectual interests. In the case of applied anthropology, the question is particularly problematic. Further, if we look at the effect of applied anthropological work on the rest of the field through time, we can see that applied work often functioned as the cutting edge of the discipline. Consequently, applied anthropologists have always been the targets of the "but is it . . ." refrain. As we permanently set aside the "but is it anthropology?"

question, we should be reminded of more relevant questions: "What is the problem?" "What are the solutions to it?" And, most important, "What are the skills and knowledge necessary to implement the solution?"

CONTENT OF THE BOOK

The book is divided into four parts. Part I, "Introduction and Overview," includes chapters intended to provide background for better understanding the core of the text, as presented in Parts II and III. Part IV of the book deals with some issues of the professional's role.

Chapter 1, "The Domain of Application," will consider both the relationship between theoretical and applied anthropology and the content of contemporary anthropologists' work situations. An explicit definition of applied anthropology is presented to give the reader more systematic and comprehensive understanding of what applied anthropologists do. The relationship between application and theory is seen as poorly understood within the discipline. Two aspects of the relationship between theory and application are stressed. First, good knowledge of theory is a necessity for the applied anthropologist because it guides research and increases the scope of applicability of the information obtained. Second, theory which is useful to the applied anthropologist will concern variables which can be acted upon. The chapter maps out a strategy for self-instruction concerning potential employment situations.

Chapter 2, "The Development of Applied Anthropology," provides a synthesis of the history of applied anthropology from the standpoint of developments in the United States. There are a number of fundamental points made in this chapter: the theoretical and applied aspects of anthropology developed simultaneously, and, to a large extent, activities in the academic realm were often motivated or at least rationalized by the information needs of governments, research funding organizations, and other policy research consumers.

The "Introduction and Overview" section of this book is concluded with a chapter on ethics organized around fundamental principles for ethical professional behavior. These principles are derived from the "Statement of Ethical and Professional Responsibilities" of the Society for Applied Anthropology. The research component of this chapter discusses the core of ethical research practice: informed consent, voluntary participation by informants, and the issue of risk. The discussion of ethics is expanded to include consideration of the conflicts which may exist between the different groups with which anthropologists work. Although most research or action situations can be carried out without facing overly difficult dilemmas, even very simple situations can turn into a labyrinth of apparently insoluble conflicts. While it is best to be prepared for these problems, they cannot all be anticipated because learning requires experience. Situations of irreconcilable conflict are easy to read about, and can even be discussed around seminar tables with some benefit, but being faced with harmed communities, betrayed colleagues, and unfulfilled contracts is quite another thing. All these complexities aside, it is important to understand that standards of ethical practice need not be viewed solely as constraints, but more importantly as good guides for effective professional action. Indeed, ethical behavior is more often than not the most effective action.

Part II of this book, "Approaches to Development in Anthropology," contains chapters descriptive of six approaches to development practice in widespread use in anthropology. The section is introduced with a chapter entitled "Anthropology in Development" that considers three topics: the anti-development critique, the historical legacy of development practices within anthropology, and a thematic discussion of what we are calling the new synthesis in this book. The development practices discussed here are addressed in chapters entitled "Action Research and Participatory Action Research," "Cultural Action," "Collaborative Research," "Participatory Rural Appraisal," "Cultural Brokerage," and "Social Marketing."

Both collaborative research and cultural brokerage seem better adjusted to complex urban environments because of their advocacy stance. Advocacy is used here as a general term for situations in which the anthropologist is directly working on behalf of community groups. This often entails working in opposition to more powerful political forces. In cultural brokerage the anthropologist serves as a link between a community service–providing institution, such as a hospital and an ethnic community which receives services from the institution. In contrast with the other approaches, the primary goal of cultural brokerage is not change per se, but increased efficiency through effective culture contact. That is, it aims at improving services for ethnic groups through enhanced communication, as well as changing the service provider and the ethnic community. Social marketing makes use of techniques derived from commercial marketing to promote new behaviors that are socially useful such as safe sex, smoking reduction, and changes in diet. These efforts benefit from the anthropologist's research skills and community knowledge.

Part III of this book is entitled "Policy Research in Anthropology." This very important aspect of contemporary anthropological practice is presented in four chapters entitled "Anthropology as Policy Research," "Social Impact Assessment," "Evaluation," and "Cultural Resource Management." The eleventh chapter provides an overview of anthropology as a policy science by discussing various application domains. A special section on using policy research data is included in this chapter. Anthropologists are both on the producing and using ends of policy research enterprises these days. In fact, one anticipates that more and more anthropologists will take on the role of policy maker as they gain experience in the agencies and firms which employ them. The next three chapters, "Social Impact Assessment," "Evaluation," and "Cultural Resource Management" provide practical instruction in the three important research areas. Social impact assessment (SIA) describes a generalized approach for doing this type of analysis. It is important to note here that SIA is usually done in response to a set of agency guidelines. Social impact assessment is most often done in response to specific federal laws, such as the National Environmental Policy Act of 1969, and consequently is limited to domestic situations in the United States. Other projects are mentioned in order to describe some of the variety of such research efforts. Chapter 13 deals with evaluation research. For certain kinds of evaluation tasks, traditionally trained anthropologists are quite well equipped. This chapter focuses on those tasks that best fit the traditional array of research skills. Basically, we can say that anthropologists are usually best prepared to serve well in evaluation of smaller scale programs or local components of larger national programs. One might also say that ethnography works best in evaluation strategies which respect qualitative data and/or are interested in the community perspective. The potential of anthropologists goes much beyond the qualitative evaluation of smaller programs. Because of this, the chapter will describe a variety of evaluation modes, including a number of case presentations. Part III is concluded with the chapter, "Cultural Resource Management." This is an area in which archaeologically and culturally trained anthropologists are very much involved. There are very close parallels between social impact assessment and cultural resource management. They are mandated by some of the same laws and share some administrative concepts.

"Approaches to Development in Anthropology" (Part II) and "Policy Research in Anthropology" (Part III), as noted above, represent the core of this text. These development and research approaches represent most of the major types of practice found in contemporary American anthropology. In addition to these activities there are many other kinds, most specific to particular new occupations for anthropologists which are an important part of the total picture. Many of these kinds of activities are commented upon throughout the text.

Part IV of this book is entitled "Being a Professional," and includes just one chapter, entitled "Making a Living." This last chapter focuses on skills which are important in anthropological practice. Most important, anthropologists need to be able to produce useful knowledge for their clients. Important communication skill areas which are discussed are report writing and proposal writing. Many anthropologists find that both skills are especially important in their jobs. Some would say they were hired because of these skills, not for their ability to do cultural analysis or ethnography. Proposal writing holds an especially enticing lure, since it often allows one to create one's own employment, either in self-organized consulting firms or for various other organizations, including universities, agencies, and firms. There are a variety of organizational skills which are treated in this chapter. In addition, this chapter also looks at the role of the consultant. Topics discussed include why people use consultants, different styles for being a consultant, and marketing your skills as a consultant.

The chapter gives practical advice on employment. The core of the chapter is about the job search and its component parts. It includes the selection of appropriate education and training experiences, selecting appropriate courses, building marketable credentials, investigating the domain of application, writing resumes, and carrying out job interviews. Survival skills after employment are also discussed. These include networking and collaboration, and skill maintenance.

NOTE ON REVISIONS

The revisions consist of various types. First, I reviewed the text line by line to determine if there were any statements that the intervening seven years had made obsolete. These were all replaced. Second, where there was a more recent statement on a particular issue, I incorporated it. Third, I deleted the chapters on action anthropology, research and development anthropology, and community development. In their place I prepared new chapters on action research and participatory action research, cultural action, and participatory rural appraisal. The chapter on participatory rural appraisal incorporates aspects of the chapter entitled "Technology Development Research" that was in previous editions. The remaining chapters in the "approaches" section have been updated. The "policy research" section was supplemented with an entirely new chapter on cultural resource management.

Acknowledgments

My first encounters with applied anthropology were at the University of Arizona. While there, I participated in the certificate program in community development as part of my MA degree program. This brought me in contact with Edward H. Spicer and Courtney B. Cleland's seminar on community development. I learned a great deal from both of them. I still maintain contact with classmates from this seminar, especially Gilbert Kushner and Chris Fry; I thank them for their support through the years. As part of this program I did a practicum in community development with the Gila River Indian Community. The practicum involved doing a manpower survey as part of a large economic development initiative advocated by the Gila River Tribal Council. I benefitted from working with other development workers, especially Burdette Morago and Milan Makovack, and members of the tribal government, including Lloyd Allison and Edison Evans. The practicum project was transforming for me. In addition to this I appreciated the opportunity to work with Harland Padfield at the Bureau of Applied Research in Anthropology of the University of Arizona. I was able to learn a great deal while working as the Director of Community Development for the Tohono O'Odham Nation. I am thankful to have had the opportunity to know Thomas A. Segundo. Tom Segundo was the Chair of the Tribal Council and one of the creators of the community development program. His commitment to the people, grasp of the development process, and sense of the people's culture was inspiring. It was a joy to work with the Tohono O'Odham community workers. They include Lupe Jose, Lawrence Juan, Alex Pancho, Charles Lewis, Wilfred Mendoza, and Ralph Antone. I benefitted from my association with a number of academic colleagues. These include Billie R. DeWalt, Kathleen M. DeWalt, Sara Quandt, Peter D. Little, Art Gallaher, Jr., Margaret Lantis, Nancy Shoenberg, and Richard Stof-fle. Also I have learned from the many students with whom I have been able to work. These include Thomas Arcury, Elizabeth Adelski, Andrea Allen, Barbara Rylko-Bauer, Satish Kedia, Carol Bryant, Tim Frankenber-ger, Jim Lindenberger, David Rymph, Carol Jo Evans, Hussein Mahmoud, Emilia Clements-Gonzalez, Scott Justice, Pamela Rao, Elaine Drew, Eliza-beth Williams, Juliana MacDonald, and Sara Alexander. I want to thank numerous fellow anthropologists for help with this and other projects: Al-exander Ervin, Erve Chambers, Elizabeth K. Briody, Marietta Baba, De-ward Walker, Dave Clements, Peter Van Arsdale, Shirley Fiske, Donald Stull, Stanley Hyland, Linda Bennett, Tom Greaves, Bryan Page, Hazel Weidman, Carole Hill, Anne McElroy, Jean J. Schensul, Stephen Schensul, Dennis Weidman, Vinay Srivastava, and Jit Marwah.

I am thankful for the love and support I have received from my wife, Jacqueline van Willigen, and my children, Anne Griffith van Willigen and Juliana Marie van Willigen.

All these people and many others have contributed to this effort.

Part I

Introduction and Overview

Chapter 1

The Domain of Application

The number of anthropologists employed to solve practical problems has increased dramatically. Rather than working in the traditional academic roles of teaching and research in a college or university, large numbers of anthropologists work for many other kinds of organizations such as government agencies, non-government agencies, and firms in a wide range of content areas. While many work for government agencies, opportunities have also developed in not-for-profit private service agencies as well as profit-making firms, including those owned and operated by anthropologists. Still others freelance through temporary contracts. These persons may describe themselves as practicing anthropologists or applied anthropologists. At their workplace they take many roles, including policy researcher, evaluator, impact assessor, needs assessor, planner, research analyst, advocate, trainer, culture broker, expert witness, public participation specialist, administrator/manager, change agent, and therapist. These roles are briefly described below.

SOME PRACTITIONER ROLES IN ANTHROPOLOGY

Policy Researcher

Policy makers require information upon which to base policy decisions. This somewhat generalized role involves providing research results to them. It may involve traditional ethnographic research or a variety of specialized research techniques. This role may be the most common and can be activated at various stages in the research process from research design to data collection. The research function is common to many applied positions, and therefore, all potential applied anthropologists need to have preparation as policy researchers. A survey showed that 37 percent of members of the National Association for the Practice of Anthropology (NAPA) reported involvement as researchers (Fiske 1991:vi).

Evaluator

Evaluator is a specialized policy research role which involves the use of research skills to determine if a project, program, or policy is working effectively or has had a successful outcome. The basic task is to objectively determine the worth or value of something. Some kinds of evaluation are called program monitoring. This role is common—the NAPA survey indicated that 31 percent reported using evaluation skills (Fiske 1991:vi).

Impact Assessor

Impact assessor is also a specialized policy research role which involves the prediction of the effects of a project, program, or policy. Impact assessment usually attempts to determine the effects of planned government projects on the nearby human communities. The information produced is usually intended to influence the design of a project, thus impact assessment often considers various design alternatives. Particular attention is paid to the unintended consequences of projects like reservoir, highway, and airport system construction. The term social impact assessment is often used to describe this kind of activity. This role is common—24 percent of the NAPA membership reported expertise in social impact assessment (Fiske 1991:vi).

Needs Assessor

Needs assessor is a specialized policy research role that involves the collection of data on public program needs in anticipation of social, health, economic, and education program design. It contributes to the process of program design and justification. This role is relatively common and is closely related to evaluation.

Planner

As planners, anthropologists participate in the design of future programs, projects, and policies. This may involve data collection and research analysis in support of decision makers. This role is not common.

Research Analyst

The research analyst role consists of interpretation of research results for decision makers of various kinds. The analyst may serve as an auxiliary to planners, policy makers, and program managers. This is a common role.

Advocate

Advocate is a label for a complex role which involves acting in support of community groups and individuals. It almost always involves direct political action consistent with the community's self-defined goals. Advocacy may be part of other roles. This is not a common role.

Trainer

Trainers develop and use training materials referenced to a number of different client groups and content areas. Often this involves preparation of technicians for cross-cultural experiences. This is a role with a long history in applied anthropology.

Culture Broker

Culture brokers serve as links between programs and ethnic communities. The role appears especially useful in reference to health care delivery and the provision of social services. Many other roles have culture broker functions attached to them. In a few cases, it is the primary role. Brokerage is always a two-way communication role.

Expert Witness

The expert witness role is usually activated on a part-time basis, mostly by those academically employed. It involves the presentation of research data through legal documents, that is, briefs and direct testimony on behalf of the parties to a legal case or as a friend of the court. This is not common.

Public Participation Specialist

The public participation specialist's role is newly developed in response to the need for public input in planning. It closely resembles the culture broker role, although it tends to occur on a case by case basis rather than continuously as is often the case with culture brokerage. The role may involve organizing pubic education using the media and public meetings. The amount of anthropological involvement in this role is increasing.

Administrator/Manager

Some anthropologists have direct administrative responsibility for the programs within which they work. These roles are usually not entry level, but usually develop out of employment in the other roles mentioned here. These are not common roles for anthropologists but have increased in the last decade as practicing anthropologists proceed with their careers. In some agencies anthropologists have become very influential because they are in charge.

Change Agent

Change agents work to stimulate change. This is a generalized role function and is part of a variety of other tasks. In some cases the change agent role is carried out as part of a specific strategy of change such as action anthropology or research and development anthropology. This role is not common.

Therapist

The therapist role is quite rare. It involves the use of anthropology along with knowledge of various "talk" therapies to treat individuals with various problems. In some cases these people refer to themselves as "clinical anthropologists." Clinical anthropologists are more often involved in brokerage roles than this very rare activity. This type of application of anthropology is not dealt with in this text to any extent.

To summarize this introduction to practitioner roles, it is important to say that the most frequent role is that of researcher. The various social action roles have great utility and potential, but are not often used. While we might associate teaching with academic employment, teaching is important in practitioner work settings. There is a general tendency for the number of roles to increase. Additional perspective on careers in applied anthropology may be obtained by reviewing the Directory of Members of the National Association for the Practice of Anthropology (NAPA) and the Society for Applied Anthropology (SfAA) (1996). This publication lists titles, employers, degrees, skills, and specializations of almost 1,500 members of the two sponsoring organizations. This is an important resource for career planning because it will give a sense about what people actually do and where they are able to do it.

Typical applied anthropology jobs will consist of many roles. Sometimes the job title reflects the role and other times not. "Anthropologist" is not commonly used as a job title. This is because most of the jobs applied anthropologists do are also available to other kinds of social scientists. Some typical applied and practicing anthropologists' job titles as shown in the NAPA/SfAA Directory of Members (1996) are advisor, archaeologist, caseworker, consultant, counselor, coordinator, curator, dean, director, editor, ethnographer, grants specialist, manager, owner, program manager, president, professor, project analyst, project evaluator, researcher, and research anthropologist. It is difficult to tell from the job title what is entailed in a particular job, of course.

CONTENT AREAS FOR APPLIED WORK

In addition to working in many different roles, applied anthropologists work in a variety of different content areas. This can be seen in the contents of *Anthropology in Use: A Source Book on Anthropological Practice* (van Willigen 1991). This volume contains descriptions of cases in which anthropology was used to solve a practical problem and is based upon materials in the Applied Anthropology Documentation Project collection at the University of Kentucky. This is a collection of technical reports and other documents prepared by practitioners. The content areas are listed below. The most frequently cited topics are agricultural development, health and medicine, and education. Most frequently cited in the survey of NAPA members are "public health and health services, agricultural development, natural resources, and education" (Fiske 1991:vi). Because of the nature of the collection process of the Applied Anthropology Documentation Project, the listing emphasizes content areas where the research role dominates. Nevertheless, it serves as a useful indicator of areas of work (see Figure 1.1).

APPLIED ANTHROPOLOGY: WHAT IS IT?

Clearly, anthropologists apply their knowledge in a wide variety of ways in many situations. Further, the extent to which their backgrounds as anthropologists can be expressed directly in their work varies a great deal. Their work is often defined by the problem and not by the discipline. In addition, new terms for the role and the work have emerged. All this makes defining the content of the field quite difficult, although still important.

We can start our discussion of definition by simply saying that applied anthropology is anthropology put to use. Given the change which is occurring in applied anthropology these days, it is tempting to leave the definitional question at that and go on to the next question. Simply asserting that use defines the field has significant advantages. The generalized and fuzzy quality of that definition is appropriate to the changing job market. Yet in spite of the utility of flexible definitions it is useful for us to think about what we do somewhat more precisely.

The conception of applied anthropology used in this book is quite general. It is viewed as encompassing the tremendous variety of activities an-

Figure 1.1
Content Areas Found in *Anthropology in Use* (1991)

Agriculture	Human Rights, Racism and Genocide
Alcohol and Drug Use	Industry and Business
Community Action	Land Use and Land Claims
Criminal Justice and Law Enforcement	Language and Action
Cultural Resources Management	Media and Broadcasting
Design and Architecture	Military
Development Policies and Practices	Missions
Disaster Research	Nutrition
Economic Development	Policy Making
Education and Schools	Population and Demography
Employment and Labor	Recreation
Energy Extraction	Religious Expression
Environment	Resettlement
Evaluation	Social Impact Assessment
Fisheries Research	Training Programs
Forestry and Forests	Urban Development
Geriatric Services	Water Resources Development
Government and Administration	Wildlife Management
Health and Medicine	Women in Development
Housing	

thropologists do now and have done in the past, when engaged in solving practical problems. The view taken here is that the various kinds of anthropological problem-solving activities are types of applied anthropology. This book is about the different kinds of applied anthropology.

Often when new ways to use anthropology emerge, the innovators will provide a name for the new practice and contrast it with applied anthropology to mark innovations so that the distinctive features are clear and one's intellectual creation is protected, at least momentarily. Early writing about action anthropology, cultural brokerage, and practicing anthropology drew this contrast even though all involved the use of anthropology and the various practitioners of different approaches shared many common interests. More recently, proponents of what is called "public anthropology" contrast what they do with applied anthropology even though both involve the practical use of anthropology in ways that appear indistinguishable. While this is a logical thing to do, it does not contribute to the idea of a shared tradition of practice.

Differences in the career and work setting can produce new terms for the activity. Practicing anthropologists often conceive of themselves as being something different from applied anthropologists. The view, more common in the late 1980s, was that applied anthropology was something that is done by academic anthropologists when doing consulting work relating to practical problems. The term practicing anthropologist may be more frequently applied to persons who are employed by firms and agencies on a full-time basis. While this distinction holds up imperfectly in use, there are some very important differences in the working conditions of these two kinds of people that lead to differences in knowledge, attitudes, and reference group. Yet the view taken here is that these all represent kinds of applied anthropology.

The term applied anthropology itself is used in at least two ways. One as a general, and generally somewhat neutral term that I take to mean anthropology in use. The best example of this is in the name of the key organization in the field, the Society for Applied Anthropology. If you look at the interests of their membership and the content of their publications, it is clear that while applied anthropology is practical and socially useful, it is very diverse, ranging from radical political action to market research for firms organized to make a profit.

Another important cause of the need to rename is the perceived way that applied anthropology was done in the past. After all, as we will discuss in the chapter on history, the name applied anthropology first referred to research in support of colonial administration in Britain. Others seem to associate top-down development strategies with applied anthropology.

While there are no previous definitions which dominate the published literature on the definitional issue, one widely disseminated statement was written by George Foster for his textbook, *Applied Anthropology* (1969). He defined the field in the following way: "Applied anthropology is the phrase commonly used by anthropologists to describe their professional activities in programs that have as primary goals changes in human behavior believed to ameliorate contemporary social, economic, and technological problems, rather than the development of social and cultural theory" (1969:54). In many ways this definition remains quite serviceable. Foster identifies the major theme in applied anthropology as "problem solution." The definition is limited in a number of ways. His use of the phrase "in programs" seems to imply that applied anthropologists do not work directly for communities. Advocacy anthropology and collaborative anthropology are kinds of applied anthropology that do just that (Stull and Schensul 1987). The definition also seems to emphasize change as the goal, while there are some examples of anthropology being used to assure stability (van Willigen 1981b).

The second usage of applied anthropology is in opposition to some other kind of practice that the person is advocating. This is a classic kind of "othering." An important cause for renaming is that applied anthropology has lower prestige than other kinds of anthropology. If you look at the discipline, the persons with the highest prestige are those that do basic research generally and write theory specifically. This pattern is quite widespread in academic disciplines generally. There may be a continual renaming of innovative applied practices to distance one's self from the perceived lower prestige of practical application.

At a general level, one can think of anthropology as having two aspects, one which is concerned with the solution of theoretical problems, and another which is concerned with the solution of practical problems. The first we will call theoretical anthropology, or sometimes basic anthropology, and the second, applied anthropology or practicing anthropology. Both terms encompass a lot of diversity. Actually, the terms theoretical and basic are problematic. Much theoretical anthropology is not very theoretical, really. We just use the term to describe its implied purpose. Basic is also a misleading term because it suggests that it comes before, or first, and serves as a basis for more practical work. As will be shown later, practical work often serves as the basis of important theoretical developments. In spite of these semantic problems, the applied versus theoretical contrast is a useful distinction.

The definition used in this text is based on review of rather large numbers of different types of anthropological practice. Considering those activities which are typically labeled applied anthropology, let us define the field in the following way: applied anthropology is a complex of related, research-based, instrumental methods which produce change or stability in specific cultural systems through provision of data, initiation of direct action, and/ or the formation of policy. This process can take many forms, varying in terms of problem, role of the anthropologist, motivating values, and extent of action involvement.

The definition used here states that applied anthropology has a broad range of products. These are information, policy, and action. In the past and in the present, the most typical product of applied anthropologists seems to be information, information which can be used to construct policy or motivate action. Action and policy are less frequently the products of the process. Parts II and III of this book deal with different types of products: action products, policy products, and information products. The situation within which these products are produced is very complex. For our purposes here we can call this situation the *domain of application.*

DOMAIN OF APPLICATION

By domain of application we mean that knowledge and technique which is relevant to a particular work setting. The domain of application includes the methodology that maps the relationships between information, policy, and action, and the context of application which includes the knowledge relevant to a particular problem area and work setting.

Application methodology consists of the intellectual operations by which applied anthropologists produce their products and have their effects. This view is consistent with the conception of research methodology presented by Pelto and Pelto (1978). It is simply an extension of that scheme to include action and policy.

Information

Information is seen as the foundation of the other two products and can exist in a number of forms. The information which we deal with can range from raw data to general theory. Mostly, applied anthropologists deal with information between these two poles. Through these methods of research we are able to move from observation, through various levels of abstraction, to more general theoretical statements. While the goal of applied work is not the production of theory, the patterns of research logic are similar to those used in theoretical pursuits.

Policy

The second product of applied anthropologists is policy. Policies are guides for consistent action. Policy can be developed in reference to a wide variety of situations. Cases of anthropologists actually developing policy are relatively rare, however. For the most part an anthropologist's involvement in the policy formulation process is as a researcher providing information to policy makers, or as an analyst who evaluates research data for policy makers. The experiences of anthropologists in this process will be discussed in more concrete terms in Chapter 2, "The Development of Applied Anthropology," and Chapter 11, "Anthropology as Policy Research."

Action

The third product is action. Here are included the various interventions carried out by anthropologists. The entire Part II of this text deals with the various action or intervention strategies which are used by anthropologists. Each one of these strategies consists of a set of related ideas about role, procedures, and values which can be used to guide action.

The three products are related in the following way: information is obtained through research, information is used to formulate policy, and policy guides action. Of course, nothing is ever that neatly rational; everything is subject to the struggles of politics. The relationship also operates in the opposite direction. The needs of action and policy often result in information being collected through research. Typically, in fact, there is a cycling back and forth through research, policy making, and action. The process of social impact assessment described in Chapter 10 is a good example. Social impact assessment is done to help predict the effects of an action taken in the future, such as building a dam and reservoir. The research is often determined by which alternative plan would have the least social cost. This information would be fed back to the decision makers and used to determine which course of action would be the best considering many factors, including the political, economic, and social. In the chapters in Part II, "Approaches to Development in Anthropology," the continual interplay between information and action is shown. In thinking about this process it is possible to be either too cynical or too naive. Think pragmatically—the process is workable.

In addition to the relationship between information, policy, and action, we can also think about these categories at different levels of abstraction. Information, policy, and action can be thought of in terms of a progression from the simple and concrete, to the complex and abstract. Anthropologists as social scientists are most familiar with this kind of relationship in terms of the linkage between observed data and general theory. The same kind of relationship exists in the realms of policy and action. The most important point is that the three realms have somewhat similar logical structures.

The general structure of the relationships across the information, policy, and action categories, and between the simple and complex levels, is shown in Figure 1.2. This figure is derived from the conception of the Domain of Methodology described by Pelto and Pelto (1978). Their model depicts aspects of the scientific research process, while the model presented here attempts to show the articulation between information, policy, and action as well as the general structure of the logic of the process.

The diagram depicts elements of a large and complex process within which the practitioner works. The work that individuals do only rarely encompasses the whole process. A typical function for an applied anthropologist would be to collect information which would be turned over to a policy maker. The policy would be used to guide action carried out by yet another person. The process is, of course, not unique to anthropology. Collaboration with non-anthropologists would be typical at various points in the process. This often requires what might be called conceptual translation. The information which is communicated may be derived from special purpose research, secondary sources, or the general expertise of the anthropologist that is involved. The point is that not everything requires or allows the execution of a research process to solve a specific problem. In some cases, what is required is the transmission of just a few informally derived facts or interpretations. Thus there is great variation in the degree of formality. In my own work in development administration, I was struck by how rapidly one could act under certain circumstances. Information flow to a policy maker can vary from a crucial fact, based on one's expertise

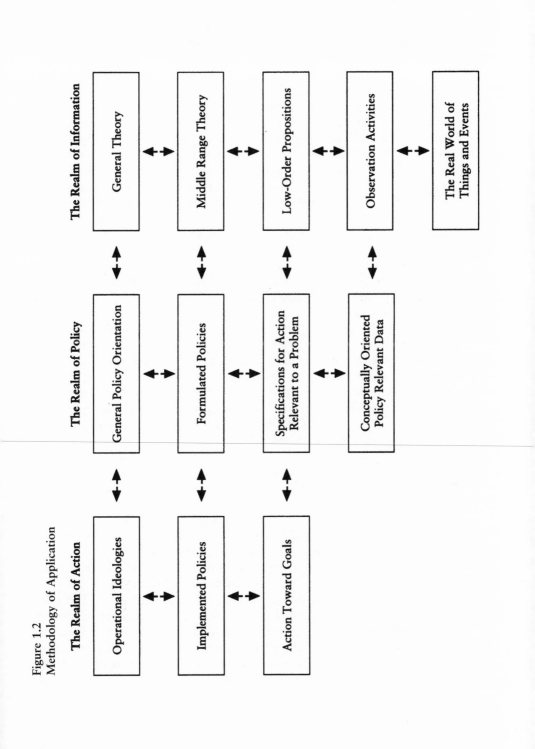

Figure 1.2
Methodology of Application

The Realm of Action

Operational Ideologies

Implemented Policies

Action Toward Goals

The Realm of Policy

General Policy Orientation

Formulated Policies

Specifications for Action Relevant to a Problem

Conceptually Oriented Policy Relevant Data

The Realm of Information

General Theory

Middle Range Theory

Low-Order Propositions

Observation Activities

The Real World of Things and Events

communicated in a meeting, to the presentation of an elaborate research report, based on a formal design. Information may also flow to the public to influence debate.

Most training that we receive as anthropologists relates to either research methodology or informational content. We receive very little training about the process of application as such, depicted here as the flow across the elements of information, policy, and action. Various aspects of this process are dealt with at various points in this text. The model of the application process and the definition presented above stress the importance of research in the whole process. The foundation of all of this is objective knowledge obtained using the canons of scientific research as a guide and standard. While this may involve special research efforts, it can also be derived from the literature or our accumulated expertise. As Sol Tax asserted, an applied anthropology which is not based on research is simply a kind of propaganda (Tax 1958, in Gearing, Netting, and Peattie 1960:415).

The research base of the application process goes much beyond that which can be legitimately called anthropology. The informational basis of applied anthropology is defined by the problem, not the discipline. If we limited ourselves to knowledge exclusively from anthropology, we could not adequately deal with the problems at hand. This is not to say that anthropology is an uninformed discipline, it simply says something about reality. Further, the information which we tend to apply has certain characteristics which allow it to be efficiently applied. Good applied anthropologists have the skill to relate information to practical problems. The discussion of anthropology as a policy science will deal with the process of knowledge utilization. There are at least three major issues or questions which are the basis of successful knowledge utilization practice. First, knowledge should be provided in reference to areas where the client can act. Telling someone about a problem on which they can not act is a waste of time. The applied anthropologist needs to be able to identify where action is possible. Second, knowledge has to be provided on time. Oftentimes action can only be effective within a specific time window. Research design has to allow for timely completion. If your goal is application, time becomes a crucial factor. Third, knowledge has to be communicated in a way which facilitates action. The basic conclusions of the process are best expressed as a recommendation for action with a justification.

In addition to the methods of application, such as effectively providing information, or skillfully converting information to effective action, the practicing anthropologist needs to know a great deal about the work context. Most important is knowledge about the particular policy area being dealt with. Each setting in which anthropologists work requires certain kinds of knowledge and experience for effective practice. It is to these practice areas that we bring our knowledge and techniques as anthropologists. In most areas of practice the anthropologist must learn a great deal from outside of anthropology in order to function in a professional manner. As mentioned above, we refer to the work context and its related knowledge as the context of application. This simple idea along with the idea of methodology of application helps focus our attention on information that is essential for being an applied anthropologist. In addition to these areas of special knowledge, we also need to understand those aspects of anthropological method and knowledge that are necessary for the work with which we are engaged.

KNOWING THE DOMAIN OF APPLICATION

The basis for effective practice is knowledge of the substantive aspects of a particular context of application. The first kind of knowledge which you should master is derived from the works of other social scientists relevant to a work context. Some content areas such as health care delivery are associated with immense bodies of literature. Other areas, such as fisheries management, are relatively limited. In addition to knowing the collateral social science literature referenced to a particular domain of application, it is also necessary to learn something of the technical basis of a particular field. If you are interested in agricultural development, knowledge of agronomy, soils, and marketing may be useful, if only to allow you to talk with your development colleagues. While not many of us can master both the collateral social science literature and a technical field in addition to our knowledge of anthropology, it is important to continually add to our knowledge of these areas.

The anthropologist's understanding of the domain of application may also be enhanced by knowledge of the legal basis for a particular area of application. In the United States, for example, many contemporary opportunities for work in various areas are made possible and shaped by federal statute and regulation. The whole social impact assessment enterprise came about through a series of laws (most notably the National Environmental Policy Act of 1969), regulations, and agency guidelines. Often, the law mandates our work. The regulations and guidelines substantially tell us how to do it. These issues are discussed in Chapter 2, "The Development of Applied Anthropology," Chapter 12, "Social Impact Assessment," and Chapter 14, "Cultural Resource Management." It is difficult to keep up with the legislative and regulatory basis for the different areas of application.

The next aspect of the domain of application for us to consider is its social organization. Here we can stress three components: the agencies and firms which hire anthropologists to do this type of work, the professional organizations established for people doing this work, and the social networks of the people employed in a particular context. It is important to identify those firms and agencies which hire people to deal with this type of work. It is especially useful to come to understand something about their hiring practices, job classifications, employment evaluation criteria, and even their previous experiences with anthropologists.

Knowledge of professional organizations is useful because these organizations often afford a point of access into the social organization of a particular content area before employment. Such organizations may have newsletters and other publications which serve as information sources.

As a student, it is difficult to tap into social networks in the area of application. As you seek employment, you will begin to build your own network. It is important in this regard to begin to collect names of anthropologists who work in a domain. This will minimally give you an indication of where and whether anthropologists are working in a specific area. It may also serve as a basis for networking. Some local associations of anthropologists, such as the Washington Association of Professional Anthropologists, provide situations at their meetings which facilitate networking. Networking provides one with a source of information about work opportunities, agency plans, and information which may lead to the establishment of more network links. You will find those who have gone before are very willing to share certain kinds of information about opportunities. Their willingness to share is based on their continued use of the same sources of information into which you are trying to tap.

Students need to systematically collect information about potential work contexts. I often suggest to my students that they prepare a "pathfinder" to a particular content area in order to guide their learning. A pathfinder is a guide to learning resources and information, and can be thought of as a road map for self-instruction. You should start your pathfinder with a "scope note" which defines the area of application. In your "scope note" you may find it useful to include reference to content, service population, and role. Some examples are water resources development with reference to social impact assessment and public input to planning reservoir construction; community development program administration among Native American reservation communities; nutritional assessment techniques as used in determining the impact of economic development; and evaluation of curriculum innovations in education in the framework of the classroom. A good pathfinder should be thought of as only a starting point. For the purposes of an applied anthropologist, a pathfinder should include information sources of the following types: guides to literature, review articles, indexing services, abstract services, major journals, newsletters, computerized data bases and websites. All of these should refer to anthropology, the collateral social science fields, and substantive technical fields. In addition, reference should be made in the pathfinder to relevant professional organizations, agencies and firms which do work in this area, and any special research facilities. A listing of anthropologists working in the content area is useful, as is a listing of the relevant statutes and regulations which are important to applied anthropologists working in the area. It is something like a career operator's manual.

SUMMARY

To summarize, applied anthropologists need to know the domain of application. This includes knowledge of the methods of application and the work context. Knowledge of method includes the practices associated with producing and communicating useful information in a policy or action setting. It can also involve various skills associated with being a development administrator or a change agent. Knowledge of the work context should include knowledge of the literature of collateral social science fields; knowledge of the substantive technical field; knowledge of statute, regulation, and policy issued from government sources; knowledge of firms and agencies which work in a content area; knowledge of professional organizations in the content area; and knowledge about which anthropologists are doing what in the content area.

It is sometimes difficult to learn the context and method of application to any great extent through course work in anthropology departments. A student with a serious commitment to be a practitioner should expect, in addition to their anthropological course work, course work in other departments, self-study, and practical experiences through internships and practica. While there are a number of training programs in applied anthropology, even these programs have to rely on a number of extradepartment resources (Hyland and Kirkpatrick 1989; van Willigen 1987), making it clear that anthropologists must expect that less of their training will fit traditional conceptions of what anthropology is. They must expect to be continually learning through their own efforts.

Start your self-instructional efforts right now. The first step is to consider your goals and interests along with an assessment of opportunities. A starting point might be to review the content areas listed in the early part of this chapter. The possibilities go beyond this list, but it is, nevertheless, an informed starting point. In addition to the content area, the knowledge and techniques needed vary with role (researchers, trainer, evaluator, planner, analyst, and so on), organizational type (public/private, profit/not-for-profit, and so forth), and service population (ethnicity, age, sex, and so forth). Define a content area for yourself which you can use as a focus for your own development and career planning. You might want to use one of the content areas listed in this chapter. Certainly, there are others that may come to your mind. Be realistic, but really reflect on your goals. This reflection process is very important, and you will find that it sets the scene for the employment process. Try to project yourself into the future. This process of planning should start now and continue through all of your training, job hunting, and employment. As you do this, your conception of your own future will become refined and more specified. This process can serve as a reference point for your development. As this process unfolds, you can increase your focus and mastery, and take better advantage of learning opportunities in your area of focus.

FURTHER READING

Chambers, Erve. *Applied Anthropology: A Practical Guide*. Prospect Heights, Ill.: Waveland Press, 1989. This text book presents a very useful discussion of work specializations in applied anthropology. Also useful for discussion of policy and policy research.

Ervin, Alexander M. *Applied Anthropology: Tools and Perspectives for Contemporary Practice*. Boston: Allyn and Bacon, 2000. This comprehensive text provides an effective treatment of research methods in an applied context.

Society for Applied Anthropology. *Practicing Anthropology: A Career-Oriented Publication of the Society for Applied Anthropology*. Tulsa, Okla.: Society for Applied Anthropology, 1978. This publication provides information on current practice in applied anthropology. Most articles are written by practitioners, many focusing on their personal experiences.

Chapter 2

The Development of
Applied Anthropology

This chapter interprets the history of the development of applied anthropology as it is currently practiced in the United States with some reference to developments in other countries. The sequence of development is divided into five periods which are defined on the basis of interpretations of the different kinds of practice done by applied anthropologists. In addition, the chapter also comments upon changes which are occurring in contemporary applied anthropology. This chapter is based upon the review of materials in the Applied Anthropology Documentation Project, as well as such published sources as Eddy and Partridge (1978b), Goldschmidt (1979), Mead (1977), Spicer (1977), and van Willigen (1991).

PERIODS IN THE HISTORY OF THE DEVELOPMENT OF
APPLIED ANTHROPOLOGY

Awareness of history does much to reduce the antipathy that exists between theoretical and applied anthropologists. Historic awareness teaches a number of important points, perhaps most important among them, that the theoretical realm is historically based on application. While this is increasingly recognized, many continue to view theoretical anthropology, inappropriately, as the genitor. The fundamental reason for this is that applied anthropology tends not to be published in traditional formats and therefore exists primarily as "fugitive literature" (Clark and van Willigen 1981). Thus, while we are continually made aware of the historic development of theoretical anthropology through the literature, the historic development of applied anthropology and its relationship to the formation of the discipline is muted by the lack of documentation. This problem is especially acute in the earliest phases of the history of the field. While some of the experiences from the past are no longer applicable in new contexts, many current activities would benefit from knowledge of the past. To paraphrase a comment made by Karl Heider in a discussion of the history of the ethnographic film, those who don't understand the history of applied anthropology will be lucky enough to repeat it (Heider 1976). George Foster expresses the importance of understanding history thus: "Current forms and place of applied anthropology within the broad discipline can be fully appreciated only with knowledge of the several stages of its development" (1969:181). As noted above, this chapter attempts to define the "several stages."

From my perspective, there are five stages: the predisciplinary stage, the applied ethnology stage, the federal service stage, the role-extension, value-explicit stage, and the policy research stage. The scheme as presented is additive. That is, general patterns of practice which emerged in earlier periods are continued in subsequent stages. The discussion of each stage includes the identification of the rationalization for the dating of the stage, a discussion of the primary patterns of practice with some examples, and a discussion of those external factors that seem to be relevant for the formation of the key patterns of practice. In reading this chapter it is important to keep in mind the fact that the discipline is also changing. Especially significant among these changes is the radical change in the scale of the discipline.

The Predisciplinary Stage (Pre-1860)

If we consider early historic sources that deal with cultural interrelationships, we find recognition of the usefulness of cross-cultural data to solve problems identified in an administrative or policy context. This is most common in contexts of expansive political and economic systems. In the case of early recorders of cross-cultural description, such as Herodotus (circa 485–325 B.C.) or Lafitau (1671–1746), their basic motivation was to provide information for some practical purpose. Virtually all proto-anthropology of the predisciplinary stage was representative of a kind of applied work. Most frequently, as in the case of Herodotus, the research was done to gather data about potential enemies or colonial subjects. In the case of Lafitau, the purpose was to inform plans for trade and marketing expansion. Later, it is possible to find examples of proto-anthropology being used to provide research data to support certain philosophical or theological positions. Although Thomas Aquinas (1225–1274) wrote about kinship and incest rules, he was attempting to support current church marriage laws (Honigmann 1976:2).

There are very early cases where cross-culturally informed administrators used their knowledge to facilitate better "culture contact." During the Middle Ages, Pope Gregory urged his missionaries to the Irish to link Catholic saints' days to pagan Irish ceremonies and to convert animal sacrifices to forms more appropriate for newly converted Catholics (Honigmann 1976: 45). Later, the most typical activities of the period included individuals appointed to carry out basic cultural research to assist in the administration of an area. A very early example of this is Francis Buchanan's appointment in 1807 by the East India Company to study life and culture in Bengal (Sachchidananda 1972). With increasing cross-cultural contact in the colonial period, more and more concern over the welfare of native populations developed. This can be observed in the establishment of such organizations as the Aborigines Protection Society founded in London in 1838 (Keith 1917; Reining 1962). The Society was concerned with both research and social service for native populations.

In the predisciplinary stage it is possible to point to a number of examples of social reformers, ministers, and administrators who were able to make use of cultural knowledge in order to carry out the tasks at hand. This includes such documented cases as the work of Hinrich Rink, who served as an administrator for the Danish government of Greenland. Rink, trained as a natural historian, contributed to the early development of self-determination among Greenland natives in the 1860s (Nellemann 1969).

There are a number of North American examples of early usages. Perhaps the earliest documented is the ethnological work of the Jesuit priest, Father Joseph Lafitau. Posted to New France as a missionary, Lafitau set about to document life in the northeast. This resulted in the publication of *Customs of the American Indians Compared with the Customs of Primitive Times* (1724). While this is framed as a theoretical work, he did engage in various practical studies. One such inquiry was his quest for ginseng, a medicinal herb in the woodlands bordering the St. Lawrence. Introduced from Asia to Europe by a fellow Jesuit, ginseng became much sought after in European markets. Lafitau attempted to find the plant in North America. To do this he sought the help of Mohawk herbalists whom he interviewed about native plant knowledge and other topics. This inquiry seemed to lead him to more general research, which contributed to his compendium on customs. He did find ginseng and became well known for this fact (Fenton and Moore 1974; Lafitau 1724).

An interesting example from the United States is the work of Henry R. Schoolcraft, one of the founders of the American Ethnological Society. Schoolcraft was retained by the United States Congress to compile *Information Respecting the History, Condition and Prospects of the Indian Tribes of the United States* (Schoolcraft 1852–1857). This imposing six-volume set is nothing if not a policy research report. It was prepared with the explicit purpose of providing reliable information upon which to base United States' Indian policy. Schoolcraft started his career as an American Indian specialist as an administrator. His professional identity as an ethnologist emerges with the development of the discipline. Because of this his career parallels changes that occur within applied anthropology.

The missionary work of William Duncan among various Northwest Indian groups serves as an example of the impact of a cross-culturally informed change agent. Working in the 1860s, Duncan made significant efforts in the area of social reform (Barnett 1942).

In this period there were some examples of the development of ethnologically informed training programs for colonial officers. Great Britain started such programs in 1806, and the Netherlands offered such programs by 1819. There is no evidence for such developments in the United States.

To summarize, contemporary anthropologists have rather little to learn about the methodology of application from the predisciplinary stage. Documentation is poor, and therefore it is difficult to develop a sense of the nature of the approaches used. The one important lesson to be learned is that anthropology in its prototypical stage had an important applied component. This contradicts the idea that applied anthropology somehow grew out of general anthropology. Later it becomes clear that the foundation of general anthropology is application and practice. The most objective view would suggest that the proto-anthropologists, for the most part, did their general interest work on the basis of what were applied research assignments. This stage ends with the emergence of anthropology as a distinct discipline (here we use 1860) following Voget's view of the history of the discipline (1975:115).

The Applied Ethnology Stage (1860–1930)

With the emergence of anthropology as a distinct discipline, the basic style of applied work typical of the next 70 years is manifested. Typically, the applied anthropologists of this stage worked as training or research specialists in support of government or private foundation–supported administrative programs. For the most part, these efforts supported the establishment of direct administrative control over native populations in internal and external colonial settings. Later in the stage, applied anthropologists carried out the same pattern of activity in the context of development programs.

It is important to emphasize that the anthropologist's role tended to be limited to providing data for policy making and problem solving. Very rarely are anthropologists involved as administrators or change agents. There were a number of administrators that became anthropologists, however. The ethnology phase is very long, and is marked by significant changes in anthropology itself. This stage covers the transition from the dominance of classical evolution theory to the structural functionalism and historical anthropology of the 1920s. The other significant process that occurs between the beginning and end of this period is the institutionalization of the discipline. That is, the basic infrastructure of a scientific discipline is formed: professional associations are organized, degree programs are established, and academic departments are formed as a body of knowledge grows and accumulates.

A fundamentally important fact that is not acknowledged in the literature on the history of anthropology is that applied anthropology serves as the foundation for the development of much disciplinary infrastructure. This can be seen in four contexts. The earliest learned societies in anthropology developed out of associations that were primarily concerned with application and social reform (Keith 1917; Reining 1962). The first organizations that hired anthropologists in the United States were policy research organizations (Hinsley 1976; Powell 1881). The first academic department of anthropology at Oxford University was established on the basis of a justification to train colonial administrators, that is as a kind of applied anthropology training program (Fortes 1953). The first use of the term applied anthropology occurred in a description of the program at Oxford (Read 1906). The first professional code of ethics in anthropology was developed by an applied anthropology organization (Mead, Chapple, and Brown 1949).

While the effects of application on the discipline were significant, the basic approaches to using anthropological knowledge remain the same throughout the period. For the most part, anthropologists carried out their research activities using an explicitly "value-free" approach. In fact, anthropologists writing in support of limiting anthropology to the style characteristic of this era often argued that their utility would be dramatically impaired if they did not approach their research from a "value-free" perspective. This was also done in conjunction with issues relating to role extension. Anthropologists argued that the anthropologist *qua* anthropologist cannot legitimately engage in roles other than the core consultant's role. This view was argued repeatedly and effectively until rather late in this particular period in the development of applied anthropology. The essence of this position is simply that when the anthropologist extends her role beyond that of researcher-consultant-instructor, she is no longer an anthropologist; she is acting as some other kind of specialist. Others stressed that involvement beyond the core role required that the value-free position often stressed had to be relinquished.

An early manifestation of anthropology in the United States took the form of the Bureau of American Ethnology. The BAE is known to us today as a basic research institute. It was, in fact, created as a policy research arm of the federal government. The first annual report notes that it was founded to, "produce results that would be of practical value in the administration of Indian affairs" (Powell 1881). The label used for this stage, "applied ethnology," was coined by James Mooney for a discussion of the BAE's commitment to policy research in the 1902 annual report (Hinsley

1976). Mooney's claims for political relevance were not hollow. His classic account of the Ghost Dance religion is described by Anthony Wallace as an early policy study done in anthropology (Mooney 1896; Wallace 1976). The creation of the BAE antedates the organization of the first academic anthropology department in the United States, at Clark University, by a number of years. The Bureau served as a model for the social research foundation of some American colonial administration experiences. A similar organization was established by the American government, in the Philippines, in 1906, which was directed by Albert E. Jenks (Kennard and MacGregor 1953). According to Hinsley, the Bureau of American Ethnology's involvement in policy studies lasted only until Charles C. Royce's study of Indian land cessions was published in 1899 (Hinsley 1979).

There are examples of privately sponsored research from this period. One such example is the work of the Women's Anthropological Society of Washington. This organization supported research into the apparently deplorable housing conditions of Washington, D.C. As an outcome of this research an organization was established to improve the quality of housing for the poor. This research was done in 1896 (Schensul and Schensul 1978).

Franz Boas, although not usually thought of as an applied anthropologist, completed some important policy research. Most noteworthy is his research sponsored by the United States Immigration Commission. He documented morphological changes in the substantial U.S. immigrant population. The research contradicted a number of racist ideas concerning the impact of immigration on the American population. Boas was, of course, a committed anti-racist. This research was published in 1910. Also related to the issue of U.S. immigration was the work of Albert Jenks at the University of Minnesota. He established an Americanization training course for immigrants in conjunction with the existing anthropology curriculum (Jenks 1921).

As early as 1864, ethnological studies were included in the colonial service training program of the Netherlands (Held 1953; Kennedy 1944). Such training was developed for the Union of South Africa in 1905 (Forde 1953), Anglo-Egyptian Sudan in 1908 (Myres 1928), Belgian territories in 1920 (Nicaise 1960), and Australian-mandated New Guinea in 1925. This type of training was not emphasized in the United States. As colonial administrative experience increased, there seemed to be more interest in ethnological training.

The British also made early and intensive use of anthropologists as government staff or contract research consultants. Anthropologists or anthropologically trained administrators provided research products ranging from short-term troubleshooting to long-term basic research. Such individuals were hired by the foreign office, colonial office, and India office, as well as the military.

During the applied ethnology period there is significant growth and development in applied anthropology. This growth occurs in certain sectors, but is, with few exceptions, limited to research or instructional activities. These developments occur most dramatically in the United States, Great Britain, Mexico, and the Netherlands. Most typically the activities consisted of the following: (1) a number of anthropologists were involved in instruction of government personnel for administrative positions in cross-cultural settings; (2) there are a number of examples of short-term troubleshooting research in which the anthropologist provided cultural data to an administration to solve a problem that had developed precipitously; in some locales, the anthropologist-on-staff seemed to be retained for this purpose; (3) anthropologists were also hired to carry out research in various problem areas at the request of administrators. These activities included national and regional ethnographic surveys, single-culture focused ethnographies, and topic-specialized, single-culture ethnographies.

During this era, applied activities made a significant and often overlooked contribution to the anthropological literature. The typical output of anthropologists during this period was research reports. If we consider the output of anthropologists hired to do problem-oriented research for the government or other sponsoring agencies, it becomes apparent that much of the distinguished ethnographic literature produced in the first half of the twentieth century was a product of applied efforts. This is particularly apparent in African and Pacific ethnography done by British social anthropologists, and North and South American ethnography done by anthropologists from the United States and Mexico.

In summary, the applied ethnology stage sees policy research and administrative training needs of governments as being an important stimulus both for early applied work and for the establishment of much organizational infrastructure for the basic discipline. Most applied anthropologists function in roles confined to research and teaching. The effects of applied anthropology on the basic discipline consisted largely of stimulating research in new areas and topics. And importantly, the potential for application was used as a justification for the establishment of many of the important academic programs.

The Federal Service Stage (1930–1945)

With the coming of the Great Depression and the New Deal, the number of anthropologists employed in application grew dramatically in the United States. This related to an apparent increased need for information on the part of government, as well as a need to provide jobs for anthropologists. It is important to note that the annual production of anthropologists was still quite small. At the same time, the academic job market was very limited until World War II. The intensification of anthropological employment in applied work reached a climax with the war. This period is named for the dominant kind of employment.

During the period of federal service, anthropologists came to work in an increasingly large number of problem areas and political contexts. Further, it seems apparent that the work of the anthropologists involved improves in quality and appropriateness. In terms of problem orientation, the research seems to initially focus on general ethnography. Later, the research typical of applied anthropologists comes to include education, nutrition, culture contact, migration, land tenure, and various other topics. This pattern is particularly characteristic of the development in British colonial territories, but, nevertheless, can be applied to describe the development of applied anthropology in the United States as well. Foster suggests at least one difference between the subdiscipline as it was practiced by its British and American practitioners when he notes "the interest of Britain's applied anthropologists in the social aspects of technological development has been relatively modest as compared to that of the Americans" (1969:194).

In the United States a number of applied research organizations were created. One of the first of these groups was the Applied Anthropology Unit established in the Office of Indian Affairs. The purpose of the unit was to review the prospects of certain American Indian tribes to develop self-governance organizations in response to the Indian Reorganization Act of 1934. Research topics included settlement patterns, education policy, and prospects for economic development (Collier 1936; Mekeel 1944; Rodnick 1936; Thompson 1956). The researchers produced a number of reports which had very little impact on the policy-making process. The Applied Anthropology Unit was created by John Collier, who had been appointed Commissioner of Indian Affairs by Franklin D. Roosevelt in 1932. Collier's advocacy of the utility of anthropology is widely viewed as crucial to the rapid expansion of federal employment of anthropologists.

At approximately the same time, the Bureau of Indian Affairs received the services of a group of anthropologists employed by the U.S. Department of Agriculture. This program, referred to as the Technical Cooperation–Bureau of Indian Affairs, carried out projects relating to economic and resource development on various Indian reservations (Kennard and MacGregor 1953). This group worked in conjunction with various physical scientists such as geologists, hydrologists, agronomists, and soil conservationists and produced various studies on the sociocultural aspects of environmental problems studied. Similar use of anthropologists had occurred in the large-scale research project carried out by the U.S. Department of Agriculture in the Rio Grande basin of the United States (Kimball and Provinse 1942; Provinse 1942). Analysis was directed at native American, Mexican-American, and Anglo-American residents of the Southwest. Research focused on the cultural factors which had influenced land use.

Involvement of anthropologists in the study of policy questions among rural American communities increased from this point well into the war years. This took a variety of different forms. For example, some anthropologists participated in the U.S. Department of Agriculture's Rural Life Studies that produced a series of six community studies that focused on community potentials for change. Perhaps most interesting among the policy researches done by anthropologists in rural America was that of Walter Goldschmidt who was involved in a number of studies for the U.S. Department of Agriculture, Bureau of Agricultural Economics. These included a study of war mobilization in a rural California county and a study of the political economy of agribusiness in the San Joaquin Valley of California. The second study produced a classic account of economic exploitation and led to Goldschmidt's villification by vested interests in California's agribusiness (1947).

During the mid-1930s, early use of anthropology in the context of nursing occured with the work of Esther Lucille Brown. In addition, pioneering work in educational policy studies were carried out in Native American education in the form of the Pine Ridge and Sherman-California vocational education surveys.

In 1941, the Indian Personality and Administration Research Project was established. For the most part this was a policy-focused basic research project which resulted in a number of useful studies of Native American reservation life, including Papago (Joseph, Spicer, and Chesky 1949), Hopi (Thompson and Joseph 1944), Navajo (Kluckhohn and Leighton 1946; Leighton and Leighton 1944), Sioux (MacGregor 1946), and Zuni (Leighton and Adair 1946). One aspect of this project made use of action research methodology which exemplifies the primary change associated with this stage. Action research was developed outside of anthropology largely by psychologist Kurt Lewin. Laura Thompson applied this technique to stimulate change in Hopi administration. Thompson's description of the technique is cited below:

Action research is normally distinguished by the following characteristics: (1) it stems from an urgent practical problem, a felt need on the part of a group, and is generally solicited voluntarily by the potential users of the findings; (2) it involves both scientists and the user-volunteers as participants in a cooperative effort— namely, the solving of the practical problem; and (3) the scientists involved normally function both as scientist-technicians and as integrative or "democratic" leaders in Kurt Lewin's sense of the term. That is, they endeavor to stimulate, draw out, and foster the talents and leadership qualities of the members of the participant group and to minimize their own roles except as catalysts of group potentialities. In their role as integrative leaders, the staff scientists train and supervise the work of the volunteer user-participant. (Thompson 1950:34)

This model for action develops in a number of different ways and continues to be used (Greenwood and Levin 1998). It serves as the basis for one chapter in the development section of the text.

Also indicative of the expansion into new research areas during this period is the work of the anthropologists associated with the Committee on Human Relations in Industry at the University of Chicago. Included among the anthropologists associated with the committee are W. Lloyd Warner and Burleigh B. Gardner. This period sees major advancements in what came to be called the scientific study of management. The most significant project was the classic Western Electric, Hawthorn Works study of the relationships between working conditions and productivity. This area of work developed very rapidly for a period of time.

The National Research Council established at least two research committees which were to have significant impacts on policy research done by anthropologists in this period. These included the Committee on Food Habits, that included Margaret Mead, Ruth Benedict, and Rhoda Metraux among others. This organization was to obtain scientific information on nutritional levels of the American population. Also established was the Committee for National Morale consisting of Gregory Bateson, Elliot Chapple, and Margaret Mead among others. This committee was to determine how anthropology and psychology could be applied to the improvement of national morale during the war.

This stage in the development of applied anthropology started in the national crisis caused by the Great Depression and concludes in the crisis of war. The intensification of involvement in application caused by World War II is astounding. Mead (1977) estimates that over 95 percent of American anthropologists were involved with work in support of the war effort during the 1940s. By way of contrast, the war in Vietnam had very much the opposite effect on anthropologists. In 1941, the American Anthropological Association passed a resolution placing the "specialized skill and knowledge of its members, at the disposal of the country for the successful prosecution of the war" (American Anthropological Association 1942:42). This effort seemed to increase the self-awareness of applied anthropologists as well as their concentration in Washington and other places.

Perhaps the most well-known war effort involvements by American anthropologists are the activities done on behalf of the War Relocation Authority. The War Relocation Authority was responsible for managing the internment camps established early in the war to incarcerate Japanese Americans. The use of social scientists grew out of the experiences of the one camp that was under the administrative responsibility of the Bureau of Indian Affairs. At that time the BIA was directed by John Collier. In response to the problems that developed at the other camps, social science programs were developed at all War Relocation Administration facilities (Arensberg 1942; Kimball 1946; Leighton 1943; Spicer 1946a, 1946b). The anthropologists who served in the camps served as liaisons between inmates and camp administration and as researchers. This involvement by anthropologists is frequently characterized as unethical, being viewed by some as supportive of an illegal and inhumane government program. If one reads their writings or discusses this involvement with them it is clear that they viewed themselves as ameliorators of a potentially much worse situation. One should read Rosalie Wax's chilling account of her experiences as a community analyst in a camp to get some feeling for the problem (Wax 1971).

In addition to the War Relocation Authority, anthropologists were involved in a variety of other programs. The Far Eastern Civil Affairs Training School was established to prepare administrators for areas which were being recaptured from the Japanese by the Allies. This operation, established at the University of Chicago, was headed by anthropologist Fred Eggan (Embree 1949). The Foreign Morale Analysis Division was created within the Office of War Information. Using various data sources this organization reported intelligence on the Japanese and other adversaries to the Departments of War, State and Navy. Some of the information was collected from internment camp inmates. Benedict's *The Chrysanthemum and the Sword* (1946) was a by-product of this operation.

During the war the Smithsonian Institution initiated a number of activities that had significant applied research components. The Institute of Social Anthropology of the Smithsonian, established in 1943, engaged in both basic and applied research projects. The applied activities included very early use of anthropological research to plan and evaluate health programs. The applied aspect of the Institute of Social Anthropology's research program developed under the leadership of George M. Foster. Contemporary applied medical anthropology was, to a large extent, shaped by the program of the Institute of Social Anthropology.

Also of interest are the various war-related compilation and publication programs of the era. These include the civil affairs handbooks published by the Chief of Naval Operations on Japanese-held Pacific territories and the *Handbook of South American Indians* published as part of a program to promote relations with Latin America. In addition to the efforts mentioned here, there were activities related to the immediate postwar period. These included research into the effects of the nuclear attack on Japanese cities (Leighton 1949), and studies of occupation problems (Bennett 1951; Embree 1946; Gladwin 1950; Hall 1949; Rodnick 1948).

It is quite clear that applied anthropology grew dramatically during this period and that the major cause was employment opportunities with the federal government relating to the depression and war. One of the products of this expansion was the organization of the Society for Applied Anthropology. Spicer refers to this as, "one of the most important events in the development of anthropology in the twentieth century" (1976:335). Now over 60 years old, the society has gone through considerable change and development through the years. In its early phases the society seemed most concerned with bringing together social scientists and administrators, reporting cases where anthropological knowledge had been usefully applied, and advocating the idea that there existed an applicable body of anthropological theory (Spicer 1976:336). An important component of the program of the Society for Applied Anthropology was the publication of the journal *Applied Anthropology* that was subsequently named *Human Organization*.

The Society for Applied Anthropology developed around local interest groups in Washington, D.C. and Cambridge, Massachusetts, and then subsequently expanded to a national membership. The changes in the Society for Applied Anthropology will be discussed in conjunction with the next two periods of American applied anthropology history. In the early days of the society's existence, most activities of the organization were directed at creating a professional identity for applied anthropologists.

This period sees major changes in applied anthropology. These include dramatic intensification of involvement of anthropologists in application and the development of a more definite professional identity through the creation of the Society for Applied Anthropology and its publications. For the most part, applied anthropology roles are still limited to policy researcher and trainer, the roles that dominate both the applied ethnology and predisciplinary stages. There are some examples of pioneering assumptions of change-producing, action-involved roles which are a striking feature of the next phase, the value-explicit, role-extension phase.

The Role-Extension, Value-Explicit Stage (1945–1970)

However interesting the historic course of the development of applied anthropology is up to 1945, it is characterized by relatively little change in the applied anthropologist's operational strategy. From the initial professionalization of the discipline, around the middle of the nineteenth century, there is little deviation from the core applied anthropology role consisting of a complex best labeled "instructor-researcher-consultant." The history of the field up to 1945 is characterized by continued elaboration of this theme. The basic pattern of the applied ethnology stage became elaborated as it became more widely accepted by both anthropological producers and administrative consumers.

It is inappropriate to suggest that the acceptance of applied anthropology was complete or even extensive. It became more and more useful, more and more important, but one senses a certain reluctance to participate in applied roles. A cadre of applied anthropologists did not develop as such, but a group of anthropologists did exist who oscillated between academic and applied appointments. Further, much employment was in service to colonial regimes (Asad 1973). This fact may have related to the historic tendency to switch back to academic careers. In any case, the radical critique of applied anthropology derives a great deal of its impact from an analysis of the anthropologists who served in these capacities (for example, Berreman 1969; Gough 1968; Horowitz 1967; Hymes 1974; Moore 1971). We are faced with an evaluation dilemma, however, for even an unsympathetic review of these efforts reveals that most anthropologists were struggling to increase the fairness and humaneness of various domestic and international colonial systems. To be sure, the anthropological perspective was more ameliorative than revolutionary, and given the power relations extant, it would seem fair to assume that the most positive impact of anthropology on colonialism could be achieved within the system. As history became reconstructed in the post-colonial period, these anthropologists took the brunt of various aggressive criticisms.

The shift in applied anthropology practice that occurs in this stage can be best understood in terms of three basic changes. First, the range of legitimate roles for applied anthropologists expanded beyond the researcher-instructor-consultant core. With role-extension came increases in the intensity of participation; that is, the number of aspects of a particular applied problem with which the anthropologist dealt increased. In a few words, anthropologists become more directly involved in implementation and intervention. Instead of merely providing information and an occasional recommendation, the anthropologists began to take increasing responsibility for problem solution. Anthropologists were no longer merely monitors and predictors of change but came to actually work as agents of change. In addition, other new roles were explored.

The second major shift occurs in terms of the extent to which anthropologists come to confront their own values, directly and explicitly. The "value-free" or, more accurately, the value-implicit approach, comes to be more openly questioned. Some anthropologists come to recognize the value-explicit approach as legitimate, after substantial debate. This means that certain anthropologists come to feel that social scientists cannot separate their work from real-world values and to do so naturally created a dangerous illusion of true objectivity. The value-explicit stance implied a willingness on the part of anthropologists to openly define goals and values for clients and client communities. This, of course, led to intense debates concerning ethics for cultural anthropologists of all types. It also led anthropologists to increased political exposure.

The third shift comes as a corollary to role extension and value explicitness. That is, applied anthropology is increasingly action-involved. This means, as suggested above, that the users of the new patterns come to be directly engaged in change-producing behavior. No longer was the role limited to the basic researcher-instructor-consultant role, but was extended to include a much wider array of action-involved roles. This change did not result in a single new approach, but a multiplicity of new approaches for applying anthropological knowledge. In addition to the retained and still important activities characteristic of the earlier stages, at least five new value-explicit, role-extended, and action-involved approaches to applications began to emerge during this period. These approaches are action anthropology, research and development anthropology, community development, collaborative research anthropology, and culture brokerage. Cultural brokerage actually appears early in the next period, as specified in the historic scheme reported here.

Action Anthropology. Perhaps the first action-involved, value-explicit approach to be developed within anthropology was action anthropology, which grew out of a University of Chicago field school organized by Sol Tax among the Mesquakie residents near Tama, Iowa, in 1948 (Gearing 1988; Gearing, Netting, and Peattie 1960; Tax 1958). The action orientation was not part of the original intent, but emerged because of the sentiments of the participating students. The "Fox Project," as it was called, consisted of a dual program of action and research which addressed a complex of ideas associated with self-determination and some more generalized research goals. Some of the key concepts of the approach are community self-determination and the idea of what might best be called interactive planning. This last idea is rooted in the work of John Dewey and is manifested in a tendency to stress an ambiguous distinction between means and ends, and to reduce the linearity of social planning. This resonates with the contemporary emphasis on participation that will be discussed later. Use of this model today is negligible. The literature produced by developers of the model is quite rich and worth reading for its applicability. Overall the approach seems quite academic today, but the underlying ideas remain useful.

Action anthropology rejects a linear view of planning. The approach used might be best termed interactive planning because of the tendency to stress ambiguous means and ends distinctions and the continual consideration of interaction of goals and action.

Interactive planning is characterized by a number of attributes. The primary proposition is that means and ends are interdependent. Ends are appropriate to means, and means are appropriate to ends. Action can be initiated in terms of means or ends. Ends and means are determined through an interactive process which is motivated by both the problem inherent in a situation and the apparent opportunities. The problem is "everything that is wrong or missing about the situation." Problems and possibilities also interact. It is obvious that the key function of the anthropologist is to discover what is the problem and what are the possibilities for change. The problem represents a complex of problems complicated by the limitations of the community and the external interventionist. Further, the capacity to solve problems is thought to increase through time. With these increases, the complexity of the problem-solutions engaged increases. These increases may be attributed to decreasing community devisiveness and increasing community integration. According to Peattie, the goals of the action anthropologist "tend to be open-ended objectives like growths in understanding, clarification of values and the like" (Peattie 1960b:301). The desired end-states are really expressions of a value stance, or as Peattie refers to them, "modes of valuing," used to analyze the continuous process.

Research and Development Anthropology. The research and development approach was first attempted in the well-known Vicos Project (Dobyns, Doughty, and Lasswell 1971; Doughty 1986, 1987; Holmberg 1958). Like action anthropology, the research and development process has both scientific and development goals. Defined technically, research and development anthropology is a means of bringing about increases in the net amount and breadth of distribution of certain basic human values through research-based participant intervention in a community. The writings of Allan Holmberg, the primary initiator, are good sources for understanding the transition toward a value-explicit anthropology. Holmberg and his associates assumed that value-free social science was unobtainable and that the research inevitably influenced the community. He argued that this tendency was better dealt with if it was made explicit and used for the betterment of the society, as well as for scientific advancement.

The goal of research and development anthropology is the wider sharing of basic human values. These values are not defined by science, but they are *discovered through* science. As will be apparent later in this chapter, knowledge of values is essential for the operation of the process. The process is, in its most general sense, a process of value achievement in which persons work to obtain certain desired ends. This is based on certain key assumptions made by Holmberg. These assumptions are "(1) that human traits are such that progress can be made towards the realization of human dignity," and "(2) that the natural order (physical nature) is such that with greater knowledge and skill, human beings can turn it progressively to the service of social goals" (Holmberg 1958:13).

The later work of Holmberg and the political scientist Lasswell deserves our attention here. These two social scientists attempted to develop what they referred to as a general theory of directed social change (Lasswell and Holmberg 1966:14). Social change was conceptualized as "a process in which *participants* seek to maximize net value outcomes (*values*) by employing practices (*institutions*), affecting *resources*" (Lasswell and Holmberg 1966:15). The social change process as the two described it involved goals, interaction contexts, and the environment. At the core were the PREWSWAR values, which were regarded as sufficiently precise and universalistic to allow systematic cross-cultural comparison. Further, the authors felt that the eight values and their related practices were the focus of specialized research disciplines. PREWSWAR is an acronym based on the initials of the eight values. The PREWSWAR values are power, respect, enlightenment, wealth, skill, well-being, affection, and rectitude. This model is not widely used today, but like action anthropology, the literature produced by model developers remains useful and very much worth reading.

Community Development. The community development approach was developed outside of anthropology in the context of British colonial administration, and the social work and agricultural extension disciplines in the United States. It is listed here because a number of anthropologists used and contributed to the approach. A widely used definition of the approach is contained in manuals produced by the International Cooperation Administration (a predecessor of the Agency for International Development). "Community Development is a process of social action in which the people of a community organize themselves for planning and action; define their common and individual needs and problems; make group and individual plans to meet their needs and problems; execute the plans with a maximum of reliance upon community resources; supplement these resources when necessary with services and materials from government and nongovernmental agencies outside the community" (1955:1). Projects using this approach often speak of concepts like felt needs, self-help, and self-determination.

The most visible contributions of anthropologists to this approach are various textbooks, which include *Cooperation in Change* (Goodenough 1963), and *Community Development: An Interpretation* (Brokensha and Hodge 1969). In addition to this, anthropologists have made use of the approach directly (van Willigen 1973; Willard 1977). The community development approach continues to be used though often renamed to stress the participatory nature of the process.

Collaborative Anthropology.[1] Action research, action anthropology, and research and development anthropology represent the first generation of value-explicit applied anthropology approaches. In addition to these approaches, various advocacy anthropology approaches developed in the early 1970s. These were supplemented by an approach called cultural brokerage around the same period. Generally, the advocacy approaches are characterized by a closer administrative relationship between the community and the anthropologist. In some cases, the anthropologist was actually hired by the local community. While this is not strictly true of the case example we are using for this type of anthropology here, the relationship between the community and the anthropologists involved was quite close. It was developed by Stephen Schensul for use in a Latino barrio of Chicago. In this case, the anthropologist worked primarily as a researcher in support

1. In the first two editions of this book, this model was called community advocacy anthropology.

of indigenous community leadership. Goals of the sponsoring organization were addressed to a limited extent. The anthropologist also provided technical assistance in training for research and proposal writing. While the role is diverse, it is somewhat more focused upon research done in support of community-defined goals. The anthropologist, although involved in the action, does not serve as a direct change agent but as an auxiliary to community leaders. The anthropologist does not work through intervening agencies but instead has a direct relationship with the community. The relationship is collaborative, drawing upon the anthropologist's research skills and the organizational skills of the community's leadership. Typically, the anthropologist's activities include evaluation of community-based programs, whether they are sponsored or managed by people from within or outside the community; needs assessments in anticipation of proposal writing and program design; proposal writing and a wide variety of generalized inputs of a less formal nature. The project was initiated in 1968 (Schensul 1973).

Cultural Brokerage. Cultural brokerage is an approach to using anthropological knowledge developed by Hazel H. Weidman (Weidman 1973). It is based on a conception of role, defined originally by Eric Wolf, to account for persons who serve as links between two cultural systems (1956). While Wolf conceptualized the role in the context of the naturally occurring roles which exist between peasant communities and the national system, Weidman applied the term to structures created to make health care delivery more appropriate to an ethnically diverse clientele. Stimulated by research findings of the Miami Health Ecology Project, Weidman created a position for culture brokers in the Community Health Program of the Department of Psychiatry of the University of Miami. These individuals were social scientists who were familiar with the various ethnic groups found in the "catchment area" of a large county hospital. Within this area, it was possible to find Cubans, Puerto Ricans, African Americans, Haitians, and Bahamians, as well as European Americans. While the role is quite diverse, its primary goal is the establishment of links between the politically dominant structures of the community and the less powerful, in a way which restructures the relationship in terms of equality.

The commitment to egalitarian intercultural relations in culture brokerage is manifested in other elements in its conceptual structure. The most important of these conceptual elements are coculture and culture mediation. Coculture is the label used for the components of a culturally pluralistic system. It is a conceptual substitute for subculture.

Cultural brokerage is a frequent component of much applied anthropology work. Much clinically applied medical anthropology focuses on this function.

The development of intervention techniques within anthropology is the most striking characteristic of this particular stage of the development of applied anthropology. Parallel with this new development is the continuation of the basic pattern of research for various administrative authorities which was characteristic of the applied ethnology stage. Much of this research received its stimulus in the early years of the role-extension, value-explicit stage from the forces put in place by World War II. These forces were substantial.

While intervention strategies were developed and used within anthropology, the most important factors that shaped applied anthropology were simple economic ones. During this phase there was a tremendous expansion of the academic job market. Persons returning from military service at the end of World War II were able to attend universities under the provisions of the "G.I. Bill." This required an increase in the number of faculty positions in many disciplines. Anthropology expanded along with others. This expansion continued through the 1960s carried by the educational needs of the children of the returned veterans. The baby boomers filled anthropology classes. According to Spicer, "It became a world of academic positions far in excess of persons trained to fill them" (1976:337). This caused a "retreat into the academic world" of substantial proportions. While economic factors associated with the expansiveness of the academic job market were important, the tendency to not take federal employment was enhanced by objections many anthropologists had toward the war the government was waging in Vietnam.

At the same time a variety of research projects motivated by basic policy questions led anthropologists to study a variety of new research areas, including native land rights (Goldschmidt and Haas 1946), land government policy toward native political organization (Gluckman 1943, 1955), ethnohistory (Stewart 1961), health care (Leighton and Leighton 1944), land tenure (Allen, Gluckman, Peters, and Trapnell 1948), urban life (Beaglehole and Beaglehole 1946), migrant labor (Schapera 1947), relocation (Kiste 1974; Mason 1950, 1958), water resources development (Cushman and MacGregor 1949; Padfield and Smith 1968), health care delivery (Kimball 1952; Kimball and Pearsall 1954), disasters (Spillius 1957), health development (Foster 1953), racial discrimination (Southern Regional Council 1961), and others.

New roles activated by anthropologists include expert witness (Dobyns 1978; Kluger 1976; Lurie 1955; MacGregor 1955; Stewart 1961), evaluator (Aiyappan 1948; Dupree 1956a, 1956b, 1958; Elwin 1977; Foster 1953; Halpern 1972; Honigmann 1953; Ingersoll 1968, 1969; Jacobsen 1973; Lantis and Hadaway 1957; Mathur 1977; Messing 1964, 1965; Pearsall and Kern 1967; Sasaki 1960; Sasaki and Adair 1952; Sorenson and Berg 1967), planner (Peattie 1968, 1969a, 1969b; Peterson 1970, 1972, 1978), as well as roles associated with various clinical functions (Aberle 1950; Landy 1961).

Anthropologists invested more effort in the documentation of sound practices for themselves and others. There were a number of manuals published in this period intended to provide guidance to development administrators, public health officials, and change agents. These included *Human Problems in Technological Change* (Spicer 1952), *Cultural Patterns and Technical Change* (Mead 1955), *Health, Culture and Community: Case Studies of Public Reactions to Health Programs* (Paul 1955), and *Cooperation in Change, Anthropological Approaches to Community Development* (Goodenough 1963). These volumes grew out of a seminar organized by Cornell University with the support of the Russell Sage Foundation to develop training materials for people working in development internationally (Bunker and Adair 1959).

An important event during this period is the development of an ethics statement by the Society for Applied Anthropology. The statement, written in 1949, was the first within the discipline. This effort has continued to the present day. Interestingly, the statement was developed in reaction to a specific basic research project rather than problems associated with application. The American Anthropological Association did not consider development of an ethics statement for about 20 years.

In summary, the role-extension stage sees anthropologists designing and implementing strategies for social change. Alongside this development anthropologists increase the array of new research-based roles. Although the social change strategies developed within anthropology during this stage appear to remain useful, their application is infrequent in the next stage of the development of applied anthropology. The development of strategies for social change within the discipline seems to be most common in the United States and Mexico. Perhaps the most important change which shaped applied anthropology during this period is the tremendous expansion of the academic job market.

The Policy Research Stage (1970 to the Present)

The policy research stage is characterized by the emergence of what Angrosino calls the "new applied anthropology" (1976). Expressed simply, this means an increased emphasis on policy research of various kinds done outside of academic employment. The typical pattern of the value-explicit, role-extension period, where the applied anthropologist would take temporary assignments of an applied nature while working as an academic, is replaced by more employment by consulting firms or as a direct-hire staff member of the agency. This kind of employment results in a dramatic increase in new kinds of research. This stage appears to be more clearly a return to the pattern of the federal service period than an outgrowth of the period before. It is different in a fundamental way, however. During the federal service period applied anthropologists returned to academia once the employment pressure was off. It appears unlikely that the large numbers of anthropologists entering the job market as practicing anthropologists now will take academic jobs in the future. They will not return because there will not be jobs for them, their salary expectations cannot be met, and they just do not want to. It is for this reason that this period is unique.

Applied anthropology of this stage is more clearly a product of external factors. There are two primary external factors: the dramatically shrinking academic job market (Balderston and Radner 1971; Cartter 1974; D'Andrade, Hammel, Adkins, and McDaniel 1975), and (at least in the United States) the creation of a wide array of policy research functions mandated by federal regulation and statute. The effect of the shrinking academic job market is substantial and increasing. An early estimate predicted that two-thirds of new Ph.D.'s produced in anthropology would find employment outside of academia (D'Andrade, Hammel, Adkins, and McDaniel 1975). Recent research on employment summarized by Elizabeth Briody shows that that the percentage of each annual cohort of Ph.D.'s that enters employment outside academia is increasing (Briody 1988:77). An American Anthropological Association survey indicated that in the 1989–1990 cohort of Ph.D.'s, 59 percent were employed outside of academic departments although most anthropologists work in academic positions (American Anthropological Association 1991:1).

Coupled with this big push factor are the pulling effects of legislatively mandated policy research opportunities. To some unspecified degree, the so-called surplus of Ph.D.'s is absorbed by other opportunities created by the aforementioned expansion in policy research. Some of the legislation which is relevant to this problem is the National Environmental Policy Act of 1969, the Foreign Assistance Act as amended, and the Community Development Act of 1974. In addition to employment directly related to these policy research needs, a very large array of new types of employment was accepted by anthropologists. Some of this employment involved research; much of it involved assuming other roles. The effects of these pull factors vary considerably. Levels of funding have varied substantially through the years with changing economic conditions, changing political styles, and periodic disillusionment with the utility of policy research.

A confounding factor in employment choice is the political attitudes of anthropologists formed by their experiences in the era of the Vietnam War. For some, employment with U.S. government agencies with overseas programs was unacceptable for ideological reasons, no matter how hard the push or attractive the pull. This, so it seems, has changed significantly as the job situation has worsened and agency programs have changed.

The changes in anthropology associated with the increase in nonacademic employment are substantial. These can be addressed in terms of three general categories: academic program content, publication and information dissemination, and social organization, as well as some general changes in style.

Academic Program Content. Starting as early as 1968 a number of academic programs specifically focused upon preparation for nonacademic careers were organized (Hyland and Kirkpatrick 1989; Kushner 1978:23; Trotter 1988). By 1994 the Society for Applied Anthropology and the National Association for the Practice of Anthropology developed guidelines for the organization of applied and practicing anthropology training programs. In 2000 a number of programs with this focus formed the Consortium of Applied and Practicing Anthropology Programs to facilitate resource sharing and cooperation (Bennett 2000). Increasingly, these programs are coming to be focused upon more specific policy areas rather than having a general orientation toward applied anthropology (van Willigen 1988). These programs tend to make wider use of internships and practica in their instructional strategy (Hyland, Bennett, Collins, and Finerman 1988; Wolfe, Chambers, and Smith 1981). The number of programs that have application as a focus have increased dramatically (Hyland and Kirkpatrick 1989; van Willigen 1985). It is conceivable that in the future a professional society will develop standards for certification and accreditation.

Publication and Information Dissemination. The most noteworthy change in publication and information dissemination was the creation of the publication *Practicing Anthropology*. *Practicing Anthropology* publishes articles which report the experiences of anthropologists in various kinds of nonacademic employment. Currently its readership is over 2000. In addition, the Applied Anthropology Documentation Project at the University of Kentucky has resulted in the establishment of a collection of the written products of applied anthropologists (Clark and van Willigen 1981; van Willigen 1981b, 1991). The increased interest in application has influenced the publication policies of the major journals. *Human Organization* shows some tendency to return to the publication of application case study materials that dominated its pages in the first decade of publication. The National Association for the Practice of Anthropology publishes a Bulletin series that features materials on application.

Social Organization. The most significant change caused by increases in nonacademic employment have been the creation of a large number of local practitioner organizations (LPOs). The first of these was the Society of Professional Anthropologists (SOPA) established in Tucson, Arizona, in 1974 (Bainton 1975; Bennett 1988). Although disbanded, SOPA served as a model for others. Local Practitioner Organizations were established at Washington, D.C.; Los Angeles, California; Tampa, Florida; Tallahassee, Florida; Ann Arbor, Michigan; and Memphis, Tennessee among other places. In addition, the High Plains Society for Applied Anthropology serves a regional constituency in the high plains. The Washington Association of Professional Anthropologists (WAPA) and the High Plains Society for Applied Anthropology (HPSFAA) are clearly the most active. WAPA publishes a newsletter and directory and regularly holds workshops at national association meetings on topics like "Seeking Federal Employment." HPSFAA has a lively annual meeting and a regular publication. Most importantly, the LPOs serve as a mechanism for effective networking in the profession.

At the national level there was considerable organizational development that has benefited American applied anthropologists. Most important is the National Association for the Practice of Anthropology organized as a unit of the American Anthropological Association. The Society for Applied Anthropology (SfAA) and NAPA are currently engaged in various cooperative activities. Canadian anthropologists benefit from the activities of the Society for Applied Anthropology in Canada, organized in 1981 (Price 1987).

Both the American Anthropological Association and the Society for Applied Anthropology have used academically employed and nonacademically employed slates for their elections for some time. Other adaptations have included changing the mix of the national meeting programs so as to increase activities relevant for nonacademically employed anthropologists and to decrease the part of the program designed for scholarly purposes. Innovations in this area include workshops for gaining skills in various policy research areas such as social impact assessment and program evaluation. NAPA has provided considerable creative leadership in this regard. The American Anthropological Association has issued a number of publications which address practical or applied issues. These include publications on the structure of training programs, done with the Society for Applied Anthropology (Leacock, Gonzalez, and Kushner 1974), the development of training programs (Trotter 1988), approaches to practice (Goldschmidt 1979), practicing anthropologists (Chatelain and Cimino 1981), and employment (Bernard and Sibley 1975). Also published were a series of training manuals in applied anthropology on various topics including development anthropology (Partridge 1984), medical anthropology (Hill 1984), policy ethnography (van Willigen and DeWalt 1985), and nutritional anthropology (Quandt and Ritenbaugh 1986).

Another potentially significant development has been the modification by the national organizations of ethics statements. The Society for Applied Anthropology approved a revision of their ethics statement in 1983. The committee was charged with adjusting the existing statement to the conditions faced by practicing anthropologists. With this in mind, the committee developed a statement that recognized the "legitimate proprietary" interests of clients in terms of the dissemination of research data, the need for truthful reporting of qualifications, and the need for continuing education to maintain skills, as well as other issues (Committee on Ethics, Society for Applied Anthropology 1983). The National Association for the Practice of Anthropology issued an ethics statement recently.

As in the two previous stages, the anthropologists working in application explore new areas of research. The growth of new areas of inquiry is dramatic. Some examples of the new developments are research into forestry (Collins and Painter 1986; Murray 1987), drug rehabilitation (Marshall 1979), homeless people (Glasser 1996), human waste disposal (Elmendorf and Buckles 1978), welfare program reform (Trend 1978b), broadcast media (Eiselein and Marshall 1976), social services in boomtowns (Uhlman 1977), educational evaluation (Burns 1975; Clinton 1975; Fitzsimmons 1975), commodity marketing (Lample and Herbert 1988) housing needs and effects (Kerri 1977; Weaver and Downing 1975; Wulff 1972), commodity-focused agricultural research (Werge 1977), wildlife management (Brownrigg 1986), radioactive waste storage siting (Stoffle, Evans, and Jensen 1987a), energy extraction (Softestad 1990), rural industrial development (Grinstead 1976), employment training (Naylor 1976), market development (Zilverberg and Courtney 1984), corrections (Alexander and Chapman 1982), building and landscape design (Esber 1987; Low and Simon 1984), fisheries (Johnson and Griffith 1985; McCay and Creed 1990); (Stoffle, Jensen, and Rasch 1981); recreational planning (Scott, DeWalt, Adelski, Alexander, and Beebe 1982; Wulff 1976); ethnography in product design (Wasson 2000), and the effects of power generation (Callaway, Levy, and Henderson 1976).

At a somewhat more general level, one can cite development in the areas of social impact assessment and program evaluation. Anthropologists were involved in some of the pioneering efforts which attempted to predict, for the benefit of planners, some of the social costs and benefits of various kinds of development projects. In domestic settings, we find anthropologists engaged in team research which developed social impact assessment manuals and standards (Maruyama 1973; Vlachos 1975). Anthropologists were involved in direct assessment of project effects (Dixon 1978; Jacobs 1977; McGuire and Worden 1984; Millsap 1978; Nugent, Partridge, Brown, and Rees 1978; Parker and King 1987; Preister and King 1987; Stoffle et al. 1987a, 1987b; Van Tassell and Michaelson 1977), and field testing of social impact assessment methodologies (Clinton 1978). Although the legislative mandate was substantially different, anthropologists were engaged in social impact assessment–related work in the context of international development. These efforts included the development of manuals for impact assessment methodology (Harza Engineering Company 1980), baseline studies to inform development planning (Brown 1980; Scaglion 1981; DeWalt and DeWalt 1982; Green 1982; Maloney, Aziz, and Sarker 1980; Werge 1977), development of regional development plans (Brokensha, Horowitz, and Scudder 1977) needs assessments (Green and Wessells 1997; Practical Concepts, Inc. 1980), social soundness analysis (Cochrane 1979; McPherson 1978; U.S. Agency for International Development 1975), project evaluations (Blustain 1982; Brown 1980; Pillsbury 1989; Williams 1980, 1981), analysis of program planning documents (Britan 1980; Collins and Painter 1986; Hoben 1980; Ingersoll, Sullivan, and Lenkerd 1981), as well as basic research into various aspects of development such as decentralization in development (Ralston, Anderson, and Colson 1981), indigenous voluntary associations (Miller 1980), and women in development (Elmendorf and Isely 1981).

The involvement of anthropologists in the evaluation of various domestic social action programs is quite common. Evaluation studies occur in a wide variety of areas, including American Indian education (Fuchs and Havighurst 1970), housing development (Kerri 1977), American Indian tribal governance (Weaver et al. 1971), employment training programs, rural education (Everhart 1975), parenting (Achatz and MacAllum 1994), alternative energy source development (Roberts 1981), innovative education programs (Fetterman 1987), alcohol abuse curtailment projects (Marshall 1979), childhood nutrition (Best Start 1994), and minority employment (Buehler 1981).

The dramatic increase in policy research efforts of various types is not associated with an increase in the use of social intervention techniques, which this chapter describes as characteristic of the pattern of application in the previous stage. There are examples of the use of action anthropology (Schlesier 1974; Stull 1979), research and development anthropology (Turner 1974; Wulff 1977), and various advocacy research approaches. The approaches based on cultural brokerage models developed by Hazel H. Weidman earlier in this stage are still in use. There are two factors that seem to have caused the reduction of this type of application: the radical critique of much of applied anthropology, and the increasing political sophistication of many of the traditional client groups of anthropologists.

A factor which will influence the future of anthropology is the changing circumstances of employment. First, the academic to nonacademic mix has changed. The nonacademic realm is quite variable within itself. The conditions of employment effect both motivation and opportunity to publish, tendency to participate in anthropological learned societies, extent of interdisciplinary orientation, and training future anthropologists. Working in a governmental organization is different from working in the private sector. There are significant differences between profit and nonprofit organizations in the private sector. The biggest differences may occur where the anthropologist owns the firm. Academic employment is also changing in many of the same ways. There seems to be a stronger commitment to consulting and, of course, many nonacademically employed anthropologists have to compete with the academics. There is an increasing tendency to take on research commitments in the policy area by academics so as to provide students with marketable experiences.

Emergence of a Multidisciplinary Tradition of Practice

In 1975 I participated in the symposium of the Southern Anthropological Society which attempted to address what the organizer, Michael Angrosino, regarded as the "New Applied Anthropology" (1976). What he referred to as new was an anthropology that relied on "short-term, contract work in public service agencies, work often involving program evaluation, and work that can often be undertaken off campus (1976:1)." The novelty of the New Applied Anthropology stimulated him to organize the symposium entitled "Do Applied Anthropologists Apply Anthropology?"

Over the past 25 years a new synthesis has emerged. This new synthesis revolves around a newly emerging relationship between anthropologists and the persons and communities they study.

Throughout this era the relationship between anthropologists and the people studied changed in many important ways. The history of the relationship between applied anthropology and the communities that they work with parallels that of the relationship between anthropologist and research community in basic anthropology. In some sense the history of anthropology, both basic and applied, is the history of the power relationships between anthropologists and the people studied. That anthropology, both basic and applied, is a product of colonializing institutions is by now a commonplace interpretation of the discipline's history. As these power relationships have changed, the stance of both basic and applied anthropology regarding the communities and people they study has changed. These changes consist of changes in anthropology's, "conceptions of (a) the object of analysis, (b) the language of analysis and (c) the position of the analyst" (Rosaldo 1993:37) and apply to both basic and applied anthropology. While the causes of the change are the same for both aspects of the discipline, the responses are different, perhaps even diametrically opposed. Anthropologists of both types find it increasingly difficult to treat the people studied as objects. The basic discipline response was to change viewpoints and think of ethnography as a mechanism for looking at our own society. The typical basic anthropological response to this essential "post-modern" dilemma is to use the ethnographic enterprise to look at themselves, to be "reflexive" as this literature says.

Ethnography is presented not as about "those studied" but a kind of "cultural critique" of the anthropologist's culture (Marcus and Fischer 1986). The adaptation implemented by some in the realm of application is quiet different. Increasingly applied anthropologists work with those studied in a collaborative or participatory mode. That is, the goals of the community are merged with anthropologists' goals. The applied anthropologist shares his or her special skills and knowledge with the community. This serves to transform the community from object to be known to a subject that can control. The perspective is consistent with critical social theory on the one hand and the modern synthesis of participatory action research on the other.

In the participatory action research mode the anthropologist works with the community to understand the conditions that produce the problems that the people face. This transformation shows the changing relationship with communities that can be traced from the early experiments with new modes of application such as action anthropology and research and development anthropology. In both these approaches, the anthropologists treated their research goals and community goals of development as essentially equal. In modes of application, such as the action research and the collaborative approaches, the salience of anthropological disciplinary goals was reduced. The applied anthropologist becomes an auxiliary to the naturally occurring community leadership.

Along with this change, the distinctions between disciplines have become much more limited. This is apparent in research methods as well as action practices. What has emerged in the action realm is a new synthesis. Most of the ideas are familiar. These include (1) local knowledge, (2) participation, (3) empowerment, (4) critical consciousness, and (5) sustainability. These are all intertwined and to an extent "scaled," i.e., they should be thought of in terms of a logical order and progression. These ideas will be discussed in Chapter 4.

SUMMARY

What is called applied anthropology has grown dramatically since the inception of anthropology as a discipline. In its growth, applied anthropology has manifested an array of tendencies. First, the applied and theoretical aspects of the discipline develop in parallel, application potentials being used as a rationale for the development of academic programs and theoretical research programs. The effect of applied anthropology on theoretical anthropology is often masked because of the nature of publication in applied anthropology and its relative lack of prestige. Second, a major effect of applied anthropology on theoretical anthropology is the stimulus of interest in new research topics and populations. This effect too is masked. Third, the development of applied anthropology is best thought of in terms of an additive expansion of research context, topics, and techniques. While there have been intervention techniques developed within anthropology, today these are infrequently applied. Fourth, applied anthropology should be thought of as primarily a product of important external forces rather than a consistent pattern of internally generated change. Mostly, the external forces are manifested in employment and funded research opportunities brought about by the needs of colonial governance, war, and foreign policy. More recently, a major external factor is the nature of the academic job market and, to a limited extent, an increase in policy research opportunities mandated by federal law.

The nature of the academic job market has resulted in the creation of a large cadre of anthropologists employed outside of academic contexts.

FURTHER READING

Eddy, Elizabeth M. and William L. Partridge, eds. *Applied Anthropology in America.* 2nd ed. New York: Columbia University Press, 1987. This volume contains a number of chapters which are useful for understanding the history of applied anthropology.

Chapter 3

Ethics

As one prepares to assume an occupational role as an applied anthropologist, one becomes increasingly concerned with standards of performance and behavior in that role. This connotes a concern for the quality of the services produced as a result of one's action, as well as concern for how and under what circumstances one produces these services. Such standards of performance and behavior are the substance of ethics. The essential core of the ethics of applied anthropology is the nature of the potential and manifested impact on the people involved.

In his important discussion of ethical issues Joseph G. Jorgensen distinguishes between the anthropologist and various other "information seekers" whom persons confront. As he notes, "Our situation is unlike that of the priest, the lawyer, or the physician, whose help is *requested by the client* and whose right to privileged communication is deemed necessary (by law, in the United States) if he is to serve his clients. In contrast, as anthropologists we *ask for the help* of our subjects and we *offer* confidentiality as an *inducement* to informants for their cooperation" (Jorgensen 1971:327).

In light of this, then, the applied anthropologist by implication would have a status distinct from the research anthropologist in terms of various ethical considerations. First, because we may have change as a goal as well as scientific understanding, we must be especially concerned about the impact of our efforts on the populations with whom we work. Second, because we may be working for an agency that is from outside or is marginal to the community, we may be forced to deal with an especially complex set of ethical concerns. Applied anthropologists typically face more complex ethical situations than other anthropologists.

Though the term *ethics* connotes an absolute standard of behavior, applied anthropologists like other human scientists both pure and applied, must, to be realistic, deal with the concept relativistically. That is to say, ethical standards are difficult enough to specify, let alone consistently apply. In each of the applied anthropologist's constituencies, we find difficult kinds of ethical requirements. That is, different ethical issues are raised in the case of applied anthropologists' relations with research subjects, project sponsors, or fellow anthropologists. The somewhat different requirements of these relationships are sometimes in conflict.

ETHICAL ISSUES IN HISTORIC CONTEXT

This is a complex period in the history of anthropology. The discipline has achieved a very high level of theoretical and methodological complexity. New areas of inquiry emerge with surprising frequency. Further change is brought about by the growth of applied activities. All this change creates new challenges and an increased concern for ethical issues. The debate has continued through the years, reaching a peak during the war in Vietnam. The tensions of that period were exacerbated by a series of ill-conceived and unethical research projects. The debate is not limited to the recent past, but has substantial time depth. As early as 1919, Franz Boas raised concerns in a letter to *The Nation* in which he accused four anthropologists of serving as spies under the guise of their researcher role. As Boas wrote,

A person, who uses science as a cover for political spying, who demeans himself to pose before a foreign government as an investigator and asks for assistance in his alleged researches in order to carry on, under this cloak, his political machinations, prostitutes science in an unpardonable way and forfeits the right to be classed as a scientist. (Boas 1919, in Weaver 1973:51)

From the time of Boas to the present, the debate continues with only a tracing of its intensity revealed in published articles, letters to the editor, resolutions passed at national meetings, American Anthropological Association ethics committee reports, and the ethics codes published by the American Anthropological Association and the Society for Applied Anthropology.

The primary issue in the ethical debate is the potential harm which the activities of the anthropologist may have on a community or a specific person. There are many important issues but this is the core of anthropology's ethical concern. This is something that an anthropologist should understand. We are inextricably linked to the communities we work with, and thereby, our actions can be continually ramified and may have serious unanticipated effects. Cora Du Bois relates an incident which exemplifies this potential in a frightening way.

Du Bois had carried out her well-known study, *The People of Alor*, in an area of what is now Indonesia, that came to be occupied by the Japanese during World War II. It was reported to Du Bois after the war that persons she had studied had innocently mentioned that they wished the Americans would win the war, because they were good people. The Alorese in question had never heard of America prior to Du Bois's field work. She reports that the Japanese heard that certain Alorese were stating that America would win the conflict. The Japanese military government rounded up the persons in question and publicly beheaded them as an example to the populace. As Du Bois notes, "There is no end to the intricate chain of responsibility and guilt that the pursuit of even the most arcane social research involves. 'No man is an island' " (Du Bois 1944, in Weaver 1973:32). However unusual this horrifying case is, it dramatically emphasizes the potential for unexpected harm our science has. Let us here engage in a discussion of some of the issues identified in the literature on anthropological research ethics.

Although there have been sad occurrences of unethical behavior by anthropologists throughout the history of the discipline, perhaps the most notorious cases emerged during the Vietnam War period. The two most frequently cited are the so-called Project Camelot, initiated in Latin America, and the various sponsored research activities carried out in northern Thailand.

Project Camelot was initiated in 1964 under the sponsorship of the Special Operations Research Office (SORO) of the U.S. Army (Horowitz 1967: 4). It was the largest grant for social science research up until that time. A quote from the prospectus of the project mailed to a number of well-known scientists provides an excellent summary of the project's intent:

Project Camelot is a study whose objective is to determine the feasibility of developing a general systems model which would make it possible to predict and influence politically significant aspects of social change in the developing nations of the world. Somewhat more specifically, its objectives are: first, to devise procedures for assessing the potential for internal war within national societies; second, to identify with increased degrees of confidence, those actions which a government might take to relieve conditions which are assessed as giving rise to a potential for internal war; and finally, to assess the feasibility of prescribing the characteristics of a system for obtaining and using the essential information needed for doing the above two things. (Horowitz 1967:4–5)

The project was ultimately to encompass studies in a large number of countries in Asia, Latin America, Africa and Europe. Initially, the activities were to start in Chile. The response to Camelot was substantial in the involved disciplines, the countries of study, and in the American political arena. In spite of the stir it caused in anthropology there was only one involved and he served as a short-term consultant. The project died a quick death and resulted in substantial interpretive literature (Horowitz 1967; Sjoberg

1967). It is difficult to identify the most important criticism in this literature and there is some criticism of its objectivity (Beals 1969).

Many persons object to the use of social science to maintain the social order in countries where there are such clearly identifiable oppressed classes. Although couched in social science jargon, the project was perceived as having a conservative bias. For example, "The use of hygienic language disguises the anti-revolutionary assumptions under a cloud of powder puff declarations" (Sjoberg 1967:48). The most strenuous objections concerned participating in research which had such strong political implications. The basic question became, should social scientists be involved in research which would facilitate interfering in the affairs of other nations? As Belshaw notes, "Within the American Anthropological Association, the reaction was immediate and sharp. Resolutions were passed condemning 'clandestine' research and research dealing with 'counterinsurgency' " (Belshaw 1976:261). More importantly, the reaction included a major study of the problem of ethics which formed the basis for Ralph L. Beals' study, *Politics of Social Research* (1969). These efforts led to the creation of the American Anthropological Association's Committee on Ethics, which until recently reviewed cases of alleged unethical behavior brought before it.

A project that had more severe implications in anthropology is the so-called Thailand Project. The exposure of this project caused a great controversy among anthropologists worldwide.

Northern Thailand is occupied by various hill tribes. These people have little political or economic leverage in the national affairs of Thailand. They have been depicted as the minority suppressed by the politically dominant lowland majority. These groups were relatively isolated although connected to the outside world through the opium trade. Opium poppies were the major cash crop. Pressure from the international community of nations on the Thai government to control the opium traffic increased. Government officials came to realize that policy makers had little information with which to develop a plan for dealing with the northern people (Belshaw 1976:264). The significance of the region increased dramatically as the Vietnam War expanded. These factors encouraged a prodigious increase in the amount of research carried out. In the early 1960s, Western social scientists "flooded" the area (Jones 1971:347), and the Hill Tribes Research Centre was established (Belshaw 1976:265). The relationship that existed between the hill people and the flatlanders was unequal. The lowlanders "tend to look down on the hill people, call them by derogatory names, etc." (Jones 1971:347). These high groups were viewed as good candidates for subversive activities and had not demonstrated loyalty to the Thai government.

Jones raises the most basic question:

Did the anthropologists who rushed into the area to do basic descriptive studies consider these political facts? It is safe to say that most of them did not. Was it an accident that the strategic and political concerns about the hill areas and the questionable loyalty of the hill people to Thailand coincided with the growing anthropological concern about the lack of knowledge of the area? Was it also an accident that, about that same time, a considerable amount of money became available for basic research on this "little known area"? The situation which developed led to a decade of concentrated research on hill people to the almost total neglect of valley culture and society. (1971:348)

As the apparent strategic significance of the region increased, the amount of research funds increased. Increasingly, scholars could make use of funds from agencies of the American government such as the Advanced Research Projects Agency (ARPA) of the Department of Defense. Research carried out on the basis of "cleaner" money, for the most part, ended up in the hands of ARPA anyway. ARPA's goals were clearly directed at counterinsurgency ends (Jones 1971:348). They were interested in maintaining the status quo and saw the utility of basic descriptive cultural data. To these ends they supported the data collection process.

ARPA wanted basic information on culture and society in Thailand, and was willing to pay to have the research done. Since most of us who have conducted basic research in Thailand have, in fact, contributed to that end, we might as well have taken ARPA's money. The question of ethics and responsibility may have little to do with the source of funding and much more with the social and political context within which the data are produced. (Jones 1971:348)

The whole presence of anthropologists in Thailand was brought under attack in 1970 by the Student Mobilization Committee to End the War in Vietnam for doing what they referred to as "counterinsurgency research." This too resulted in a major crisis in the discipline which seems to have intensified interest in various ethical concerns. It is clear that the conflicts generated during the Vietnam era concerning ethics contributed a great deal to the understanding of our responsibilities. The process which these discussions developed was very painful and disturbing. In retrospect, many respected scholars were unfairly accused, yet the increase in understanding may have been worth it.

THE PRIVACY ISSUE

The fieldwork process is based largely on overcoming the boundaries which exist between the personality of the researcher and that of the informant. We call this breakdown of protective boundaries "rapport building." Through the building of rapport, we erode the informants' tendency to protect their private personalities. It is possible, even probable, that with the development of rapport, the informant provides information that could be damaging to them, if not properly protected.

Why do people give us information? Many do so because they value the goals of science. However, in many cases the goals of science are irrelevant or unknown to them, and they may be responding for a whole range of other reasons. These might include their own standards of hospitality, their perceptions of the anthropologist's power, and their own need for recognition and attention.

We must be wary of any tendency to use whatever power and prestige the anthropologist might have to produce positive responses in informants. Clearly, it is possible to use our relative power to obtain data. One might even argue that "rapport-building skills" are in fact the most insidious deception.

We often give our research subjects assurances about anonymity, yet our capacity to protect the information is not absolute, although one might argue that it is reasonably assured. We don't have the legal right to claim that our information is privileged. Anthropologists' legal status is not unlike journalists whose data and data sources can be subpoenaed. Yet, the ethical standards of the discipline, and more recently the legal requirements of federally funded research, seem to suggest that absolute control is possible. These conditions cause us to work as if we had absolute control over access to our data. In applied research settings, control of the use of data may be in the hands of the sponsor rather than the researcher.

We value our research and its products. It is possible to build substantial justification for the continuation of such research efforts. The question is, however, what costs must individual research subjects bear in order for the research to go on? The respondent's costs include loss of opportunity, loss of control of data, as well as any physical risks.

THE ISSUE OF CONSENT

Perhaps the paramount issue in the ethical debate is the issue of consent. That is, our discipline should expect that its practitioners carry out their activities with the permission of research subjects. That is to say, the anthropologist must ask the question, "May I do this?" Further, the informant must know the circumstances in which the question is asked. It is only with adequate knowledge that the subject can give permission in a way that is ethically meaningful. Sufficient knowledge is a relative concept to be sure, but, nevertheless, would include an understanding of the purposes of the research activity; the identity of the funding agency and its goals; the final disposition of the data; and the potential impact the data would have on the individual. Further, the informant must understand that his or her participation is voluntary. Special procedures are required for consent to be given in these cases. Such are the components of what is referred to as "informed consent."

Informed consent is the foundation of ethical research. Much impetus for formalizing ethical issues, such as informed consent, has come from the medical research area. This impetus is derived from the real and immediate risk of much medical research which uses human subjects. Further, many of the most abusive human subject research projects have been carried out by medical researchers. The abuses of medical research and other disciplines have led to increasing public concern. Associated with this concern is an increased government involvement in the ethical dimension of large-scale federally funded research projects. Most individual research projects which are considered for federal funding must be evaluated in terms of key ethical issues such as informed consent. In spite of this concern, there is still a significant amount of ambiguity concerning these issues. Let us present here a widely applied definition of informed consent. This definition of informed consent was provided by the Board of Regents of the State of New York in 1966. It provides clear guidelines for medical investigators, though it could also be used for anthropologists.

No consent is valid unless it is made by a person with legal and mental capacity to make it, and is based on a disclosure of all material facts. The federal government defines some populations as vulnerable and not able to give informed consent. These include the underaged, mentally handicapped, institutionalized or incarcerated, persons under risk because of the illegal status or activities, people who can't read, and people who are ill or physically handicapped. Any facts which might influence the giving and withholding of consent are material. A patient has the right to know he is being asked to volunteer and to refuse to participate in an experiment for any reason, intelligent or otherwise, well-informed or prejudiced. A physician has no right to withhold from a prospective volunteer any fact which he knows may influence the decision. It is the volunteer's decision to make, and the physician may not take it away from him by the manner in which he asks the question or explains or fails to explain the circumstances. (Langer 1966:664)

Though "informed consent" is rather easy to specify as a requirement, it is sometimes very difficult to achieve. Part of our task in establishing the conditions of informed consent is to convey the implications of our research when we may not fully understand these implications. The type of research populations we, as anthropologists, deal with tend not to be in the position to adequately recognize the implications of our research. As Jorgensen notes,

because our research is often conducted among illiterate or semiliterate who have scant knowledge of the uses to which data can be put, we are doubly obligated to spell out our intentions and not to exploit their naivete. The extent to which we must explain our intentions will vary with the problems we address and the knowledge possessed by the host population. Our host populations, in particular, will vary greatly in their understandings of the implications of the ways in which research conducted among them could damage their own interests. I am not suggesting that it will be easy to apprise them of everything they ought to know, nor to make them immediately understand all they ought to know. The anthropologist himself is often naive about the implications of his own research. (Jorgensen 1971: 328)

The fact that anthropologists tend to use inductive research designs also causes a certain amount of difficulty in legitimately achieving the goal of informed consent. Anthropologists create strictly deductive research designs infrequently. With such designs, the ultimate range and breadth of a research project can be more easily determined. In the field, topics grow and change. A question is raised by these changes: how and under what circumstances does consent have to be obtained again? Does consent to carry out one aspect of the research imply that consent is given for other aspects of the study? Oftentimes, the researcher begins his or her project with noncontroversial topics, and then, slowly changes focus to the more controversial, for the very reason that if the latter topic had been broached during the initial stages of the research project, the anthropologist would have been run off.

This represents a difficult problem. There are those that suggest that "consent should be requested for the research ends that are anticipated"(Jorgensen 1971:328). This may be difficult in certain social contexts. The goal of informed consent implies that the research activities are carried out without deceit and misrepresentation. To quote Jorgensen:

I accept the premise that anthropologists, by the very nature of their dedication to free and open inquiry and the pursuit of truth, cannot condone deceit in research. If the anthropologist seeks truth, exposes falsehood, feels an ethical obligation to others of his profession not to compromise them or make their own legitimate research suspect, and feels he has a right and a duty to honor the obligations he has made to his informants in requesting their help in giving him information about which they are protective, he cannot assume a masquerade at all. (1971:329)

THE UTILITY ISSUE

As suggested above, anthropologists' research means that certain costs will accrue to the research subject and thereby to the subject community. In most cases it would seem that the loss of time to the informant is inconsequential. Most humans have sufficient leisure to allow some interaction with a social scientist. Further, it seems in most cases the research efforts of anthropologists will tend not to harm informants if the data is properly protected. Yet there are cases where the work of the anthropologist caused harm.

The most important idea here is that information can be used to control people; that is, knowledge is power. That phrase has become meaningless because we rarely take time to examine the mechanism by which knowledge is used to control people. Just how anthropological data plays into the hands of an exploitative, multinational corporation, an oppressive, totalitarian organization, or a secret intelligence agency is not clear. It is difficult to find out given the fact that it isn't even clear how more "righteous" organizations make use of such data. The implications of the potential for harm, however, are so serious that we must develop our position in terms of the *potential* for harm rather than the real probabilities.

When we do this, we are confronted with a number of serious problems. In most cases in pure anthropological research, the costs of research accrue to the researched, whereas most of the benefits accrue to the researcher. At least it seems improbable that given the normal research process in anthropology, research subjects will receive any significant benefit from the enterprise. These communities are rarely equipped to use such data; the topics selected by the researcher are often irrelevant to the information needs of the community, and the researcher rarely provides information to the community. This kind of research might be construed as the ultimate kind of anthropological self-indulgence, if it weren't so common. The Dutch applied anthropologist Gerrit Huizer refers to this self-indulgent anthropology as hobbyism (1975:64). As he notes,

It seems as if the most immediate purpose of the research is the satisfaction of a rather arbitrary curiosity (or urge for knowledge) of the social researcher. The satisfaction of this urge according to the rules of the game of scientific effort and the passing on of the knowledge gained to others determines the career and promotion of the research worker. (1975:64)

The remedy for this problem is the active and conscientious consideration of the interests of the research population in the research design process. Huizer notes, however, that

the research could possibly serve the interests of the people investigated or even remedy their distress, hardly occurs to most social scientists. Such a thing might occur by chance, but generally the interference with the realities under investigation is seen as disturbing or dangerous for the scientific quality of the research. (1975: 65)

Huizer advocates a close identification between anthropologist and research subjects so that the interests of the subject population may be protected.

The best treatment for this problem is the direct negotiation of the content and goals of the research design between researcher and community. The negotiation may result in modifications of the research procedure so that objectionable procedures may be removed. But, more importantly, the project can be modified to help meet the information needs of the subject

community. It may be simply required that the research design remain un-
changed but that reporting requirements be changed so as to improve the
community's access to the research results. Other alternatives might mean
"piggybacking" community research needs on the researchers' topic, selecting a community-defined topic as the primary focus of the project, or
providing another kind of service in lieu of research. The point is that the
utility of a project to the community is a relevant ethical dimension that
can be addressed. In applied research these issues may be simplified in the
sense that the research design and goals are determined by, or through,
negotiation with the client community.

The question remains, however, *who* is the client community and who
are its representatives? Oftentimes applied anthropologists must work on
research problems for clients who, although they serve a community, are
not truly representative of the community. Ethical issues must be dealt with
most carefully in this situation. The anthropologists must consider the impact of their behavior when they are acting as agents of service organizations, development agencies, or political action groups. In cases where the
client group is part of the community, the extent of representativeness must
also be considered. It is not always clear to what extent subgroups such as
the "leadership" elite are representative of the total community.

THE COMMUNICATION ISSUE

There is a great deal of tension in anthropology concerning the ethics of
publication. This multidimensional problem is particularly relevant to the
ethical concerns of the applied anthropologist. As applied anthropologists,
we are faced with complying with diverse standards of information dissemination. As scientists, we are obliged to communicate results so that others
may share in our contribution to knowledge. The research process is
thought to end only with effective communication of research results, the
assumption being that there is "an immortal open record of research results
where all scientists are able to present their results for the benefit and scrutiny of their scientific peers" (Price 1964:655). Though it seems that applied
anthropologists tend not to emphasize the publication of their applied results, they are motivated like most scientists to get things on the record for
a wide variety of rather intense motivations. These motivations include the
lure of immortality in print, the publish-or-perish tenure struggle for those
who are employed in academic jobs, and the need for nonacademically
employed anthropologists to establish some academic credentials so as to
maintain the possibility for academic employment, if they so choose. Publication by practicing anthropologists can serve to increase personal influence in the domain of application.

The potential applied anthropologist author faces a number of problems.
First, few journals are actually geared up to publish materials which have

applied relevance. Applied research results sometimes have limited appeal for the general social science audience. Oftentimes the components of an applied project that see the light of publication are not those parts that were significant in accomplishing the goals of the project. What often gets published are those components that have an academic cast to them. There isn't even a consistent tendency to document or archive materials produced in the course of applied anthropologists' activities. These deficiencies of information exchange seem to limit the cumulative improvement of applied anthropology.

This is by no means the most crucial issue applied anthropologists face in the realm of publication and the communication of information. The primary issue is the extent to which the applied anthropologist can make information public. As applied anthropologists, our employers often have some control over the disposition of the research results. The problem also occurs in the realm of physical science as Price notes,

Historically, there has been a very interesting contrast between the literature ethics of basic science and those of technology. In basic science, the motivation is always for the most complete publication that will ensure the payoff, of recognition of the contribution of the individual scientist and his reward by eponymic fame, Nobel prizes or similar honors or at least by appreciation. In technological research and development, with profit or military ascendancy substituted so largely for honor, the effort is toward publication only as an epiphenomenon, not as an end product. (Price 1964:655)

All researchers are enjoined ethically to control the release of collected data. For example, it is absolutely necessary to maintain the anonymity of our research subjects. No matter what our relationship is with a client, we must maintain the privacy of the informant. Our job is not to collect data about individuals for other individuals. But even if we are capable of maintaining the anonymity of informants, serious ethical problems remain. The most difficult kinds of ethical problems are caused by research in which the anthropologist, in a clandestine manner, researches a community on behalf of another group or agency. The researcher may either mask his researcher role, his real questions, or any working relationships that he might have with a third party.

ETHICS IN APPLICATION[1]

The ethical dimensions of one's behavior must be taken into account in the application process. Unethical behavior can cause serious harm to the work of an applied anthropologist if care is not taken to protect the relationship with members of the community with whom work is being done.

1. The authors of this section are Mahmoud Hussein and John van Willigen.

Two important ethical concerns confront applied anthropologists working in development. These are (1) accountability and responsibility and (2) quality (Gardner and Lewis 1996). The first raises issues of empowerment, and the argument is to whom is the development anthropologist accountable and responsible? Certainly not to the policy makers and the rich, because this will jeopardize the role of the poor and the marginal in the development process. The question of quality is raised here to show how it can be insured in a short time frame that an applied anthropologist spends in the field. Closely tied to this is the issue of the "fly in, fly out" tendency that does not guarantee the quality of work.

Another ethical problem regarding anthropologists' involvement in development projects is the question of the terms of involvement. At what stage of the development process should the anthropologist be involved? This concern is important, especially when the project is poorly designed (Gardner and Lewis 1996). The role of an applied anthropologist can be that of an expatriate working in a country or a site abroad. This can lead to the taking up of scarce employment opportunities and also use of the locals as subordinate staff (Gardner and Lewis 1996).

Honesty in applied anthropology is essential. Unqualified professionals, wearing gowns of experts (what Chambers calls "chameleon consultants"), sometimes pose as development consultants (Chambers 1997). Problems of behavior and attitudes can cause harm to the credibility of anthropology as a discipline and the anthropologist as an agent of development and change. Facilitators and trainers have sometimes been slow in learning not to dominate, especially in participatory development (Chambers 1997).

Numerous mistakes are made in the field, which include dominant and superior behavior, rushing through the development process without taking time to earn trust and build rapport, sticking to routines and disregarding other options, and bias against some sections of the community, especially women, the poor, the old and the vulnerable. Other ethical problems include poor or no compensation for people's time, effort, and help, the failure to honor pledges made, and the arousal of expectations, expectations which are seldom met (Chambers 1997).

The overall credibility of the applied anthropologist rests on good behavior and conduct. All aspects of ethics discussed above shed some light on the importance of dealing with research or development subjects in a mutually respectful manner. When ethical standards are upheld, it will produce the desired results of insuring the quality of applied work, and this will surely earn the discipline reputation for effectiveness. It will also uphold the role and status of the applied anthropologist as a facilitator, researcher, and advocate of participatory development.

GUIDES TO ETHICAL PROFESSIONAL PRACTICE

For our purposes, the most useful statements on ethical practice for application are the statements of the Society for Applied Anthropology and the National Association for the Practice of Anthropology. These statements were written with reference to the work circumstances of the applied or practicing anthropologist. The statement of the Society for Applied Anthropology is included below as a guide. Approved in 1983, the statement applies to the membership of the society, although it will serve as a guide to others (Committee on Ethics, Society for Applied Anthropology 1983).

STATEMENT ON PROFESSIONAL AND ETHICAL RESPONSIBILITIES, SOCIETY FOR APPLIED ANTHROPOLOGY

This statement is a guide to professional behavior for the members of the Society for Applied Anthropology. As members or fellows of the Society we shall act in ways that are consistent with the responsibilities stated below irrespective of the specific circumstances of our employment.

This statement is the fourth version of the Society's ethics statement. It was modified in response to concern about the increase in the number of anthropologists employed in applied roles outside of universities. This statement is not associated with a system of certification or licensure. Because of this, the society's Ethics Committee is not equipped with sanctions against unethical behavior.

1.) To the people we study we owe disclosure of our research goals, methods, and sponsorship. The participation of people in our research activities shall only be on a voluntary and informed basis. We shall provide a means throughout our research activities and in subsequent publications to maintain the confidentiality of those we study. The people we study must be made aware of the likely limits of confidentiality and must not be promised a greater degree of confidentiality than can be realistically expected under current legal circumstances in our respective nations. We shall, within the limits of our knowledge, disclose any significant risk to those we study that may result from our activities.

This paragraph states the basic components of ethical research practice. These are voluntary participation, informed consent, and confidentiality. This is supplemented with a reference to risk. One point must be emphasized: disclosure of sponsorship is especially important in research that has a practical effect. Individuals who are asked to give consent must be made aware of sponsorship so that they can better calculate their own interest in reference to the goals of the sponsoring organization. The paragraph contains reference to the fact that in the United States the promise of confidentiality from a researcher will not protect against a legal subpoena. Researchers are not legally protected as are physicians. We are more like journalists in this regard. Risk is primarily viewed in terms of the physical or psychological risk associated with a research procedure as applied on an individual basis. The risks which are generated by social science research tend to be psychological, political, and economic. These risks should be disclosed.

2.) To the communities ultimately affected by our actions we owe respect for their dignity, integrity, and worth. We recognize that human survival is contingent upon the continued existence of a diversity of human communities, and guide our professional activities accordingly. We will avoid taking or recommending action on behalf of a sponsor which is harmful to the interests of a community.

This paragraph is clearly keyed to social survival. The view taken here is that cultural diversity is adaptive and the destruction of it reduces the species potential to survive. Thus, the scheme is not based upon a relativistic conception of what is right or fair, but on a fundamental view of what behaviors relate to and support survival of the species. The last reference to community interests is important to the action-taking anthropologist especially. The statement means that in a basic sense, even though employed by an organization, a basic overriding responsibility toward communities exists.

3.) To our social science colleagues we have the responsibility to not engage in actions that impede their reasonable professional activities. Among other things this means that, while respecting the needs, responsibilities, and legitimate proprietary interests of our sponsors we should not impede the flow of information about research outcomes and professional practice techniques. We shall accurately report the contributions of colleagues to our work. We shall not condone falsification or distortion by others. We should not prejudice communities or agencies against a colleague for reasons of personal gain.

This paragraph addresses that area which produces the most difficulty in ethics—relationships with colleagues. While the entire research community benefits from the free flow of information, sponsoring organizations may have legitimate needs that may result in restrictions on the flow of information. We should not engage in unfair competition with a colleague.

4.) To our students, interns, or trainees we owe nondiscriminatory access to our training services. We shall provide training which is informed, accurate, and relevant to the needs of the larger society. We recognize the need for continuing education so as to maintain our skill and knowledge at a high level. Our training should inform students as to their ethical responsibilities. Student contributions to our professional activities, including both research and publication, should be adequately recognized.

People who train applied anthropologists have the obligation to remain up-to-date in their skills. Further, persons offering training in applied anthropology need to continually consider the needs of society in terms of the training which they offer.

5.) To our employers and other sponsors we owe accurate reporting of our qualifications and competent, efficient, and timely performance of the work we undertake for them. We shall establish a clear understanding with each employer or other sponsor as to the nature of our professional responsibilities. We shall report our research and other activities accurately. We have the obligation to attempt to prevent distortion or suppression of research results or policy recommendations by concerned agencies.

This paragraph points to one of the important uses of ethics statements, the protection of the employee from requests for the performance of unethical practice. The best protection is "up-front" discussion of the constraints. This may serve as a means for supporting the applied anthropologist in cases where the agency which employs him is suppressing or distorting research results.

6.) To society as a whole we owe the benefit of our special knowledge and skills in interpreting sociocultural systems. We should communicate our understanding of human life to the society at large. Restated in simple terms, we need to communicate to the public anthropological knowledge which will be useful to them and provide positive influences on their lives.

CONCLUSION

The ethical concerns of applied anthropologists are complicated by the fact that their work is intended to have a practical effect. Ethics for action are closely related to ethics for research because our action and policy products are rooted in research. The foundation of ethical research practice can be conveyed in a few words: confidentiality, voluntary consent, and risk disclosure. Action and policy must, for ethical reasons, be initiated in reference to community interests as well as the interests of sponsoring agencies. At this point applied anthropologists must be self-policing from the standpoint of ethics because the discipline does not have a mechanism for certification of individuals or accreditation of training programs.

Ethics need not be considered as constraints, but as guides to effective practice. That is, through ethical practice more effective action and policies can be developed. Why is this so? The primary reason is that relationships between researchers and those researched are made more regular and predictable. Further, the long-term potential of these relationships is enhanced. Thus, we all have a stake in ethical practice. It is important that each applied anthropologist share in the responsibility.

FURTHER READING

LeCompte, Margaret D., Jean J. Schensul, Margaret R. Weeks, and Merrill Singer. *Researcher Roles & Research Partnerships*. Walnut Creek, Calif.: AltaMira Press, 1999. This volume, part of a larger series on research methods, includes an introduction to research ethics including institutional review boards.

Part II

Approaches to Development
in Anthropology

Chapter 4

Anthropology in Development

Participatory development is a process in which the individuals and groups of a community work together on problems that they see as important in order to benefit their lives in some way. The process may both help a group achieve its goals and increase its capacity to achieve goals in the future. Although this process is a typical aspect of the life of healthy communities, there is potential that the process can be made more effective with the assistance of a trained practitioner of participatory development practice. The presence of a trained practitioner may be useful for increasing the rate of development activity, reducing internal conflict, and expanding the resource base. Participatory development practitioners can contribute to effectiveness by providing community facilitation skills, special knowledge of particular areas of technology such as education, public health and agriculture appraisal techniques, and linkages to the resources outside of the community.

Part II of the book includes chapters on various participatory methods. These include action research and participatory action research, cultural action, participatory rural appraisal, and collaborative anthropology. There are other methods which could be included. Cultural brokerage and social marketing are not usually thought of as participatory methods, but in fact they have a strong commitment to the same values.

The methods used are consistent with an anthropological perspective on the development process. This consistency includes concern for the meaning of the development process to the persons most affected, the members of

The authors of this chapter are John van Willigen, Elaine Drew, Carol Jo Evans, and Elizabeth Williams.

the communities undergoing development. As authors we place a value on "bottom up" processes that facilitate people to action that produces sustainable improvements in conditions of life in communities. The foundation of the process is respect for local knowledge.

There was a significant increase in the amount of anthropological involvement in the development process starting in the aftermath of World War II. At that point onward anthropologists were involved in a number of ways. These include serving as researchers in the development project planning and evaluation process, the developing of models for development action, and actual implementation of development. The first of these is the most frequent.

Before we begin these chapters that describe different approaches to development, we wanted to discuss concepts that we see as underlying contemporary development anthropology. In addition, we wanted to review the critique directed at contemporary development because this impinges on anthropologists involved.

ADDRESSING THE DEVELOPMENT CRITIQUE

The process of development entails societal change and the intentional activities necessary to bring such change about (Gardner and Lewis 1996). A suitable general definition states that development is "conscious pursuit of certain objectives with a view to increasing welfare" (Sandford 1983:4). This process may occur in any aspect of community life including economy, education, public health, nutrition, and so forth. While development implies something desirable, the process often has a negative aspect. Often large-scale economic development can increase social inequality that supports the interests of those who own property. Negative ecological consequences can also occur making environmental sustainability an important issue in development. There are also unintended consequences. A minimal cost of development is the opportunity cost. Doing two things at once is difficult.

The idea of development is closely tied to the nature of twentieth-century history. The ascent of technology and science in Europe inaugurated a new age of rationality, enlightenment, and the expansion of capitalism. One of the mechanisms of this process was imperial expansion and colonialism. The natives, or the colonized, were referred to as backward and irrational while, on the other hand, the colonizers were "rational agents of progress and development." This line of thinking led to the emergence of modernization theory, which emphasized the modernization of the natives out of their "traditional" ways. Industrialization and urbanization were the key processes in modernization. The antithesis of modernization theory was dependency theory, which was more concerned with the nature and causes of the "underdevelopment" of poor nations. Dependency theory emerged with a discussion of unequal exchange, inequitable distribution of resources across nations, and the ways in which such inequitable relations foster the dependency of poor nations on wealthier ones.

Modernization scholars of the 1960s saw development in evolutionary terms. They felt that countries had to "progress" through certain stages before they could be considered "developed" (Rostow 1960). Among other things, Rostow explored the factors that lead to developed or underdeveloped conditions. According to his analysis, development was equated with economic growth. A country that successfully goes through the various stages described by Rostow can be categorized as developed whereas those who are in the process can be described as developing.

Others argue that development of some wealthy countries produces underdevelopment. According to Escobar (1995), development is a process that has been produced historically. He argues that the period immediately after World War II saw an emergence of the concept of underdevelopment that was associated with the countries of the South (formerly referred to as underdeveloped), especially those in Africa, Asia, and Latin America. Underdevelopment was associated with poverty and backwardness, and this view, Escobar argues, emerged from the United States and Western Europe who regarded underdevelopment as a problem inherent in the countries of the South and therefore deserved immediate and concerted action to deal with it. New strategies were developed to cope with the problem of underdevelopment.

Gardner and Lewis (1996) point out that global problems of poverty and inequality cannot be explained by either modernization or dependency theories. Despite the tremendous contribution of these approaches to our comprehension of development, the South is still lingering in the seas of poverty, high rates of illiteracy, malnutrition, and political instability.

Furthermore, economic growth is often implicated in the development process, a point that is upheld by many development agencies including the World Bank (Gardner and Lewis 1996). Measurement of development is based on indices such as the Gross National Product (GNP) and per capita income. The argument in this case is that as the economy grows, there will be a corresponding growth in other sectors, such as education and health, thus positively affecting social indices such as infant mortality rates, illiteracy, and malnutrition (Gardner and Lewis 1996). This school of thought posits that as the economy grows, there will be a benefit to all citizens in the form of better education, better housing, and better health. This is the so-called "trickle-down effect." The shortcoming of this assumption is that the trickle-down process is slow and not pervasive. Unequal benefits of development are widely recognized. Therefore, the goals of development practitioners are often geared toward increasing equity in the distribution of benefits.

For example, in the development literature throughout the 1970s there was a focus on basic human needs with emphasis on poverty alleviation. This orientation in development program design involved what is commonly called "targeting." This view emphasizes societal welfare as compared to industrialization and modernization. The targeted beneficiaries were the masses of people living in countries of the South who were living without basic human needs. The target group was the vulnerable in the society such as small farmers and women-headed households (Gardner and Lewis 1996). The focus in this period was therefore to provide people with necessary help so that their standards of living could be improved. It is important to note that in this process, the attention was not on empowering or enabling the beneficiaries to provide for themselves, nor was the focus geared toward involving the local people in identifying and solving the constraints they faced in their efforts to secure livelihood.

Due to inherent drawbacks in development approaches of the past decades, there was an emerging consensus in the late 1980s and 1990s that saw development as a process that needed full participation from the local people. This approach held that local people should be the driving force behind any development initiative in their areas. The guiding premise was that "They know better than anyone else what is good for them and what their urgent needs are." Subsequently, they should have the opportunity to express their needs, desires, and solutions. Participatory approaches in development have indeed influenced many individuals and groups to rethink their roles regarding the whole process of development. Advocates of the participatory view emphasize the crucial need for involvement of the local people in the development process. Not only should local people be involved, they should be involved as problem identifiers and as main actors and decision makers. The foundation of this thought is the fact that the local people know the complexity, diversity, and dynamism of their environments better than the "outsiders" (Chambers 1997). Drawing from this theoretical premise, participation becomes a viable and promising way of development in rural as well as urban areas throughout the world in both the wealthy and poor countries. According to Chambers, there is a growing consensus on the goals of well-being for all: secure livelihood, enhancing the capabilities of the people, equity for all (especially the poor, weak, vulnerable, and exploited), and sustainable changes in the economic, social, institutional, and environmental domains of everyday life (Chambers 1997).

THE FOUNDATION IN IDEAS

Use of these ideas occurs in many disciplines. Anthropology has contributed to the development of these ideas and continues to make use of them. These include local knowledge, participation, empowerment, conscientization, and sustainable development.

Local Knowledge

This idea is now widely used in development circles and refers to knowledge and practices enmeshed in a local community. It is used in contrast with "expert knowledge" which is the technical information brought to the situation by trained outsiders such as agronomists, sanitarians, physicians, or foresters. It is sometimes referred to as indigenous knowledge (IK) or indigenous technical knowledge (ITK) although this label is thought of as somewhat confining to the extent that indigenous implies being limited to knowledge that is locally generated. It can also be referred to as "traditional knowledge" although this label suggests that the knowledge is unchanging. Local knowledge is dynamic and is continually tested and adapted to local needs.

Discussions of local knowledge often emphasize the role of systematic observation and experimental practices that are found in every community. Within development practice there has been a shifting of perspective away from the privileging of the knowledge of technically trained persons from outside the community to the valuing of the knowledge of the community itself. For example, in agricultural development, "instead of starting with the knowledge, problems, analysis and priorities of scientists, it starts with the knowledge, problems, analysis and priorities of farmers and farm families" (Chambers et al. 1989:xix).

While anthropologists have always been concerned with "local knowledge," explicit concern for this emerged little more than two decades ago in the development arena. This involved a reconceptualization of local knowledge. This went against the widely held view that "local knowledge" was uniform, static, and invalid, and that "expert knowledge" could provide an adequate foundation for development. More and more researchers realized that local knowledge systems were very much like the expert systems. They were dynamic, experimentally based, and were valuable for understanding how things worked. Increasingly, local knowledge came to have a role to play in the development process. Increasingly, researchers emphasize the fundamental similarities between the sciences of all the people of the world.

Success in development programs often requires paying attention to local knowledge. Local knowledge–based developments were often more sustainable. There are a number of reasons for this. Basing a project on local knowledge often means use of locally available, lower-cost resources rather than more costly materials brought into the community from outside. Local knowledge–based projects are usually better understood by the community and therefore more easily managed by them. Local knowledge–based projects can be more easily adapted to local circumstances. Emphasizing local knowledge in project planning can increase the likelihood that the project addresses local needs and circumstances. There may also be a decreased potential to create dependency on the part of the community. The use of a local knowledge–based approach is necessary to achieve participatory development.

As the development community has become more sensitive to the importance of local knowledge, there has also been increased economic exploitation of the producers of local knowledge. Critics of pharmaceutical companies that do "bioprospecting" in places like Amazonia say that the producers of "local drug knowledge" do not get adequate compensation. There has been more and more concern about protecting local knowledge as intellectual property (Greaves 1994).

Participation

What is participation? It can be represented by many words: involvement, representation, cooperation, and so on. But what is the true meaning of participation. Is it involvement? Is it representation? Is it cooperation? After all, the powerful can force the powerless to be involved in certain activities. Anyone can claim that she or he represents a certain group of people. Through various strategies, those in positions of power can often coerce others to cooperate. Again, is that participation?

Understanding the values or characteristics attached to participatory activities can help us understand its meaning. Self-determination is an important component. A participatory viewpoint requires one to understand the situation within which one operates and the role one plays in it. Participation derives from one's own consciousness and determination and awareness of the system.

Development anthropologists can strive toward a more democratic process, but must recognize at the start that no relationship is completely neutral. In order to strive toward a mutually beneficial and equitable relationship during the development process, practitioners can act ethically and responsibly to reduce risks and negative unintentional outcomes. Anthropologists do not deny as anthropologists the personal benefits of our own participation in such projects (financial, professional, political, and so forth). Instead, they start from the premise that participatory research is truly collaborative and as such, all collaborating parties ideally receive some benefit, whether material or nonmaterial.

Participation of the intended beneficiaries of development projects in the development process is widely advocated by most national and international development agencies. Because of this the word participation often appears in the literature on development agencies. Indeed some widely used techniques include "participation" in their names (see for example "participatory action research," "participatory rural appraisal," "participatory technology development," "participatory learning and action," "participatory impact monitoring," and "participatory monitoring and evaluation").

There is considerable difference between agency rhetoric and the extent to which development is participatory at the level of the local community. The extent to which a development effort is participatory can vary considerably. Participation ranges in a continuum that includes information sharing, consultation, collaboration, and finally, empowerment. Organizations that are committed to participation in their development programs may vary substantially. There will be a difference between the participation programming of a non-governmental organization like Oxfam and that of a large, quasi-governmental bureaucracy like the World Bank. Some have spoken about "pseudoparticipation," as occurs when community members are asked to ratify decisions made by the program managers rather than actually designing the projects (Uphoff 1991:478).

Participation is sometimes thought of as a new way of doing development, even trendy. Concern about participation of local people in the development process has existed for a very long time. There are clear antecedents in the mass education movement in the late 1940s. Rhetorically, participatory approaches are contrasted with approaches in which planning and implementation decisions are made by persons outside the community, usually by professional technicians or governmental bureaucracies. Because of this, people speak pejoratively about "technocratic" or "top down" development. A technocratic approach places little value on local knowledge and the capacity and potential of local organizations. This means that a participatory approach will tend to place a high value on local knowledge and organizations.

Participation almost has to involve local community organizations, either those which are established or newly constituted. There has been research done on the characteristics of community organizations that are more effective in participation (Uphoff 1991:496). Informally operated organizations seemed to work better than more formal ones. Organizations that work to share decision making through horizontal linkages seemed to work better. Size was a significant factor. Organizations that had linkages to governmental organizations did not tend to have better results. Organizations that were established by local leaders seemed to work better than those established by outsiders. In this regard often what is authentic participation in decision making by established traditional groups like a community council can be not very democratic. Sometimes women and poor people are not really part of the process.

Participation can occur at various stages of the project cycle and all sectors of a project. Participation can occur during research done in anticipation of project design, in project implementation, in benefits of the project, and in project monitoring and evaluation. One should look for the extent to which beneficiaries actually allocate resources to get a feeling for how participatory a project is.

There are a number of ways of ensuring participation of beneficiaries in project design and implementation:

1. *Have Explicit Goals and Designs.* The extent of participation must be made clear from the very beginning of the project. This should be done in such a way that it is acceptable to all persons involved.

2. *Have Realistic Expectations.* The goals of participation should be realistic. It is important to be sensitive to the time requirements of different segments of the project cycle. A fixed deadline can often be very disruptive to effective participation.

3. *Have an Organizational Framework.* Participation occurs in an organizational framework. This framework may be provided by existing local organizations. If these groups are inadequate or insufficient, culturally appropriate organizations need to be designed and supported. Development efforts may, if properly designed, result in strengthened organizations.

4. *Have an Adequate Resource Base.* There should be adequate financial investment to support participation.

5. *Be Concerned about the Whole Project Cycle.* Participation needs to occur during the entire project cycle from design to evaluation. (Cernea 1991a:465–466)

An important possible outcome of the participation process is empowerment.

Empowerment

Empowerment is a process whereby individuals or collectives of individuals move from a state of being simply acted upon to one in which they are initiating and directing control over their lives. Stated more succinctly, empowerment, as defined by Rappaport (1984:3) is, "the mechanism by which people, organizations, and communities gain mastery over their lives." An elusive concept, having developed out of the "social action" ideology of the 1960s and the "self-help" movements of the 1970s, empowerment is often best understood by what it is not—powerlessness, helplessness, hopelessness, and disenfranchisement, or those conditions in which an opinion is held that one's behavior cannot determine or control the outcomes that one seeks. Empowerment is the antithesis of these powerless states of being.

Empowerment, as a process of becoming, involves the cognitive and behavioral development of individuals or groups over a period of time. More specifically, empowerment entails the systematic and progressive cultivation of participatory skills and political understandings of those formerly without power. Incorporating individual's experiences, the process of empowerment develops within individuals and groups an awareness of the manifestations of powerlessness in their lives. The process of empowerment often results in people increasing their understanding of how such social and political inequities are institutionalized and impact them. This is the process of conscientization. Once awareness and understanding of the sources and forms of powerlessness are acquired, the next step in the process of empowerment is providing the individual or group with the tools necessary to address their own powerlessness.

Conscientization

Conscientization means the development of critical awareness of the structures that cause one's current circumstances. Brazilian educator Paulo Freire developed his method of conscientization, or the development of critical consciousness, as part of an effort to help Brazilian farming families learn to read and write (Freire 1997:17). More specifically, it is "learning to perceive social, political, and economic contradictions, and to take action against the oppressive elements of reality" (Freire 1997:17). Freire's program became popular in Brazil because people were learning to read and write in six weeks, while also learning their capabilities to change oppressive structures which kept them poor. Freire's main contribution to the literacy training was not speed, but helping poor Brazilian villagers overcome the feeling that they were too ignorant to learn (Werner and Bower 1982). In this work he discovered what he describes as the "culture of silence" of the dispossessed and poor who are too ignorant and tired to change the hegemonic forces which keep them poor. It became clear to him that the whole educational system was one of the major instruments for the maintenance of this culture. He believed people had the power as individuals to attain a critical consciousness of their own being in the world, to recognize and understand historic forces influencing their place in the world, and develop the ability to change that world. His pedagogical method consisted of naming the problem, reflecting on the problem, and then acting on the problem.

Sustainable Development

Decreasing poverty was an important goal of many development programs funded by organizations such as the World Bank and bilateral agencies like the U.S. Agency for International Development. With the advent of the environmental movement came an increased governmental concern about environmental impacts. This in turn influenced development programming. In response to this, the idea of sustainable development emerged. This complex idea was given more concrete focus through the World Commission on Environment and Development (also called the

Brundtland Commission), which was established by the United Nations in 1983. The commission defined sustainable development as "development that meets the needs of the present without compromising the ability of future generations to meet their own needs" (Brundtland Report 1987:43).

The issue of sustainability has come to be expressed in a wide range of themes in addition to economic development. These include biodiversity, climate change, soil and water conservation, efficient and renewable energy use, air quality, solid waste, population planning, forestation, and alternative agriculture. Increasing discussions about sustainability have come to recognize the environmental problem in terms of a complex web that includes the environment, economic equity, and social integrity. The concern for equity and poverty reduction addresses the concern about political sustainability as well as more narrowly conceived environmental concerns. Equity issues are especially important, given their tendency to associate environmental concerns with elite interests.

Increasingly the organizations that fund development projects structure their programs and policies to address the long-term environmental impact of their projects. As a result, there is more concern about sustainability issues in project planning.

SUMMARY

The development anthropologists of today make use of a complex array of ideas that were nascent when anthropologists were first involved in development activities directly in the 1950s and 1960s. They function as part of a complex of practices and ideas that have emerged starting in the 1970s and include the ideas that are the core of this chapter. These are local knowledge, participation, empowerment, conscientization, and sustainable development. Previously anthropologists made use of approaches to development that were from within the discipline. These included research and development anthropology and action anthropology. Though not widely used, these approaches represented effective means of achieving goals of development within the context of the anthropological worldview. These approaches were major departures from the traditional role of the anthropological researcher that most anthropologists still think of as a core of the experience of being an anthropologist. What has emerged over the last two decades is a complex of ideas and practices that are not part of a particular discipline. These ideas develop and change in response to the challenges faced by practitioners. Contemporary development practices, like contemporary research practices, are influenced by many and owned by none. Because they are good ideas, they are widely used. Much of the current tradition of practice has been very heavily influenced by anthropology. It may be because of this that anthropologists are comfortable with the ideas and practices. The following chapters of Part II present various approaches used by anthropologists working in development.

FURTHER READING

Chambers, Robert. *Whose Reality Counts? Putting the First Last.* London: Intermediate Technology Publications, 1997. The works of Robert Chambers are foundation texts for a person committed to participatory development.

Brundtland Report. World Commission on Environment and Development. *Our Common Future.* Oxford: Oxford University Press, 1987. This document is frequently cited in discussions of sustainability.

Chapter 5

Action Research and Participatory Action Research

Action research (AR) and participatory action research (PAR) are methods of research and social action that occur when individuals of a community join together with a professional researcher to study and transform their community in ways that they mutually value. The idea of cogeneration of understanding is often part of AR and PAR discussions. The "community" for an action project can be a neighborhood, village, school, organization, or any social group in which members want to enact some change. This broad definition of community gives AR and PAR potential to deal with many different kinds of problems in many different settings. For example, PAR has been used to develop nonviolent alternatives to tribal infighting among the Enga of Papua New Guinea (Young 1997), to provide HIV prevention education to women in San Francisco (Stevens and Hall 1998), to examine a worker cooperative complex in a small Basque city in Spain (Greenwood et al. 1992; Whyte and Whyte 1988), and to support business development in Norway (Greenwood and Levin 1998).

In discussing AR and PAR it is important to note that some writers make a clear distinction between AR and PAR while others treat the two terms as more or less synonymous. It is useful to sort through the issues. The term action research was used first. Participatory action research is historically derived from action research. Early action research literature continues to be useful to participatory action research practitioners. The idea of PAR emerged to stress the participatory and non-dominating orientation of practitioners and to separate the practice from examples of co-optation of the approach by the business community. Greenwood and Levin draw

The authors of this chapter are Elaine Drew, Wini P. Utari, and John van Willigen.

a good example of this from industrial management. They say "One way of achieving the currently fashionable goal of total quality management is by involving the work force more fully in the life of the business. This is often framed as increasing participation, and recently, some conventional organizational development consultants have begun calling their work PAR" (Greenwood and Levin 1998:180). Greenwood and Levin talk about both under the rubric of AR (Greenwood and Levin 1998). While we maintain the terminological distinction, our view is essentially identical to Greenwood and Levin.

DEVELOPMENT OF THE APPROACH

Kurt Lewin coined the term *action research* (Greenwood and Levin 1998: 17). He was a social psychologist whose interest was focused on social change. Greenwood and Levin see "Lewin's work is a fundamental building block of what today is called AR" (Greenwood and Levin 1998:19). His ideas emerged in a series of applied research projects done in the 1940s.

AR has very early linkages to anthropology. During his service at the Bureau of Indian Affairs, John Collier called for anthropologists to support action research (see, for example, the work of Laura Thompson 1950). In addition to Collier's work, Lewin himself worked in association with Margaret Mead in the American Food Habits Project. As applied anthropology gained more formal recognition in the discipline, AR was promoted as a way to work against the "professional expert model." In other words, applied participatory research worked to minimize the authoritative power of the researcher and grant legitimacy to the local knowledge of community members. While early "participatory research" was not always linked to action objectives, it did make an attempt to include community members in the research process—from data collection through analysis and sometimes in publication.

Action research, according to Lewin, "consisted in analysis, fact-finding, conceptualization, planning, execution, more fact-finding or evaluation; and then a repetition of this whole circle of activities; indeed a spiral of such circles" (Lewin quoted in Kemmis 1980:3). Lewin also put forth the idea that research should be evoked by the needs of people for a particular action, and that the research techniques should be integrative of a wide variety of tools able to accomplish that action. The core idea of AR is that research will be more valid and there is a greater likelihood of it being used by a community when the community has meaningful participation in the research process (Argyris and Schon 1991:86).

KEY CONCEPTS

Research

One of AR's strengths as an approach is its process leads to the generation of new and powerful knowledge. The knowledge constructed during the inquiry process leads to social action, and the reflections on actions also lead to the construction of new knowledge. Parallel with Lewin's criteria on judging a good theory, AR uses "workability" (defined as an ability to support practical problem solving in real-life situations) to judge the credibility/validity of good knowledge.

Participation

Participation has a strong value in AR. Participatory process is understood to create a strong commitment to the knowledge generation process and enable participants to take some responsibilities in increasing their control over their own lives.

Action

AR is a research with a social agenda. It aims to alter the initial situations in the direction of a more self-managing, liberated state. The action grows out of the research experience. In contrast with most applied research, the users of the research are the same as the researchers. This makes knowledge use much more likely.

THE PARTICIPATORY ACTION RESEARCH PROCESS

The PAR process begins when members of a community recognize some problem they want to change. Once the problem is presented to a professional researcher either by community members, an extension agent, another researcher, or an agency, she or he begins communication with community members. At this preliminary stage, the professional researcher should work to gain thorough knowledge of the community in question by doing a complete literature review and answering a few basic questions: What is the context of the community? What is the political organization? If the community is governed by particular individuals, will those individuals grant access to their community for a PAR project? Have other development projects been attempted in this community before? How might the successes or failures of those projects impact the potential for success for another development project? In what venues might the researcher introduce herself/himself to the community? Questions such as these represent a general reconnaissance on the area of general interest. Anthropological research methods such as ethnography, participant observation, interviews, field notes, archival analysis, and case studies often form the basis of this initial exploration.

Both AR and PAR place a high value on local knowledge. According to Greenwood and Levin, "AR is based on the affirmation that all human beings have detailed, complex, and valuable knowledge about their lives, environments, and goals" (1998:109). This contrasts with scholarly knowledge of academic experts in that it is part of people's actual lives. The action researcher serves to bridge everyday knowledge and the knowledge of the "expert" by engaging them in a cogeneration process. Greenwood and Levin call this "cogenerative learning" (1998:110). This has two potential positive outcomes. The local community can be enhanced, and the goals of the researchers can also be served.

Typically, the PAR process includes problem identification, information gathering, mobilization of community members who are affected, collaborative analysis and critical reflection, collaborative planning, action, and new reflection. Despite the linear representation, these stages do not occur in a neat and orderly progression, but often occur simultaneously. In fact, many PAR practitioners envision the PAR process as an ongoing spiral of action and reflection. Furthermore, participation occurs at every level of the PAR process. Thus, the stage referred to as "mobilization of participation" simply refers to the continuous efforts of current participants to gain and sustain representative participation and interest.

Identify Problems and Constraints

If a community has not already identified a problem for a PAR project, members working with a professional researcher can utilize several strategies to generate themes for evaluation. Of course, the decision about which strategies to apply should be made by the community. One strategy members might apply is an exploratory questionnaire. In this questionnaire, the researcher working with key informants constructs basic questions about community needs, usually regarding a variety of domains, such as health, agriculture, environment, economy, education, and so forth. The questionnaire can be mailed, hand delivered, or simply asked informally and noted as members talk to other members of the community.

Once a problem has been identified, the researcher along with community members can begin to discuss how they want to acquire more information. For example, members of a community may decide to conduct more formal, in-depth interviews with other community members, attempting to gain a representative sample of the community if it is large, or a complete sample if it is small. Informal interviewing and participant observation often yield important information for professional and community researchers to share with other participants. Focus groups can also help to gauge the level of interest, resources, and constraints for various problems.

If more than one problem is identified for action, the facilitator may implement several techniques to help members prioritize their action objectives, such as pair-wise ranking. The goal of this phase is to work with community members to define a PAR project.

Participation

Once a problem has been identified and targeted for PAR, community members along with the professional researcher continue to seek out additional support and resources from members. At this stage, a community may also seek out the advice of technical experts from outside the community. Here, it is important to remember that participation can take many forms: individual communications with the professional researcher or other community members, group discussions or focus groups, joint committees, and/or task forces. The form, frequency, and duration of participation will depend on the context of the PAR project. After all, the "degree of participation achieved in any particular project is the joint result of the character of the problem and environmental conditions under study, the aims and capacities of the research team, and the skills of the professional researcher" (Greenwood et al. 1992:175). No matter what form of participation is utilized, it is necessary for the researcher to clearly define what she or he means by *participation*. As Whyte, Greenwood, and Lazes suggest, "[s]ome aspects of those descriptions can be buttressed by measurement: how many people were involved in the participation process, how often and over what period of time they participated in it, how many proposals for change were initiated by [subjects themselves] . . . how many proposals were actually implemented" and so on (Whyte et al. 1991:52).

Collect Data

Data collection actually begins with the very first conversation about the PAR project. During data collection, participants become researchers themselves as they continue to dialogue with other community members and begin to gain a deeper awareness of the problem. Data might include interview transcripts, fieldnotes, literature reviews, seminars, focus group results, archival research, and so on. Some participants might also utilize reflective personal journals as important sources of data. Also during data collection, participants may seek out the advice of other professionals (economists, bank officials, extension agents, public health officials, and so forth) to gain specific or technical information.

Critical Reflection

As research participants begin to dialogue about their situation, they enter into the process of critical reflection. Throughout this process, members examine and construct general themes then evaluate and reconstruct those themes from a more critical perspective. This phase is difficult to define, as it tends to be a more abstract psychological process of individual and community awareness.

Planning

Planning emerges from the solutions proposed by participants. Plans for action also include discussions of how much participation is needed, how to obtain necessary resources, and plans for continuous evaluation.

Action

Action occurs when local participants and other collaborators begin to put the plan into action such that the improved social situation occurs.

Evaluation—New Reflection

Participants observe the action and continue to dialogue about the positive/negative outcomes. Participants may even become critical of their original plan and reconstruct a new plan. The cycle of social change continues with simultaneous action/reflection. The cycle continues until the group is satisfied with the outcomes. Usually a PAR project will go through two or more "PAR cycles." However, it is not unrealistic for a project to continue indefinitely in this fashion.

THE MONDRAGON INDUSTRIAL COOPERATIVE AR PROJECT IN THE BASQUE COUNTRY: A CASE STUDY

The Mondragon Cooperatives, located in the highly-populated and industrialized Basque region of Spain, are well-known examples of industrial democracy and worker ownership and participation. Because of their size and success as labor-managed organizational alternatives to advanced capitalism, Mondragon is the subject of substantial writing and analysis by social scientists (Greenwood et al. 1992; Whyte and Whyte 1988).

The financial structure of the cooperative and its membership is an important part of the Mondragon story. Each worker-member pays a fee equivalent to a year's wages; this funds the worker-owner's "capital account" and defines the person's economic stake in the cooperative. The participants receive pay and increments to their capital account. These dis-

tributions are based on economic performance of the cooperative and capital needs of the organization. Pay distribution is based on a job
classification. The ratio of top-paying jobs to low-paying jobs is low by
American standards at 6:1. As part of this, the "managers" are paid less
than they would be under typical capitalist organization. The managers are
elected by the workers to four-year terms and are subject to recall (Greenwood and Levin 1998:43).

The cooperatives were founded in the 1950s with five leaders and thirteen coworkers. Currently there are nearly 200 cooperatives with over
30,000 worker-owners involved in the production of industrial robots, machine tools, semiconductors, computer circuit boards, household appliances
such as refrigerators, electrical and plumbing supplies, and foods. They also
offer various services including cooking and janitorial services. The AR
project took place within the Fagor Group the largest of the many cooperative groups.

A team, including anthropologist Davydd Greenwood, was involved in
a four-year AR project which was focused on solving some of the cooperative's problems. The project started with a consultation between the
Fagor director of personnel and William Foote Whyte, and later Greenwood. This resulted in the development of some proposals to do research
on the cooperative. In a general sense the project was to increase the social
research capacity of the cooperative. The cooperative already had economic
research capability that was well developed.

AR started with mutual visits. Greenwood taught a summer course in
AR. The AR team consisted of second generation cooperative members.
The underlying question had to do with the problems of integrating new
members into the ideology of the organization and the adaptability of the
coop. Much of the early work of the team focused on reading the relevant
literature on the cooperative. Greenwood describes aspects of this part of
the process: "We explored the constant use of dichotomies to stereotype
desired and disapproved behavior in the cooperatives and to contrast the
cooperatives with ordinary businesses" (Greenwood and Levin 1998:144).
The team developed approaches that helped them better understand the
cooperative through research practices that were consistent with cooperative principles. The research was "self-managed, open-ended and practically
useful" (Greenwood and Levin 1998).

The process by which this emerged was difficult. There were misunderstandings about roles. Initially, at least, the Fagor members of the team
expected that Greenwood would be more directive and that he would express an expert's role. Instead, "His goal was to develop a research mindset
through which members could learn new things about themselves, find
counterintuitive information, and develop action plans that linked these
findings to appropriate actions" rather than to simply come in and do the
research (Greenwood and Levin 1998:45). In this way Greenwood worked

to overcome the rest of the team's traditional conception of social research. The path out of this situation involved reading and reflecting on the existing literature on Mondragon. The AR team disliked this literature, feeling that it was a misrepresentation. Greenwood advocated that they needed to take charge of the depiction of themselves. This is where the project actually started.

This said, it is important to note that the team learned many social research techniques as well as produced a reinterpretation of itself. "In particular, the team came to believe that organizational culture in Fagor set the terms of conflict and contradiction in the group, and that the strength of the system was not found in absence of conflict but in commitment to broad goals and a set of rules of debate" (Greenwood and Levin 1998:45–46).

The process is research based. Much of the research consisted of focus groups and long series of interviews with the most alienated. Selection of the persons to be interviewed was an important part of the process. The data collection concluded with "a series of focus groups in which the team members subjected their most important values about cooperative life to open questioning: participation, solidarity, and the freedom of information" (Greenwood and Levin 1998:46). The research actively sought conflicts and contradictions in Fagor and found them. They concluded that the concern that experienced members had with new members was misdirected and even self-serving. They discovered that many of the problems grew out of the practices of the personnel department rather than a failure of new members to get it right. Many of the practices of the administration were inconsistent with the cooperative principles of the organization.

PAR FOR PRIMARY HEALTH CARE DEVELOPMENT IN A PHILIPPINE COMMUNITY: A CASE STUDY

Since the World Health Organization's Alma Ata Declaration in 1978, primary health care (PHC) has been the governing agenda behind global health development programs. Particular PHC programs took various shapes depending on the agency or sponsor. The PHC strategy meant a de-emphasis on urban-based, high-technology, and curative medical care. Instead, attention was redirected toward community-based preventive health programs that would rely on low-cost, appropriate technologies to meet the basic health needs as defined by local people through participatory processes (Coreil and Mull 1990:xiii). This subtle departure from top-down policies demonstrated the incorporation of social science research that had long affirmed the importance of community involvement to the long-term success of PHC projects.

Since PAR includes community participation throughout the development process, and since participation and motivation among community members often increases sustainability, PAR may provide successful strategies for implementing sustainable PHC in various communities. Today, many PHC planners are gearing their projects toward high community participation and "bottom-up" development.

Funded by Canadian sources, the De La Salle University Research Center in the Philippines conducted a PAR project among a forest-dwelling people inhabiting the rugged interior of the island Mindoro province in the Philippines. The nearly 6,000 Hanunoo live in the grassy woodlands of the southeastern part of the island. Settlements tend to be relatively small, usually with five or six one-family dwellings each. The Hanunoo have been characterized as a monogamous, bilaterally structured society with both men and women participating in locally important economic activities, and mainly shifting agriculture (Conklin 1975). While both women and men are regarded as complements of each other, particularly in terms of subsistence and general economic production, the gendered division of labor among the Hanunoo has a significant influence on the local health care system.

In terms of subsistence activities, Hanunoo women do much of the farming: weeding, planting, and burning (although decisions about the location of the plot are to be made by the husband). In terms of community decision making, women tend to have less power than men. However, since women are the primary caretakers of the household and of the children, the domain of health care has been constructed primarily as a woman's area of authority.

Health planners observing these local structures of authority, and taking into account the recent movement in PHC development toward the empowerment of women in local communities, decided to approach the Hanunoo women for training as health care workers. Researchers thought that women would be empowered by their new roles as local health care workers, particularly since they would be in charge of planning, managing, controlling, and assessing the collective actions of community members.

Among the Hanunoo, the biggest health concerns were poor nutrition, sanitation problems, and a lack of basic health care. The overall quantity of food consumed is low and strongly influenced by the seasons. During the months of June through September, families may eat very little or go without food. Sickness itself is attributed to two general domains of causation: the evil spirits that inhabit the landscape around them, or natural explanations such as injury from an accident, insect bites, or burns. Local healers usually prescribe herbal remedies for "natural" ailments, but rely on good spirits to help them cure someone who has become the victim of an evil spirit.

The PAR project was conducted to evaluate the effectiveness of establishing a community-based health care system through training of local members, the use of indigenous knowledge and resources, and active participation from the community in planning the new health care system. The reason that the development researchers applied PAR is because they wanted the program to be culturally appropriate and to take into consideration the local social, political, and economic dynamics of the community to maximize sustainability and capacity building. Researchers hypothesized that if they worked within local structures and coordinated the participatory action research with local members, that a decentralized system of health care could encourage cooperation among the members and provide the best chance of fully realizing better health in the community.

Two villages that had not been visited by other health personnel during the previous year were selected to participate in the study. The project was conducted through three general phases. The first phase consisted of gathering information within the community to gain general knowledge of the local health conditions and get members' input in priority health concerns. This phase also helped the "outsiders" to understand local constructions of sickness and healing, or what medical anthropologists call "ethnomedicine." The second phase of research centered around the actual formulation and implementation of the PAR project. The third phase began after 15 months and focused on an overall evaluation and assessment of the project and its strengths and weaknesses. In order to evaluate the success of the new health care delivery system, researchers utilized household surveys and an assessment of local health workers who had been trained during the project. As a result of this last phase, researchers hoped to learn valuable lessons and to then be in a better position to make recommendations to other PHC planners about the sustainability and replicability of PAR projects for PHC development.

During the initial phase of research, four local healers were identified who became part of the research team. These healers discussed local perceptions of nutritional status, sanitation, and local desires for basic health services. Meanwhile, clinicians were invited to participate in the study to examine household members in the village to gain a general sense of the variety of health problems within the community. Among the problems were high infant mortality, upper respiratory infections, skin diseases, parasitism, malaria, and nutritional anemia. Sanitation was extremely poor in the villages, with most of the household members using the bush for defecation and open springs and streams for their water supply. Waste was disposed of mainly by open dumping of garbage.

Once researchers had gained information working with local community members, they decided that a community-based health program would have the best chance for success. Since researchers were working from a PHC perspective, they contacted the Ministry of Health. A committee made up of a ministry representative, the medical consultant, a public health consultant, and a project nurse was formed to create a manual. The manual targeted key information about basic health care and consisted of sketches of daily life. After the manual was reviewed and approved by the committee, the project nurse and the local midwife were trained to become trainers in their communities. At this time, community assemblies were held to find out what the community at large regarded as its primary health concerns and what they also considered as possible solutions. During the assemblies, the communities selected 30 women to become *Doktor sa Barangay* (DSB) on the basis of their interests and perceived abilities.

The DSBs were then trained by the nurse and the midwife through lectures, hands-on instruction, and practicum. The DSBs were then assigned to particular areas of the region as field workers, while the nurse maintained the central health facility for consultation with the DSBs as well as her own clinical duties.

As more women became interested in the role of the DSB, the number grew to 37 women only four months into the project. At the end of the 15 months of project implementation, researchers conducted an assessment of the PAR project through local interviews with health workers, household surveys, survey of the village health committee members, and a skills assessment of the DSBs. The results revealed a slight improvement in sanitation facilities, a slight reduction in childhood mortality, and an increase in basic awareness of disease etiologies. Researchers also noted a reduction in the prevalence of upper respiratory infections, skin diseases, anemia, malaria, and pulmonary tuberculosis.

Since the project required the participation of the Ministry of Health, the project was constrained from the start. However, as Osteria and Ramos-Jimenez point out, PHC is based on three general components: community participation, voluntary village health work, and appropriate technology. "Part of the failure in getting the community to participate . . . arises from trying to impose an alien bureaucratic notion of participation rather than seeking to achieve it through the traditional structure of the village" (Osteria and Ramos-Jimenez 1988:227). Of course, community participation does not automatically ensure that all local needs will be met. After all, the services are usually geared toward basic needs and may not immediately enhance the preventive measures needed to maximize community health in future generations.

From the overall project assessment, the researchers realized several key areas of concern: the selection of voluntary health workers, community participation, training, incentives and rewards, supervision, and support. Since women were already in charge of household health care, the use of volunteer women from the village—as well as community participation at large—was considered central to the overall implementation of the PHC project. Since the project was collaborative throughout all phases of the action research, researchers hoped that the "resulting increase in cooperative interaction would lead to a more united community and act as a catalytic force for further development efforts as it creates a sense of responsibility to act on the expressed needs for using indigenous knowledge" (Osteria and Ramos-Jimenez 1988:229). Researchers also realized some of the unintended consequences of the PHC project.

Since the households were set far apart (due to the use of shifting cultivation), women had little motivation to visit the households. Furthermore, since women are the primary caregivers in the household, women had very little time to devote to an outside job before the job became burdensome. The instructions for local health workers assume that a few local members will be able to manage a wide range of functions—home visits, environmental sanitation, providing a safe water supply, first aid for injuries, treatment of simple and common ailments, health education, nutrition, maternal and child health, family planning, and record keeping. Certainly it is absurd to think that these women could take on such tasks and still take care of their households, their children, their husbands, and their farms.

Women's morale was also affected by the lack of confidence that some local households had in their abilities as DSBs. Furthermore, training the women was difficult due to language barriers and low literacy level. And finally, the village health committees made up of local members were harder to establish than initially thought because local members were not as interested in sustained activities.

Clearly, the project among the Hanunoo has its problems. However, as a result of the project, Osteria and Ramos-Jimenez argue that perhaps PHC planners will realize that the "disparity between the magnitude of the results expected and the meager resources and efforts expended is considerable: too much is expected from too little input." This advice basically means that PHC planners need to take seriously the problems surrounding community motivation, resources, incentives, and rewards. In this case, women were probably the best candidates for DSBs due to the pre-existing role of women as managers of family health. However, since women are already heavily burdened with work, taking on the role of DSB on a voluntary basis necessarily means that the DSBs can only work part-time. "The best solution to encourage sustained activity seems to be the incentive scheme for the voluntary worker—that is, the provision of nominal payment or payment in kind" (Osteria and Ramos-Jimenez 1988:231).

Furthermore, health workers need to be supported by an entire network of community members, including technical, supervisory, referral, and logistic support. An important ethical consideration here lies in the fact that community members—particularly the very poor members—come to expect the provision of basic services. When those expectations are not met, the community begins to lose faith in the abilities of the health system and it eventually fails. If PHC is to be successful, it needs to take the PAR approach seriously and work to gain full participation. Furthermore, the process needs to be much more collaborative and cogenerative as opposed to some model of the "health care system" being imposed from the top-down.

SUMMARY

Action research and participatory action research represent a useful array of practices that address local needs in a constructive, capacity-building way. The AR and PAR literature is rich and consistent with the community orientation of anthropologists. Anthropologists have contributed to the development of these approaches since they were originally developed. The process will tend to incorporate local knowledge and address local needs by its cogenerative nature. The action research traditions inevitably link research and action. There is a substantial use of these approaches in many different settings.

FURTHER READING

Greenwood, Davydd J. and Morten Levin. *Introduction to Action Research: Social Research for Social Change.* Thousand Oaks, Calif.: Sage, 1998. This is an invaluable contemporary statement on action research and participatory action research. The stance is both intellectually reflective and practical.

WEB SITE

http://www.parnet.org/.

Chapter 6

Cultural Action

Cultural action is a process directed at changing the relationships between poor people and power elite. People are poor because of the political economic structures that exist in the world. It takes an essentially cultural approach to deal with the factors which cause poverty and powerlessness. The word "cultural" refers to the fact that the process deals directly with the community's knowledge and understanding about their situation. The essence of cultural action is the process by which a community, through reflection and study, can better understand those factors which cause their predicament and through this understanding achieve a release from these circumstances or their own liberation. It is highly participatory and focused on increasing self-determination in the context of cultural dominance and oppression. This approach is sometimes called radical or liberation pedagogy.

Some of the ideas that constitute cultural action are widely used in contemporary education in America. Direct use by anthropologists is far more common in Latin America than in the United States. Nevertheless Freirean thought is part of community development discourse in the United States. What is rooted in Brazilian radical thought is in part now mainstream innovative educational practice on most American college campuses. It can be seen in the emphasis on critical thinking, and active and participatory learning.

Portions of this chapter were published in Cultural Action: Theory, Process and Practices, *High Plains Applied Anthropologist* 16(1):9–18, 1996. The authors are Barbara A. Cellarius, Deborah Crooks, Patricia Kannapel, Juliana McDonald, Cynthia Reeves, and John van Willigen.

DEVELOPMENT OF THE APPROACH

The *cultural action* approach was developed by Brazilian educator Paulo Freire (1921–1997) as a means for liberating illiterate Brazilian peasants from oppression by the elite. He came to the approach through his own life experiences. The approach is also called Freirean method.

Freire was born in Recife, Brazil, to a middle-class family. Though middle-class, he did experience poverty as a young person during the Great Depression of the 1930s. His father died while he was young which made it necessary for him to be a family bread winner. This experience was formative in his development. He was trained in law but choose a career in education. Elza Maria Costa de Oliveira, to whom he was married, was an important influence on his life. She was a teacher. Through her commitment to assisting the poor through education, his own consciousness was raised. He came to learn about *Catholic action* and *basic church communities*, ideas associated with liberation theology (Taylor 1993:22).

Freire expressed the idea that domination, aggression, and violence are intrinsic parts of social life. This is often expressed in terms of race, class, and gender but can also be based on religious beliefs, political affiliation, national origin, age, and physical or mental disabilities. His ideas were first put into practice among the very poor people of the impoverished northeast of Brazil. He was successful in bringing literacy to hundreds of poor farm families. He soon became the director of Brazil's national literacy program which became very successful. He was attacked by the right-wing, land-owning elite. Freire was forced into exile following a military coup in 1964. He developed his mode of practice further while working with poor farmers in Chile (1964–1969). His ideas are described in his classic statement on radical education, *Pedagogy of the Oppressed* (1970) and many other volumes. He established the Institute of Cultural Action in conjunction with the World Council of Churches in Geneva, Switzerland. His return to Brazil was in 1990 under a general amnesty declared by the government. Paulo Freire died in 1997. His work continues to influence educators, anthropologists, and other social scientists.

The reason his approach came to be widely used is that Freire and his associates did not just teach literacy in a decontextualised way but emphasized the relationship between literacy and participation in the political process. This helped the poor see their own potential and capacity. Literacy, instead of being unobtainable, is something that everyone can aspire to.

KEY CONCEPTS

Cultural action incorporates a large number of special terms that reflect a specific view of the world and understandings about how the structures of the world can be changed. Many of the terms are derived from Marxist thought and resonate with critical social theory. While this terminology is useful, the meanings are often obscured by convoluted prose that seems to be intent on creating jargon meaningful to a specific intellectual community.

The Freirean view sees the world as consisting of dominating power elites and the people they oppress. Oppression is associated with poverty and distorts the knowledge and understanding poor people have about the world and the reason for their place in it. This is the process of alienation. As the elites control wealth they also control the understandings the poor have of their situation. Another way of saying this is that the elites control the content of the culture of the poor. Under these circumstances the culture of the poor becomes inauthentic because it is basically structured by the power elites. This line of thinking illustrates Freire's use of the basic ideas of cultural anthropology. For example, Freire uses the idea of culture in way that is consistent with the way that it has been used in anthropology. Culture consists of what humans have constructed both material and immaterial—buildings and artifacts on the one hand, and ideology and symbols on the other. The key task of cultural action is to make it possible for oppressed people to take control of how they are depicted.

The concepts of humanization and authenticity are central to Freire's thinking and to the method of cultural action. Humanization is a process in which one becomes truly free and authentically human. Authentic humans control their own culture. Freire believes that this should be the ultimate human occupation. To be human is to be neither oppressed nor oppressor. Although elites in a society may see themselves as more "human" than others, Freire argues that their humanness lacks authenticity. By virtue of the fact that they oppress others, the elites cannot be truly free nor can those who are oppressed be free as they are complicit in their own oppression. According to Freire, authentic humanness and authentic freedom cannot be achieved by simply attaining a higher status in a corrupt system; they can only be obtained by throwing off that system so that both freedom from oppression and freedom of oppressing can be obtained.

Freire gives this example: a peasant moves through the system to become a landowner. The peasant has internalized the oppressive aspects of the system by taking on the landowner's attitudes and behaviors. Although the peasant has achieved a measure of freedom in that he or she is no longer a possession or object in the inventory of the landowner, authentic liberation has still not been achieved. The individual who now possesses material, whether in the form of people or material items, is still denied freedom. Conditions of humanity are not achieved.

Freire's philosophy has straightforward implications for education. Educating others to take part in a dehumanizing system accomplishes little more than the maintenance of the status quo. Freire calls for a humanizing pedagogy that is constructed through a dialogue between student(s) and teacher(s) that is based on relevant topics. The topics are not imposed by others, but are generated by the students themselves. This allows the students to move beyond the dehumanizing system in which knowledge is defined and controlled by the elite to the creation of a system in which knowledge is defined by all and controlled by none.

Under these terms, the process of humanization is freely negotiated among all parties, by coequals, enabling all to achieve their own authentic humanity. According to Freire, this process should be the same whether applied to education, research, or revolution. Truly liberating education, research, or revolution requires that all are active and equal participants *in* the process, not simply objects *of* the process. When this occurs, authenticity and humanness are achieved.

Freire's ideas about education reflect his thoughts about humanization. He conceptualizes two approaches to education: the banking approach and the problem-posing approach. The banking approach, traditionally used in schools and academic settings, is an act of depositing knowledge, with the teacher as depositor and the student as depository. The teacher is viewed as the holder of knowledge while the student is viewed as an empty receptacle. The role of the teacher is to fill the student with knowledge by narrating content to them. The role of the student is to listen and memorize the content presented. Freire sees an underlying motive in the use of the banking approach: the dominant class indoctrinates the subordinate class with its view of reality and stifles any creative powers within the subordinate class that might lead it to recognize true reality and rise up against the elites. Banking education is an important mechanism for the production of alienation.

The problem-posing approach, in contrast, is characterized by a student-teacher partnership in which the two engage in dialogue and reflection, each learning from the other, each teaching the other. Problems of human beings and their relations to the world are presented for reflection by both teacher and student. Students discuss, or dialogue in Freire's terms, these problems with the teacher, engage in critical thinking in order to arrive at an understanding of the problems, develop solutions to those problems with that understanding, and then implement a plan of action using those solutions.

In Freire's view, the problem-posing approach is revolutionary in that it does not accept a static view of the past and present, nor a predetermined view of the future. It also does not assume superior knowledge on the part of the teacher. This approach assists teachers and students in recognizing that their situation is not a matter of unalterable fate but is instead a problem that can be understood and solved.

This first goal of radical pedagogy shows the relationship between thinking and acting that should exist for change to occur. Conscientization is defined as "learning to perceive social, political, and economic contradictions, and to take action against the oppressive elements of reality" (Freire 1970:19). It is the process of developing consciousness that has the power to transform reality. Conscientization can be thought of as a method of liberating education that humanizes its participants. It is an intentional process of critical awareness of the world, and those who become conscientized "are able to discover the reason why things are the way they are" (Gadotti 1994:166). Poverty, illness, and other problems have structural causes. A conscientized person understands the structures that cause poverty and illness to be.

Conscientization is different from "consciousness raising" which means the promotion of preselected information about a specific topic consistent with the interests of the people doing the speaking. The idea of consciousness raising implies a kind of cultural superiority (Berger 1974).

Conscientization involves the process by which people discover the experiences that have structured their world. In the terminology of Freirian analysis these are represented as generative themes. Generative themes are codifications of aspects of the reality that people face every day of their lives. These generative themes are a large class of knowledge about the particular situation that the people find themselves in, and may be found in words, phrases, expressions, characteristic ways of speaking, of composing verses, and of talking about the world (Gadotti 1994:19). Generative themes emerge through a dialectical process which takes place between the facilitator and the people from the community. These themes are ideas, concepts, expressions that are known to the people. They are selected for investigation because of their relevance to their lives and their capacity to generate the ability of the people to confront the social, cultural, and political reality in which they live. The themes must suggest and mean something important to the people of the community. Through the study of these generative themes, two goals of radical pedagogy may be attained: conscientization and praxis.

Praxis is thinking about and acting upon the world around us. It is the process by which the cultural world is created and the physical world is transformed. The world exists because humans are conscious of it and this consciousness of self and of the world is what makes humans unique and different from all other species. In order to exist, to be in the world, humans must act upon and transform the world. The purpose of humans in this existence is to act in ways that will create a full and rich life for both individuals and for the collective group. Humans are capable of thought and action, which are both at the heart of the meaning of praxis.

Through action and thought, humans can solve the problems of their immediate existence. By solving problems, history is made, and humans are aware of the history which they have created. Humans recognize their past in this history, are aware that they are creating history, and have the ability to create the history of future generations. This framework of the realization of past, present, and future is part of the definition of human existence.

Praxis consists of both thought and action. It is not enough to mouth the words of propaganda, to mimic the words of teachers or revolutionary leaders. Thought must create a real change in the consciousness of the individual and of the collective group. Freire makes the point that thought and action are concurrent and should not be thought of as a step-by-step process. This is a qualitative change, an awareness of the world, and a conscious effort to change, to transform the conditions of life.

PROCESS OF CULTURAL ACTION

Cultural action involves people defining problems based upon their view of the world and their situation. The process involves a team composed of a facilitator, who acts only to guide the activities, a number of investigators or educated experts who are typically from social sciences such as anthropology or sociology, and the local people who act as co-investigators at all stages of the process. The groups formed in this way have been called "culture circles" or "reflection groups."

The people discuss their problems in the culture circles. This involves the conscientization or "awareness raising" discussed earlier (Werner and Bower 1982). This is an open-ended group dialogue process. The group is formed by those that share a problem and a facilitator. While this is an educative process, it doesn't involve the flow of information from the teacher as expert to the class. It is not based on the "banking" approach. The questions raised in the dialogue do not have predetermined answers. The group works to better understand the problems they are facing. Each group member's perspective is given equal value. It is best when everybody takes part in the process.

Werner and Bower offer the following advice on leading a discussion group (1982:16). They suggest:

1) encourage all persons to take an active part; 2) assure them that they are among friends and are free to speak their own thoughts; 3) advise them to listen carefully, and avoid interrupting each other; and 4) warn them not to simply accept what another person says, but to think about it carefully, or analyze it. (1982:16)

It's not a matter of just saying all of this. The leader has to genuinely believe that each person in the group possesses relevant and valid knowledge. The questions that are used to stimulate discussion need to be truly open-ended. Discussion is often stimulated by facilitators by using words, pictures or objects. These stimuli need to be familiar and understandable to the people. The jargon of technical fields or leftist politics should be avoided. Facilitators need to welcome criticism. It is said that to "accept a sincere attack on your own ideas" should be taken "as a sign of successful leadership" (Werner and Bower 1982:34).

This is the basis for everybody learning from each other. The distinction between expert and novice is erased. The questions should foster the view that through the discussion group they can act and exert control on the world around them. Part of this is to increase the feelings of self-worth and feelings of strength within the group. This is difficult to do. The life experiences of oppressed people make it difficult to change their consciousness. "This is especially true with persons who have learned to silently endure their misfortune and who accept society's view of themselves as powerless, ignorant and hopeless" (Werner and Bower 1982:26).

Freire found it useful to focus on specific words, things, and situations. In the course of the discussion some words and phrases are repeated. This repetition suggests that the ideas behind the words are important parts of the consciousness of the group. For example poor people may continually refer to the idea of "slum" where they live. This may be done uncritically, indicating an acceptance of the conditions of life there. This can be discussed with the circle facilitator focusing on the meaning of the slum, how slums come to be slums, and the reasons members of the circle experience poverty. In this way they develop a critical consciousness about their lives. Slum becomes a generative theme, an idea that can be used to produce critical understanding of a situation.

This process is much more workable if it is done in the context of learning of practical skills. Freire's original work did involve awareness raising to be sure, but it was done in the context of poor people learning to read and write. Consciousness without context is difficult. Werner and Bower say, "to be most effective, educational methods that increase self-confidence and social awareness should be built into all aspects of training programs and community activities" (1982:18). There is sometimes the temptation to do the conscientization in the Freirian mode but to revert to a top-down, expertise-driven mode when presenting technical information. As they work on generative themes, this deep level of involvement of the community allows those involved to be better able to act on the themes to cause change.

The process involves three areas of investigation which compose a concurrent, iterative process, and not a linear, step-by-step process (Taylor 1993:73).

Naming

The first part of the process is to identify or "name" the problem on which work will be done. The initial phase involves informal meetings between the cultural action facilitator and members of the community. The facilitator will live with the community in order to develop an understanding of their culture. What is the question under discussion? The problem is defined by community members, reflecting their perceptions of the world in which they exist. The facilitator must enter into a dialogue with the people in order to know their objective situation and their perceptions of the situation. The meetings between the members of the community and the cultural action worker are informal. From this dialogue, the generative themes are identified.

Reflection

The generative themes are reflected upon. Reflection involves thinking about the situation and trying to explain it. The situation of the people is seen as a living code which has been developed through the generative themes and is to be decoded or deciphered. Instructional materials in the form of photographs, posters, reading texts, and so on are produced which are based on generative themes. Through the use of such materials the investigator represents the themes to the people in a systematized and amplified form. The images of "codifications" depict the generative themes in an attempt to stimulate thinking about the situation. These materials are used as the basis of reflection and should be organized so as to offer various possibilities of analysis. In this way, links can be made between the various themes, and the people are able to examine the historical-cultural context of the themes. This process of decoding develops a critical consciousness of the situation that may then lead to the development of strategies of action meant to transform the situation.

Action

The process becomes concrete. The group identifies possible routes of action to change the situation. What options are there becomes important. Action involves cooperation, unity, and organization. Facilitators and the people of the community together must create the guidelines for action.

CASE: CULTURAL ACTION EMPLOYED IN EDUCATION AND COMMUNITY DEVELOPMENT

Anthropologist Sebastiao Rocha and a group of teachers frustrated with the low-quality school system of their region founded the Centro Popular de Cultura e Desenvolvimento (CPCD) in Belo Horizonte, Minas Gerais, Brazil. A not-for-profit, non-governmental organization, the center promotes popular education and community development through educational programs for poor people. The starting point of the process is the culture of the communities with which they work. The culture of the participants is the raw material of their action programs. They focus on the development and use of innovative methodology, training of educators, and encouragement of community participation. Their program reflects the pedagogical ideas of Paulo Freire. Participation is important. Participants include "children, adolescents, adult men and women, not as mere beneficiaries or objects of our interest, but citizens and partners of all the processes and stages of the projects" (http://www.cpcd.org).

Minais Gerais is a state in the impoverished southeast of Brazil. There the current economy reflects the historic dependence on gold mining and the collapse of this industry. The people of the region have high unemployment and long-term dependence on employment in mining. Because of the history of labor practices in the highly capitalized and economically volatile extraction industries, there is less tendency for these people to participate in the political process.

CPCD has created and manages a large number of different projects located in various cities of the region. In Curvelo the community of learning project focuses on training people of the local community to train others. This project was to result in the training of 250 community agents of education. The Bornal de Jogos project focuses on education through play. The project results in the fabrication of large numbers of games and toys that relate to motor development, reasoning, reading/writing, and mathematics.

One of their projects *Ser Crianca* ("To Be a Child") won first place in a UNICEF program for recognizing achievement in education and participation. This program provided an innovative education program for children and adolescents 7 to 14. There are over 500 participants at three locations in the region.

Brazilian public schools only provide half-days of classes. *Ser Crianca* supplemented this with a daily program during the students' after school hours. Perhaps more important than these activities is that *Ser Crianca* provides a place for children "to speak and be heard" (Walbran 1999). This idea is at the core of Freirian methods. In the project, Freirian methods are most clearly expressed in the methodology of the circle (or wheel). The circle is an alternative to the traditional hierarchical pattern found in schools. Children form a circle at the start of each session during which various things are done. They plan the day's work, share news from home, discuss goals. Circles are also used for conflict resolution and to establish goals. More generally, the circles build a sense of community. A child can call for a circle to discuss a wide range of issues. These may include sexuality, family violence, and the challenges of living in a small town in the interior of a developing country (Walbran 1999). The circle removes the pedestal which protects the teacher and forces them to examine their own values. The approach facilitates critical thinking, including thinking about the political implications of the education process. CPCD teachers are given special training to deal with their role in the circles. The approach is the antithesis to "banking education" in which the authoritative teacher makes deposits of information in passive students.

Teacher training is an important part of the mission of the center. The methods of *Ser Crianca* are taught to groups of teachers from outside the program. The strategies of the program are applied to teacher training itself. Teachers are engaged in play activities and share in the production of toys and other aids to learning. Teachers are encouraged to develop professional solidarity.

In the program, participants plant and care for the school's organic garden and prepare foods from the garden for the school's lunch. This involves reading and writing about recipes from the kitchen. They have a small factory for toys where they make toys out of recycled materials. Participants have made large numbers of educational games. They also have gardens and produce jams and jellies using fruit they raise without harmful chemicals.

CPCD has disseminated projects to other regions of Minas Gerais, other Brazilian states, and two other countries namely Mozambique and Guinea Bissau.

SUMMARY

Cultural action is an approach that is widely used to achieve educational goals in many different settings. While it was developed in the context of very poor communities, the ideas have been applied in a wider array of settings. The core of the process is a dialogue of community members done with the help of a facilitator. The goal of the dialogue is that participants better understand the factors that put them in their current situation. The approach results in the people of the community having an enhanced sense of what they can do to improve their situation. They are liberated from the negative images that the wealthy have placed upon them. Although often couched in a political rhetoric that appears to create distance with many readers, elements of the approach are now very widely used on college campuses.

FURTHER READING

Freire, Paulo. *Pedagogy of the Oppressed*. New York: Continuum, 1970. Freire was a prolific author. *Pedagogy of the Oppressed* is a classic in the radical education literature. It is a logical place to start reading.

Chapter 7

Collaborative Research

Collaborative research anthropology is a process in which researchers, program developers, and community members are networked to do research for "joint problem solving and positive social change" (J. Schensul and S. Schensul 1992:162). Although collaborative anthropology is primarily a research activity, the anthropologist is also involved in change-producing action. The anthropologist serves not as a direct change agent but as an auxiliary to community leaders. It is important to the success of the process that the relationship between the community and the collaborating anthropologist be direct. Because of this, little collaborative research is done through intervening agencies.

DEVELOPMENT OF COLLABORATIVE RESEARCH

Collaborative research anthropology was developed by Stephen Schensul and Jean Schensul within the context of community programs in Chicago, Illinois and Hartford, Connecticut (J. Schensul and S. Schensul 1992). The initial project was done by Stephen Schensul in the Mexican-American community of Chicago (Bell, Schensul, and Just 1974; S. Schensul 1973, 1974, 1978; S. Schensul and M. Bymel 1975; S. Schensul and J. Schensul 1978). This program was originally focused on community mental health but grew to include many aspects of community welfare. These programs were diverse and included "bilingual education, maternal and child health, mental health, community-based mental health training, substance abuse, child abuse, sports and recreation, and gang-prevention work" (J. Schensul and S. Schensul 1992:167). Through encouragement and modeling provided by the Chicago program, a number of other projects were initiated.

These included an advocacy project for Mexican-American women (Stern 1985) and an advocacy research project focused on access to perinatal health services (Gaviria, Stern, and Schensul 1982).

In the late 1970s Stephen Schensul and Jean Schensul initiated a series of collaborative research projects in Hartford, Connecticut. As part of this process a number of community health organizations were developed (J. Schensul 1982; S. Schensul 1981). Subsequently a number of collaborative research projects were done in conjunction with these organizations, especially Hartford's Hispanic Health Council. These projects were focused on long-term community planning in health, health education, demography and minority recruitment to health careers, evaluation of community-based projects (Pelto and Schensul 1986), training community members in research (J. Schensul and Caro 1982), community needs assessment, innovative program demonstration (J. Schensul 1987), and development of culturally appropriate health education programs. These efforts served to link many community and governmental organizations and resulted in an increase in the research capacity of the ethnically diverse communities of Hartford.

There have been large numbers of research projects funded by many different local, state, and federal agencies. The research designs and methods of these projects tended to combine qualitative and quantitative data. Projects often used ethnographic research as a foundation for projects to develop rapport and increase cultural appropriateness. The projects used diverse research techniques including key informant interviews, focus groups, and surveys, among others. Studies often used probability samples and when necessary, quasi-experimental designs. That is, they used statistical analysis frequently and comparison groups and/or multiple time series measures when necessary. Community involvement in design and real concern about knowledge-utilization are defining characteristics of the approach. Elements of the research methods used can be obtained by reading the books of the seven-volume *Ethnographic Toolkit* (J. Schensul and LeCompte 1999). The authors of these books draw many examples from collaborative research projects in which they were involved.

KEY CONCEPTS IN COLLABORATIVE RESEARCH ANTHROPOLOGY

A key concept is collaboration, collaboration between anthropologists and community leadership focusing on the former's research skills and the latter's information needs. The primary reference group of the collaborative anthropologist is the community. Collaborative anthropology is an involved-in-the-action process. It is based on two fundamental assumptions. First, "Anthropological research should provide information to the population under study which contributes to the development of the community and the improvement of community life" (S. Schensul 1973:111). The research effort is often focused on the community's immediate research needs with provisions for "direct, immediate and localized" feedback. Further, the research is not intended to make a contribution to the generalized pool of scientific knowledge. A second basic assumption is that "programs for community development and improvement are most successful and effective when they are conceived and directed by knowledgeable community residents" (S. Schensul 1973:111). This assumption indicates the belief that an anthropologist's potential for success in assisting a community to achieve its goals is enhanced by working in collaboration with the community rather than an external agency. In this setting the research team works to make community-defined social action possible by providing research results that support community efforts.

The collaboration part of the process is expressed through community organization linkages. Collaborative research is conducted in "partnership with those most invested in the problem and its solution" (J. Schensul and S. Schensul 1992:162). Emphasis is placed on linking organizations that have little or no research experience with those that are experienced researchers. Inexperienced groups might include "schools and day care centers, community organizations, businesses, neighborhoods, ethnic groups, unions, and other community-based groups" (J. Schensul and S. Schensul 1992:162). These kinds of groups could be linked with universities or nonprofit research organizations.

Collaborative linkages can be initiated by either the community or the researcher. A community group may ask for research assistance to help in advocacy of their goals. They can also seek this relationship to help evaluate one of their programs or help to set agendas. Researchers may initiate the process because they need the expertise of the community for their work to go forward. They may need participation to gain access. The participation of the community may be necessary for the funding agencies (J. Schensul and S. Schensul 1992:162). A mutually sustaining relationship may emerge which results in considerable growth in the process. Organizations serve their constituencies better, the groups gain political power, and community skills are built. This occurs in addition to the ostensible purpose of the specific project.

The nature of the specific project grows out of the relationship developed with the community. This relationship is multistranded and contingent upon many of the rapport building skills characteristic of anthropological fieldwork. A substantial period of time is necessary to develop effective collaboration because of the need to develop trust and understanding in the context of complex political activities. A key to effective collaboration is the manifestations of commitment on the part of the researcher. The researcher has to be prepared to allocate a significant amount of time to the process. The relationship between the collaborative research anthropologist and the community is best if it is sustained.

THE COMPONENTS OF SUCCESSFUL COLLABORATION

For successful collaboration to occur, a number of principles should be followed. The relationship between researcher and activist must be symmetrical and coequal. The activists must work as co-investigators on collaborative research projects. The *principle of parity* is based not so much on democratic values, but on the fact that the activist is knowledgeable of the community and its needs, which is essential for meaningful collaborative research. Further, it is through parity that the research and data utilization skills are most effectively conveyed. It is intended that through collaboration the activist becomes a better producer and consumer of research results.

Success in collaboration is also enhanced by *community control of research operations*. Community representatives must determine if a specific research project, and its related methods, is appropriate to community needs. Community control implies an informed and involved constituency. Community control also implies a substantial amount of reformulation of the research effort during implementation.

The effectiveness of research collaboration is enhanced by wide sharing of the research effort. The sharing of effort helps insure that research will be useful to the community and its action plans. Sharing of the research effort also increases the research skills of the community.

The recipients of research results are the activists and the community members. Dissemination of results in traditional academic channels is a secondary consideration. The primary function of the research effort in collaborative terms is the furtherance of the developmental and political goals of the community. Communication of research results outside the community can only be done if it is in the interests of the community. Review of research results by community activists prior to dissemination in public contexts is advisable.

A major factor relating to the success of the collaborative research effort is the extent that the research done is an expression of community goals. Thus, real collaboration is only possible where there is substantial ideological sharing and agreement between anthropologist and activist. The quality of the collaboration is evaluated through analysis of its positive impact on the community, not its impact on the discipline of anthropology.

Researchers in collaborative relationships with a community need to be parsimonious. They must be able to identify research goals in such a way as to allow quick satisfaction of community informational needs. This means that research techniques must be time-effective. The collaborative anthropologist should be able to work quickly. Theoretical elegance that does not serve the goals of the community is viewed as unproductive in collaborative projects. This type of research makes use of various techniques that contribute time economies. These include large research teams, highly focused research instruments, and clear conceptualizations of research purposes. Consistent with time-effectiveness *and* the basic ideology of collaboration is direct community participation in the research effort. And, in fact, most instructional activities in this approach relate to making community members into competent researchers. The developers of the collaborative model have clearly conceptualized the contrast between applied and theoretical research, and have through their efforts, made a significant contribution to the development of anthropological methodology.

THE COLLABORATIVE ANTHROPOLOGY PROCESS

The collaborative anthropology process is conceived as having a series of steps (S. Schensul 1973).

1. Development of Rapport and Credibility of Applied Research

The initiation of the collaborative research process is seen as having three critical elements. These are "the presence, influence, and insight of an applied social science researcher, the participation of skilled knowledge-oriented activists, and an issue or problem of passionate interest to a group of individuals, institutions, or agencies" (J. Schensul and S. Schensul 1992: 180).

Traditional anthropological fieldwork approaches are very useful for developing working relationships and rapport. It also serves to develop in the researcher an operational understanding of the total setting of the problem as it is defined collaboratively.

2. The Identification of Significant, Indigenous Action Programs

The participant-observer, anthropologist-as-advocate attempts to establish a preliminary understanding of community priorities as they are related to the organization of existing and potential programs. This understanding will provide a basis for decisions that the anthropologist must make concerning involvement. The involvement process is, of course, based on some value-explicit decisions. As Schensul notes,

Unlike the traditional fieldworker, the researcher's own value system plays an important part in the kind of action he will seek to facilitate. Rather than avoid this issue, the researcher must balance the values and attitudes of the people in the community with his own ways of looking at the world before he commits himself to any program. (S. Schensul 1973:113)

3. The Negotiation of Cooperative and Reciprocal Relationships between the Applied Researchers and the Action People

This process is most successful when the potential contribution of research to the community is quite well understood. Associated with this is the need for a clear identification of the motives of the researcher. The researchers and activists must both participate in the negotiation process. This process is calculated to produce a clear indication of the community's research needs. Additionally, the process, which increases community sensitivity toward the utility of research, can result in increased access to information in the community on the part of the researchers.

4. Initial Participation in Specific Action Programs

This step often results in the collection of case study material relevant to specific programs. The researcher should stress "rapport development" and "program assessment" in this period. Baseline data is also collected, which is useful for long-term program evaluation.

5. The Identification of Specific Informational Needs of the Action People

Participation of the community is an important factor that determines the extent of use of the research. Stephen Schensul makes a recommendation concerning this part of the process: "We have found that research results have a higher probability of being useful when people in the community who are involved in programs play an important role in the development of research concepts and strategies, and when community and program people help in the collection and analysis of data" (S. Schensul 1973:114).

6. Meeting the Needs of Long-Range Research Plans

In addition to meeting the short-term informational needs of the community, the anthropologist should develop a set of long-term research goals. These goals are more closely identified with the type of operations typical of the "theoretical" anthropologist, yet these long-term operations are also important to the goals of the community. Through these efforts the researchers create a data base which may meet the short-run informational needs of the community. Short research projects often serve as practice for the long-term research projects.

7. Formalized Research and Data Collection Operations

As the process proceeds, less reliance is placed on the informal research strategies, such as participant-observation and key informant interviewing. As specific informational needs are identified, research operations become more structured and formal. As community members come to participate in the research effort, the process becomes more highly structured.

8. Analysis of Data

Analysis techniques must be time-effective. This is a crucial attribute of the process. As Stephen Schensul notes,

Unlike more academically based research, the time within which research results are produced is vitally related to their usefulness. The "involvement in the action" strategy requires the development of procedures for the rapid analysis of data utilizing simple and easily manipulated techniques. At the same time, more sophisticated techniques are used to serve less pressing action needs as well as the long-term research goals. (S. Schensul 1973:116)

9. Data Dissemination, Evaluation, and Interpretation

The results of the research are rapidly disseminated. If the information is not effectively communicated, even the most "significant" results will not have "significant" impact on the situation. The researcher can increase communication effectiveness by increasing the number of media of presentation. Results suggest that the least effective means of communicating is the typical technical report. An anthropologist who is concerned with communicating with his clients should use a variety of presentation techniques. It is suggested that the anthropologist be an aggressive and innovative communicator. The dissemination process is thought to influence the outcome of the process significantly in that "disseminating data to community groups allows criticism, evaluation and assessment of the results to be rapidly fed back to the researcher" (S. Schensul 1973:116). The results of research, good or bad, are "exposed to scrutiny" in the community.

The collaborative researcher must be committed to creating an effective organization between researcher and community. The bases for defining community are flexible, and vary from project to project. Some examples are a geographic area, a network of programs, a specific ethnic population, and the community associated with a particular school. The initial process is one of networking through key informants. This then may serve as the basis for linking activists and their organizations. Through this a potential network of collaborators can be identified and organized. "The first important criterion for success is the selection of an experienced or knowledgeable facilitator" (J. Schensul and S. Schensul 1992:181). This person needs to be knowledgeable of the communities involved and committed to community involvement in the policy process. "The second criterion is inclusion" (J. Schensul and S. Schensul 1992:181). Organizations that are relevant to the problem should be included. In some of the projects in Hartford, the number of organizations included in the project got to be quite large. It is important to be prepared to demonstrate the importance of research in the research-action process. In addition, incentives need to be included to sustain participation.

COLLABORATIVE RESEARCH IN CHICAGO'S MEXICAN-AMERICAN COMMUNITY: A CASE STUDY

The case focuses on work done by Stephen Schensul among the members of the Mexican-American community on the lower west side of Chicago. His involvement grew out his employment in a community mental health program that had a mandate to serve the ethnically diverse population of the neighborhood. The neighborhood has "an overwhelming Mexican cultural orientation. Restaurants, taverns, groceries and supermarkets providing Mexican foods and services dominate the entrepreneurial activity" (1973:108). The intensity of Mexican-American residence makes it possible for persons to be employed in Spanish-speaking contexts. The resident Mexican-American population represents three types of individuals: immigrants from Mexico, *Tejanos* (that is, Chicanos from Texas), and Chicago-born Chicanos.

Collaborative research developed out of Schensul's increasingly close relationship with community leaders and increased distancing between him and the mental health program. Initially Schensul conceived of his role as a provider of research services to improve the understanding of the mental health program's staff of the neighborhood they were to serve. This approach did not work well. As Schensul and his team's knowledge of the community increased, so did their "contacts." This tended to legitimize them in the eyes of the mental health program's staff as anthropologists and they became increasingly free to participate in the affairs of the community. This was expressed through what was called the community research unit which was part of the community mental health program.

The unit was able to get involved in its first survey project, which involved identification of characteristics of the school population. The school project, which developed in conjunction with school staff, was to provide information that would lead to improvements in parent-school communication. Specifically, the project intended to determine through parental interviews the nature of family, social, and economic life in a neighborhood and to discover the parents' attitudes toward the school. In addition, the research intended to determine the nature and attitudes of the teacher population as this relates to teaching Mexican-American children, and to determine the basis of the student's response toward the school situation. The research procedure used interviews, home visits, and student records applied to a random sample.

The research produced a number of interesting results that improved the researchers' understanding of the community. Through the survey they found that they had grossly underestimated the size of the Mexican-born population of the total Chicano population. The research indicated that the parents had strong preferences for bilingual and bicultural education. Although the research had little impact on school administrators, the researchers learned some lessons about effectively conveying data to program administrators.

The school survey was followed up with a similar study of a Catholic school that served the same neighborhood. The research found that the Catholic school families were residents in Chicago longer and were more bilingual. They also seemed better off socioeconomically and educationally. The Catholic school's administration offered the researchers greater opportunities to communicate to the parents. This included a session in which the researchers were allowed to address a meeting of the parents' association. The researchers used a number of different techniques including handouts of summary tables, Spanish translation, overhead projections, and parental feedback. The parents were especially interested in the demographic aspects of the study.

For a number of reasons, the research did not have any significant impact on the community or the school. The researchers felt the schools were unresponsive to this type of research because of control from outside the community, nonindigenous staff, and little interest in orienting programs toward the community. The school research had left the research team frustrated and dissatisfied.

The team's energies came to be directed at the research needs of a settlement house funded by the Presbyterian Church that served one of the neighborhoods in the corridor. Preliminary research indicated that the settlement house played an important role in the community as a meeting place for various community groups. The research for the settlement house was to focus on the "block clubs" that the settlement house was attempting to develop in their service area.

Relationships with the settlement house were quite good, based on the interaction with persons at the center that occurred during the initial period of participant-observation. Without any specific goals in mind, the research team began negotiation with the staff of the settlement house to determine the nature of the research. The team was to interview residents and perform the necessary work to carry out a census survey. Significantly, the anthropologists were to be in contact with the block team leaders and residents in order to provide feedback of research results to decision makers.

The researchers assigned to each block were quickly drawn into the action of the block club development teams. The researchers assisted in getting community improvement petitions filled out, organizing community activities such as street dances and fiestas, and doing attitudinal research concerning community needs. The researchers also carefully documented residents' participation. The initial efforts improved researcher understanding of the community. This, coupled with the high-quality interpersonal relations that developed, did much to facilitate the application and development of the collaborative model.

As the research progressed there was a shift in emphasis from general, area-wide research for the purpose of generating basic demographic data to problem-focused, block-specific research. There were a number of issues examined. One block was faced with a problem characteristic of many American neighborhoods, a zoning change. The research team assisted in the collection of data that was useful in the resistance process. The team worked to communicate the nature of the threat to the community. They also documented the nature of the participation that was useful for further projects.

Initially, the group seemed successful in resisting the change. Unfortunately, the zoning change was approved at a meeting held by the zoning commission that was not announced in the community. Some months later the new construction took place. The anthropologists were somewhat disillusioned by this. In any case, it was a lesson in big-city politics.

The experience on the zoning project led to decreases in the participation of the research team in the community mental health program. The team became increasingly concerned with the research needs of community groups and justified their approach in terms of the preventive component of the community mental health approach. At this point they "discovered" collaboration. Although community mental health programming was intended primarily to provide mental health care directly to patients, a certain portion of resources could be allocated to alleviating community-based causes of mental health problems, such as bad schools or little economic opportunity.

The approach was successfully applied in a number of different contexts following the somewhat fortuitous "discovery" of the approach. A selection of these projects will be reviewed here. The projects selected were related to community needs and the developing data base of the research team. Additionally, the team came to be more and more tied to formally established community organizations. One of these organizations was ALAS (Alliance Latino-Americano para Adelante Social) which was one of the first and most active community action groups. ALAS dealt with a number of crucial issues which faced Chicanos nationally and locally. More specifically, this meant increasing the quality of bilingual and bicultural programming in the Chicago school system. They were especially interested in augmenting the Teaching English as a Second Language (TESL) program. The action research team supported the efforts of ALAS in this and other realms.

Commando Anthropology

Initially, the involvement in the bilingual education issue took the form of an ALAS organized "commando raid" to assess the quality of TESL programs in the schools of the area. With no forewarning 11 separate research teams entered the schools of the community at precisely 11:00 in the morning. Each team was equipped with a data collection schedule. The teams attempted to identify the extent and quality of the TESL programs. The project revealed the fact that TESL classes were limited in time and were often not held. Additionally, TESL classes were often run by untrained substitutes or non-Spanish-speaking teachers. The space allocated to the program was determined to be of low quality. The general conclusion was that the TESL program did not meet program guidelines.

The data derived from the process of "commando research" were organized and used to support the filing of a suit with the Illinois Civil Rights Commission. The "raid" showed that it was possible to do good research under severe time constraints, if speed was planned into the research project.

THE COMMUNITY RESEARCH UNIT AND EL CENTRO DE LA CAUSA

The staff of the Eighteenth Street settlement house in the barrio had become increasingly concerned with the quality of recreation, social, and educational services that they offered. The situation had become critical because of the physical deterioration of existing community facilities. To improve the situation the settlement house staff attempted to develop a new youth program to deal with what the other social service agencies called "hard-core kids." These individuals were simply not welcome at the existing social service programs. The situation called for an alternative kind of facility. This alternative was to take form under the name of El Centro de la Causa. The key organizer was a street worker who developed a following among local gang members.

The group found an old parochial school which was not fully used. With a group of volunteers, the building was cleaned and renovated. A recreation program was organized and soon a group of Chicano students were able to offer some classes on various Chicano topics. Various local businessmen were able to make contributions. Some clinical services were also offered at the center. The center also drew a number of new participants. As participation increased so did the services offered. El Centro began its first "fund raisers" in 1971 with a community fiesta and carnival. Three years later, El Centro had a $400,000 budget. The staff had been successful in acquiring funds from outside the community. Their fund-raising success was related to their skill as well as the changing relationship between Chicanos and the federal government. In the case of El Centro, these grants took the form of a drug treatment program and a mental health paraprofessional training program, as well as various other education, youth, and other social service programs. Increasingly, El Centro became a focal point for the political activism that was to sweep the Chicago Chicano community.

It was in conjunction with the program at El Centro that the collaboration was most effective. The research team's activities grew, expanded, and increased in complexity. Their relationship with El Centro was multifaceted in that it included a wide range of activities and responsibilities.

While the ultimate goals of the collaboration must be in the hands of the community leaders, the researcher has to be involved in all phases of the action. This implies that the anthropologist using this approach activates a number of roles beyond that of researcher. The El Centro project made use of the anthropologist's research skills very early, but soon these activities were supplemented. Members of the research team participated with activists in strategy planning and policy making. The team was also given the responsibility of providing historic documentation, and a major role in "facilitating communication with outside groups" (S. Schensul 1974: 205). The team's involvement included "identifying potential sources of funding, participating in meetings with representatives of a number of institutions and funding agencies, using research data on health, mental health, drugs, drug use, youth organizations, community structure, and demography in reports and discussions in which the community "case" was presented, and "collaborating with community activists in writing formal proposals for funds to private institutions and federal funding sources" (S. Schensul 1974:206).

Through the research team, El Centro was better able to present its case to relevant agencies. The developing data base of the center collected by the team was useful in preparing proposals which served to legitimate the presence of the research team. The data which proved useful was quite variable, including such things as ethnographic studies of Mexican folk medicine found in the literature, data relating to evaluation of local health care facilities, and information dealing with sources of additional grant funds. Although research skills are important, they can only be made useful through an ability to communicate. The researchers were the means by which the community could express its ideas and plans. "The applied researcher must demonstrate the ability not only to describe the research results, but also to write effectively and economically about program structures, treatment plans, training schedules and other components of community programs" (Schensul, 1974:206).

Increasingly, the team was drawn into all aspects of program operations and management. This related to a general tendency of the researchers and the activists to become more and more alike. The researchers were taught action skills in organization of the community and bureaucratic manipulation. The activists learned to be competent researchers. Ultimately, they could develop research protocols and analyze research data.

As the program at El Centro increased in complexity, the team was called upon to carry out more focused research. Often a staff member would communicate a specific research problem in conjunction with a program development need.

For example, the youth service staff decided that, before developing a program that would be based on their own preconceptions, they needed a survey of youth attitudes and behavior. Together, we constructed an extensive questionnaire that was eventually administered to more than eight hundred youngsters (aged thirteen to fifteen) in the community. (Schensul 1974:206)

Similar activities developed in association with a program of treatment for Chicano drug addicts.

Research skills increased and the team developed a good workable understanding of the collaborative process. The team discovered that a key to research success was to negotiate research methodology with staff and activists. According to Stephen Schensul, negotiation "can increase the relevance of the information collected, make activists more receptive to the resulting data and create more sensitivity to the inevitable problems and delays in data collection" (1974:207). The team also attempted to carry out research both in terms of long-term and short-term needs so that each short-term project would result in an increase of their data base. The effectiveness of this approach increased as the team learned how to better predict future information needs. The team discovered that the well-designed, methodologically clean project often did not meet the needs of the situation. The results were often not available at the correct time. At times, in order to be effective, the researchers had to go into a "quick and dirty" mode.

As the relationship between the researchers and the El Centro activists improved, there came to be an increasing focus on internal research activities. This grew out of a need to institutionalize the research effort of El Centro. In response to this, an internal research unit was created. The unit engaged in a number of significant research problems.

The team continued to work through El Centro. Their efforts became directed at a wide range of increasingly concrete action programs. Each was addressed to specific needs identified within the Chicano community. El Centro de la Causa continues to be involved in social action in Mexican-American neighborhoods in Chicago today. Anthropologists continue to collaborate with the organization.

SUMMARY

Collaborative anthropology represents a set of anthropological activities that are well adapted to working in direct relationship with community organizations as opposed to working through an intervening agency. The role of the collaborative anthropologist is focused on the expressed needs of the community, usually expressed through its leadership. Usually this involves work as a researcher, research trainer, and proposal writer. Collaboration does not usually call for the anthropologist to be directly involved in change-producing decision making. The collaborative anthropologist is, as Schensul says, involved in the action, but as an auxiliary to community leadership. Collaboration means using one's research skills to support the attainment of community goals. This simple, but very useful idea can be expressed in many ways. The case presented here represents a good model of the collaborative role. It is clear that the collaborative anthropologist must be able to reduce somewhat his or her use of the discipline as a reference group. The reference group is the community. Professional achievement is measured in reference to the community's achievement of its goals. This is not an easy task, but when it occurs it can yield powerful satisfactions on the part of the anthropologist, while increasing community capabilities. While there are a number of skills which are useful to the anthropologist working collaboratively, proposal writing often is crucial. This can both help achieve the goals of the community and provide the means for the continued involvement of the anthropologist.

FURTHER READING

Schensul, Jean J. and Stephen L. Schensul. Collaborative Research: Methods of Inquiry for Social Change. In *The Handbook of Qualitative Research in Education.* Margaret D. LeCompte, Wendy L. Millroy, and Judith Preissle, eds. San Diego, Calif.: Academic Press. 1992. This provides a historic overview and summary of the important aspects of collaborative research.

Stull, Donald D. and Jean J. Schensul, eds. *Collaborative Research and Social Change: Applied Anthropology in Action.* Boulder, Colo.: Westview Press, 1987. The volume contains good documentation on a number of projects involving collaboration.

Chapter 8

Participatory Rural Appraisal

One of the most useful methodological developments in applied anthropology in the last 25 years are the models for doing useful research more rapidly. At this point there are a wide variety of techniques being applied in a variety of different contexts. This chapter is focused on the use of these approaches in the realm of agriculture. There are examples from public health, nutrition, and housing, among many other sectors. One of these methods is participatory rural appraisal.

Participatory rural appraisal (PRA) is one of a family of participatory research methods widely used to plan or assess development projects and programs. PRA is an important part of the tool kit of the contemporary development professional that enables "rural people to share, enhance, and analyze their knowledge of life and conditions, to plan, and to act" (Chambers 1994:953). Through PRA and with the cooperation of community members, development professionals can discover and document local conditions that are relevant to planning programs and projects that are culturally appropriate and consistent with local needs and priorities. As a method PRA is consistent with the historic pattern of anthropological research practice. Many anthropologists have contributed to the development of the method.

PRA utilizes a large number of data collection and documentation techniques within the context of a strong commitment to participation. The specialized techniques done by community members include mapping the

This chapter is written by John van Willigen and Hussein Mahmoud. John van Willigen has used rapid assessment in an agricultural development setting in Kentucky and Aceh Province, Indonesia. Hussein Mahmoud participated in PRA projects and training at Egerton College in Kenya, where he is a faculty member.

institutions or physical setting of a community and constructing seasonal calendars, health and wealth rankings, and rating community preferences (Rietbergen-McCracken and Narayan 1998). These data collection practices are richly innovative and useful in many contexts. PRA can be used in a wide range of sectors such as natural resource utilization and management, poverty assessment, agriculture, health and nutrition, urban needs assessment, and food security (Chambers 1994).

WHY USE PRA?

The development literature documents a large percentage of failed projects. One way that the rate of success may be increased is by understanding the community circumstances of the project. This can be carried further by having the community actually be involved in the planning process. PRA can increase the potential that the project is suitable for local conditions and is culturally appropriate.

Achieving success in development is quite difficult. One source is the lack of enough reliable information with which to plan the project. Research can be defective in a number of ways. First it can be framed in terms of the concepts and priorities of persons from outside the community or expressed in overly technical language so that it is difficult to apply. In this way local needs and concerns are not addressed. Second, research can be delivered too late. Time effectiveness is an important aspect of having an impact. Third, the research may be done by specialists who are not in very effective communication with either the community or the research users.

The use of PRA increases the likelihood that the research will reflect the understandings and priorities of the community. When doing PRA it is very important to keep these general goals in mind. There is always a concern that PRA is done for its own sake or perhaps done with too much attention to formal requirements of a set of steps or processes. Technical manuals about the PRA process can be dangerous because they encourage rote learning, ritualized performance of PRA, and imposition of outsider perspectives on communities (Chambers 1994:116). The key is "use your own best judgement at all times" (Chambers 1994:116). Always remember what the point of this is.

Because of the increased range of application of PRA, the label participatory rural appraisal has become a misnomer (Rietbergen-McCracken and Narayan 1998). To start, PRA practice can vary a great deal in terms of quality of participation, ranging from information sharing through consultation, collaboration, and empowerment. The technique is used in urban as well as rural settings. The approach is used for an increasing variety of purposes beyond that of appraisal of a community's situation prior to design and implementation of a development project.

PRA's practical applications are evident in many fields. The sectors identified by Chambers (1997:119–122) are:

Natural resources management including watersheds, and soil and water conservation; land tenure and policy; forestry; coastal resources and fisheries; people, parks and biodiversity; community plans. Agriculture including farmer participatory research; livestock and animal husbandry; irrigation; integrated pest management. People, poverty and livelihood including women and gender; selection [for program participation]; livelihood analysis; participatory poverty assessments. Health and nutrition including health (general); food security and nutrition assessment and monitoring; water and sanitation assessment, planning and location; sexual and reproductive health. Urban needs assessment; community participation; urban poverty and violence.

Other areas of PRA applicability and acceptance mentioned by Chambers include adult literacy, children, education, emergency and refugee problems, and participatory management and evaluation.

We have cited a few specific examples that are documented in recent published literature. These include PRA being done with forestry cooperatives in Vietnam (Bardolf 1998), village planning in Indonesia (Mukerjee 1998), women in development planning in Morocco (Gandhi 1996), urban poverty and violence in Jamaica (Moser and Holland 1995), risk analysis in fishing in South India (Ramesh, Narayanasamy and Boraian 1997), and poverty assessment in Kenya (Narayan and Nyamwaya 1996).

DEVELOPMENT OF THE APPROACH

PRA was a development out of the rapid appraisal methods used in development planning. Rapid appraisal methods emerged under various names in the late 1970s and had gained widespread acceptance among those working in agricultural development.[1] These rapid assessment procedures were known by various names including informal survey (Rhoades 1982), reconnaissance survey (van Willigen and DeWalt 1985), *sondeo* (Hildebrand 1980), and perhaps the most widely used term, rapid rural appraisal (RRA). These methods spread from what was largely a tropical agriculture arena to other contexts. A similar approach, rapid assessment procedure (RAP), came to be used in health and nutrition (Scrimshaw and Hurtado 1987).

THE RRA PROCESS

RRA represents a middle ground between ethnographic practice and survey methodology. RRA's main thrust lies in its ability to enable outsiders

1. Chambers uses the International Conference on Rapid Rural Appraisal held at the University of Khon Kaen in Thailand in 1985 as an indicator of widespread acceptance of the method (Chambers 1997:112).

to learn from insiders (Chambers 1983) in a rapid and reliable way. Some of the general properties of reconnaissance surveys are described below.

An important component of the RRA process is the collection of secondary data. This may include reports on previous research projects, local statistical sources, maps and aerial photographs, satellite images, as well as the usual articles and books. While training Indonesian agricultural scientists in RRA, we had them go to a government agency, Kantor Statisik to find relevant data on the villages within which they were going to do their field work. We have found highly specific information about some places where we have done RRA on the Internet. While secondary data is important to the process, it is important to use it critically. RRA, in part, was developed to overcome the problems caused by the problems associated with the use of this kind of data.

Interviews are often carried out by "information users" themselves rather than enumerators as often occurs in survey research. Usually interviews are done by teams. The teams themselves will consist of persons of different disciplinary backgrounds. For example, in work with Kentucky farmers, the larger team included anthropologists, sociologists, agronomists, horticulturalists, soil scientists, animal scientists, and extension workers. The interview teams of two to three persons usually included a social scientist, an agricultural scientist, and usually an extension worker. The persons grouped in the teams changed everyday. The daily rotation increased the cross-disciplinary learning. This part of the process is very valuable. The interviews tend to be much more interactive than the interviews associated with typical surveys. Kentucky farmers would often ask the participating agricultural scientist questions about farming practices and would get advice. While the interviews are usually guided by topical outlines, the interviewers modify the line of questioning in response to what is being learned in the interview. Needless to say, formal interview schedules in which each question is presented in a strictly standardized format are not used. Documentation usually involves the compilation of simple "jot notes" that may or may not be expanded later. Some technical statements on the process go so far as to say that written field notes should not be used (Hildebrand 1980) and one should rely on "head notes."

The selection of people to interview is purposeful rather than random. Often a quota approach is used. Let's say the RRA is being done to help understand farm production constraints in a specific region in order to design improved agricultural technology directed at dealing with the constraints. In cases like this, the research planners might develop a quota matrix so that farm households of different income levels and ecological zones might be contacted. In using RRA with Kentucky farmers, we conceptualized different types of farmers based on what we knew about Kentucky farm communities and came up with a "rough cut" of four different farming systems. These were small grain producers, dairy farmers, and tobacco and livestock producers. These categories combined with concern for ecological diversity were used to select the early persons to interview. As we learned more, we added "retirement farmers" to the mix. The initial categories were derived from our experiences in these types of communities and consultation with people from the community like agricultural extension agents.

Data collection is dynamic and iterative. It's like ethnography: as you observe and interview key informants, you learn. What you learn changes what questions you ask. Survey methods require you to consistently ask the same questions in the same way from start to finish. This is one of the reasons why RRA is so enjoyable. When you are doing it you are continually learning. For example, in our work with Kentucky farmers, we soon discovered that the farmers had no problems with getting "production credit" so we stopped asking about it. In order for the data collection process to be dynamic and iterative, data analysis has to start right away. The foundation of data analysis is research team group discussions that occur frequently. The group consists of all the people that were involved as interviewers. These sessions result in the preliminary conclusions that reshape the inquiry for the next day.

As the RRA is completed, it may result in a more elaborate survey. In fact, sometimes RRA is done specifically to inform a survey. Later in this chapter we will discuss this approach in the context of a specific program in Peru. In that case they used the term "informal survey" (Rhoades 1982).

RRA AND PRA COMPARED

RRA and PRA are closely related, yet they are different in significant ways. When we think of RRA, I think first of rapid and reliable research done by research scientists. The role of the outsider is central to the process and consists mostly of eliciting information. Early discussions of this approach stress lower cost, rapid completion, and making use of information. RRA was conceived as an alternative to the formal standardized survey. An important motivation for the development and use of RRA was avoidance of the cost and delay caused by most other research methods rather than participation as such.

With PRA we think of participation of the men and women of a community in the appraisal that occurs prior to a development effort. Instead of experts making sense of their field notes and memories, visualize typical community members diagramming a village's physical resources using a stick to scratch maps in the compacted soil under a tree at the center of their village. The role of the outsider is primarily as a facilitator and far less central than in RRA.

The purposes of these approaches are very similar. Both are intended to improve understanding of a particular place and the people who live there to help plan or evaluate a project. PRA represents a development out of RRA. While some literature seems to critique RRA as being insufficiently participatory, I think it is best to retain both techniques in one's personal tool kit. RRA continues to provide a time and cost effective method for understanding communities on their own terms. Nevertheless, as Chambers reminds us, RRA "entails outsiders obtaining information, taking it away and analyzing it" and therefore it can be thought of as extractive (1997: 113).

PRA has many of the same goals but places much greater importance on community participation in the research process. The PRA approach gradually became more widely used. It is important that it combined various participatory approaches that were developed previously. Concern about participation was part of the discourse of development practitioners for a long time. It become part of the concerns of those using RRA in the 1980s. At the Khon Kaen Conference participants discussed something that they called "participatory RRA." Chambers sees "five streams" that influence PRA. These are "action-reflection research; agro-ecosystem analysis; applied anthropology; field research on farming systems; and rapid rural appraisal (RRA)" (1994:106). These content areas continue to influence PRA.

In "action-reflection research," Chambers combines two overlapping categories. These are participatory action research (Fals-Borda and Rahman 1991) and the critical consciousness idea of Paulo Freire (Freire 1970). These contributed to the idea of "personal commitment and empowerment" to PRA practice.

Field research in farming systems done by various disciplines influenced the development of PRA. Farming systems research became increasingly participatory from its beginnings. In Chambers' view this research tradition helped people understand the complexity, diversity, and risky nature of many farming systems; the knowledge, rationality and innovativeness of poor farmers; and farmer's substantial capacity to experiment and to do their own analysis (1994:110).

Agro-ecosystem research provided many analytical tools for PRA. These methods use aspects of systems, space, time, flows and relationships, relative values, and decisions in their approach. These include "visual representation and analysis; transects (systematic walks and observation); informal mapping (sketch maps drawn on site); diagramming (seasonal calendars, flow and causal diagrams, bar charts, Venn diagrams); and innovation assessment (scoring and ranking different actions) (Chambers 1997: 109). All these practices are not very technical and assist in seeing relationships. The method, initiated in Thailand in the late 1970s, grew and spread to other areas of the world. Agro-ecosystem analysis encompasses much of ecological as well as system properties, and this makes it appropriate to be adopted by participatory approaches that endeavor to empowering rural communities in resource utilization and management.

Farming systems research recognizes the capability of farmers in understanding their complex environments through performing experiments, appraisal, and analyses. It is the recognition by farming systems approach of farmers' awareness and capability of understanding their environment which PRA borrowed and instituted in its methodological procedures. It is imperative to acknowledge the fact that farmers are well acquainted with their diverse and unpredictable situations and environments. The contribution of farming systems to the progress of PRA is particularly notable.

All of these emerging research practices were influenced by anthropology. The participant observation and intensive, long-term fieldwork of social anthropology are consistent with the research needs of rural development (Chambers 1997). These aspects of anthropology were very appealing to users of participatory approaches. Applied anthropology recognizes local knowledge, distinctions between emic and etic perspectives, and the value of learning from local people that is so much a part of the motivation of those committed to participatory approaches.

THE PRA APPROACH

PRA has gained popularity and wide acceptance as a development approach in many rural as well as urban settings in many different countries. It is, like RRA, a viable alternative to questionnaire surveys. Conventional questionnaire surveys, besides involving high costs in time and money, are sources of delays in learning and gathering information that is misleading or not used (Chambers 1997). PRA attempts to overcome this shortcoming in several aspects, including aid in gaining insights in local scenarios, identifying social and economic differences, monitoring and evaluation, and employing quantitative analysis.

PRA opens up new avenues of participatory development in which local people's capabilities are not only enhanced, but also appreciated. Furthermore, in the PRA approach the value of relaxed rapport is cherished; diagraming and visual sharing are employed in data capture and analysis; and the power of sequences of methods is put to use. In the PRA environment, researchers are trained in such a way that communication with the local people is enhanced in ways that facilitate understanding of one another, and local people are encouraged to define problems in their own terms. This develops a relaxed environment of learning from each other, that is, between the researcher and the informant. This kind of training has been lacking among engineers, economists, and agriculturalists, and the results have been poor communication that often led to failure and abandonment of projects (Gardner and Lewis 1996). In the past, development processes have been constrained in many ways that the PRA approach attempts to solve.

The rapid spread of PRA has generated problems. The first problem is quality control, which is believed to have caused extensive problems. This involves what Chambers calls "chameleon consultants," whose numbers have been on the rise, and who pretend to be competent in PRA training and consultancy while the truth is that they possess very little or no knowledge of PRA methodology (1997). He calls them opportunistic consultants. This jeopardizes the quality of PRA approach, which has become a requirement in many donor- as well as bilateral-funded projects. Secondly, problems of behavior and attitudes are looming in PRA circles. In this regard, PRA facilitators and trainers sometimes have been slow in learning not to dominate. The third problem involves field practice and ethics. Numerous mistakes are made in the field, which include dominant and superior behavior, rushing through the PRA process without taking time to earn trust and build rapport, sticking to routines and disregarding other options, and bias against some sections of the community, especially women, the poor, the old, and the vulnerable. Other ethical problems include little or no compensation for people's time, effort, and help, a failure to honor pledges, and raising the expectations of the people, which are seldom met (Chambers 1997). Gardner and Lewis (1996) examine how the PRA approach can be abused in practice. They particularly question the problem of time, and their main concern is how the PRA approach can gain insights into a community's functioning in about two weeks when an anthropologist would need at least a year to understand the various aspects of community life. The particular question raised here is how can we capture diverse community issues in such a short span of time? It is true that some issues may be overlooked in a rapid assessment, but on the other hand, with participation of the community concerned, important insights and issues can be learned in a relatively short period of time. Frequent visits to the site can help overcome the problem of time.

In PRA, theory is articulated with practice, and moreover, PRA is based on the philosophy of "handing over the stick" to beneficiaries (Chambers 1994). PRA promotes practical engagement with local communities in ways that encourage openness to complexity and diversity. PRA also addresses the question of decentralization and empowerment. Its distinctive nature lies in its concentration on changing conventional professional behavior in a top-down setting to enhancing and supporting analysis and action by local people, empowering those who are peripheral and weak (1994). Chambers writes that PRA "has three foundations or pillars: the behavior and attitude of outsiders, who facilitate, not dominate; the methods, which shift the normal balance from closed to open, from individual to group, from verbal to visual, and from measuring to comparing; and partnership and sharing of information, experience, food and training, between insiders and outsiders, and between organizations" (1997:104–106). In essence, PRA seeks to empower the marginalized sections of the community, which include women, minorities, the poor, the weak and the old, as well as the vulnerable (1997:104–105).

PRA METHODS

Semistructured interviewing is central to the PRA process. Like RRA practices, interviews are based on a flexible interview guide. The interviews themselves should be somewhat conversational to allow the introduction of new topics. Interviews can be carried out either with persons from the community, persons with specialized knowledge, key informants, or randomly encountered or systematically selected groups. Interviews are often done in teams of two to four persons. One person will serve as the note-taker on a rotating basis.

Participatory mapping is extensively used in PRA. In addition to documenting the physical attributes of the community, the maps also reveal a great deal about how people perceive the community. Local people and the PRA team engage the process in public. This may involve scratching the map on the ground or drawing it with chalk on a large sheet of paper. This process attracts many people who participate in a useful debate. Discussion of the completed map is an important part of the process. The map needs to be recorded of course. There are many different types of maps used. These include historical maps done to document and discuss changes, and social maps used to chart different kinds of households or sections of the community.

PRA often involves inquiry into the different groups and organizations within a community. This is often referenced to decision making and power associated with a problem area and accomplished through a mapping process. In this case Venn diagrams (perhaps drawn on the ground) are used to show both relative importance (through size) and relationships (through the extent of overlap). This can be done in a group context or individually. The mapping process can be used to address questions about change by comparing past and present. Goals can be explored by comparing the present with a desired future.

There are several different techniques used to identify local views of problems and their relative importance. Using a small group discussion format it is possible to simply have the participants list and rank community problems. A somewhat more complex approach is pairwise ranking. This involves writing problems down on cards and then having the facilitator hold up problem cards two at a time and ask which of the two is most important. Participants are asked to compare. Their responses are recorded on a matrix (all problems x all problems). The problems then are listed in terms of the number of times they were selected as most important in the comparison. If done in a group the ranking procedure can be linked to a discussion of how the problems can be solved.

Similar approaches can be used to rank development alternatives. A matrix can be established in which the primary alternatives are listed on one side of the matrix and the comparative dimensions are listed on the other. Some examples of things to compare include income-generating activities, various health care possibilities, or different crops. Not all alternatives or preference dimensions can be listed because of time and space constraints. A ranking done during a PRA with a group of village women in India serves as an example (Mascarenhas 1992). They were asked to rank their preferences for seven different income-generating activities (brick making, producing certain agricultural commodities, gathering firewood, and shoemaking). These were then rated using a 1 to 5 rating system in terms of time consumption, potential profits, labor, credit availability, and difficulty of the work.

The construction of seasonal calendars can be done in PRA. These are useful for understanding the economic cycle and often help identify difficult periods of the year like the "hungry times" found in some places. Group participation in the discussion process that leads to the calendar improves the quality of the result. A wide range of data can be included in the calendar. These can include "rainfall, crop sequences, labor demand, availability of paid employment, out-migration, incidence of human diseases, expenditure levels, and so on" (Rietbergen-McCracken and Narayan 1998). This may be very important for project planning purposes. The seasonal calendar can be cross-checked throughout the field work.

In order to put these practices in context, we have selected for discussion the Farmer-Back-To-Farmer Model. Both RRA and PRA have been used in this context under various names.

THE FARMER-BACK-TO-FARMER MODEL: A CASE STUDY

Farmer-Back-to-Farmer (FBTF) is an approach to farm technology development which is based on close collaboration between farmers and the technology developers. This means that the technology development process starts with joint researcher-farmer identification of the problems that can be solved through technology and ends with on-farm evaluation of the resulting technical solution with full farmer participation. Between the start and finish of the process, there is continual farmer-researcher collaboration. In general terms it is consistent with the worldview and values of farming systems research (Shaner, Philipps, and Schmehl 1982) is similar to a perspective called "farmer-first" (Chambers, Pacey, and Thrupp 1989). The FBTF process incorporates rapid assessment techniques.

The FBTF approach was developed by anthropologist Robert Rhoades and agricultural technology designer Robert Booth as part of the technology development program of the International Potato Center (CIP) in the early 1980s (Rhoades and Booth 1982a). Today the FBFT model serves as the basis for the work of the Sustainable Agriculture and Natural Resource Management—Collaborative Research Support Program (SANREM CRSP).

The key to understanding FBTF is a statement by Rhoades, "Successful adaptive interdisciplinary research must BEGIN and END with the farmer, farm household, and community" (Rhoades 1984:33). Most researchers always have a set of research questions which if they had some money they would set about working on. They do not necessarily start the process by finding out what is needed. Usually the research questions taken up by agricultural researchers are planned outside of the context of the farmer community without much reference to the consequences of the research.

The FBTF model consists of a "potentially recycling" series of four "targets or goals" (Rhoades 1984:33). The diagram of the process shows this. These targets are diagnosis, identifying solutions, testing, and adaptation (Rhoades 1984:33). The process starts with understanding the problems that farmers have. As these problems come to be better understood, technological innovations are developed that solve the problem. The development and testing of the technology is done under conditions as much like the farmer's situation as possible. Much is done on farms with intense participation of farmers. The process starts with the researcher learning about the circumstances of the farmer. In the farmer-back-to-farmer approach there is emphasis on understanding the viewpoint of the farmer. It requires "putting oneself as much as possible into the farmer's shoes to understand how they view the problem in both technical and socio-cultural terms" (1984:35). This early phase involves a wide range of different research methods. These include rapid appraisal (called informal surveys), formal questionnaire-based surveys, farmer field days, farmer advisory boards, and participant observation. Participation of the researchers in the life of farmers is important. Rhoades advocates that "scientists work hand-in-hand with farmers in their fields in exchange for information" (1984: 35). Each of the different participants, farmers and scientists, contributes to the process based on their skills and knowledge.

In highland Peru potatoes are the staple food and market crop. A CIP anthropologist studied post-harvest storage. Potatoes are subject to potentially significant losses. He found that the farmers' conception of post-harvest loss was different from the researchers'. For one thing, the researcher found that farmers were less concerned than he was with the deterioration of potatoes for household consumption or marketing. People use the potatoes for a variety of things in spite of what the researchers regarded as post-harvest loss. The farmers did not look at post-harvest deterioration of potatoes for the market in the same way as the researchers. According to a CIP staff member, "We scientists often perceive technical problems through different eyes than farmers. Losses to us were not necessarily losses to farmers"(Rhoades 1982:129). All potatoes were used in some form—fed to animals, or dried for storage.

It turned out after extensive diagnostic work in the communities that the CIP came to understand that farmers *were* concerned with post-harvest losses of *seed* potatoes. The traditional mode of storage resulted in extensive sprouting while in storage. Removing sprouts increased the amount of work for farm households while it decreased the quality of the seed. Improvement of storage of seed potatoes became the problem that the researchers and the farmers came to share.

Traditionally the farmers stored all potatoes, whether for seed, marketing, or consumption, the same way—in a dark room. Dark room storage was implicated in the sprouting. The designers proposed the use of diffuse light storage.

In diffuse light, sprouting is suppressed. It is not possible to use diffuse light storage for market or consumption potatoes because the light causes "greening." Greening renders potatoes unmarketable and inedible but still useful as seed. The green is chlorophyll produced by the potato to get ready to grow as a plant. Also produced in the greening process is the alkaloid *solanine*, a natural pesticide which is poisonous. The experiments demonstrated that diffuse light storage reduced sprout length, improved tuber quality, and increased yields.

At this point many things remained to be done to implement this technology. The anthropologist attempted to identify low-cost ways that storage could be achieved. He did not advocate modifying the traditional dark room storage technology. He conceived of the storage of seed potatoes under the veranda of the traditional highland Peru home using experiment station seed trays. Potatoes stored in this way were also subjected to a yields test and performed well. Field research indicated that the solution would not be adopted because of the cost of the seed tray innovation. The storage system was redesigned for a lower cost. The evaluation indicated that the system was widely used at various sites in Peru and in 25 other countries in Latin America, Asia, and Africa (Rhoades 1984).

Methodologically the FBTF model is flexible and adaptable to the local situation. Under these circumstances it is clear that this approach builds on local knowledge rather than replacing it. Solutions are not found on the "shelf" of the scientific technology producers. The "solutions" that are available are inconsistent with the problems. As FBTF process-based solution emerges there has to be continued contact between the technology producers and the users, the farmers. Rhoades speaks of "constant on-the-spot" exchange which was so apparent in the potato storage case (1984: 35). This can involve redefinition and abandonment of ideas. It is important to maintain this exchange to continue to link the researchers at the experiment station with the farmers. They work together to solve problems. When a solution is developed, the process proceeds to testing and adapting.

The farmer acts as an advisor to the process of fitting the newly developed technology to local conditions. This reverses the classic top-down approach in which some expert tells the farmer what to do. The initial testing and adaption then proceeds to "on-farm trials" as was done to identify the impact of the storage strategy on yields.

The FBTF approach involves turning the farmer into a researcher. The products of the process are evaluated in three ways: agronomically, economically, and socioculturally. In the case of potato storage, the farmers wanted it to be cheaper.

Part of the evaluation process is to compare the new technology to traditional methods. Further, the developed technology is evaluated on-farm with the participation of farmers to see if it will work. Involvement of farmers in on-farm trials can be difficult in many parts of the developing world because farmers may defer to the prestigious status of the researchers. The circle of the process is closed with follow-up evaluations. The key here is observation of the innovation in the context of use by the farmers in the natural setting of their farms. There should be concern about the impacts of the adoption. As Rhoades says, "data must be collected on the reception of the technology by farmers, the ultimate judges as to the appropriateness of a proposed technology" (1984:36).

As indicated at the beginning of the discussion of FBTF the approach is used as a guiding principal by the SANREM CRSP. SANREM, based at the University of Georgia, is a participatory natural resource research, training, and information exchange program. It focuses on development and dissemination of information to support decision makers who use natural resources in sustainable ways. Currently SANREM has conducted research for sustainable development in Burkina Faso, Ecuador, the Philippines, Cape Verde, and Morocco. Funded in 1992 for an initial ten-year period by the U.S. Agency for International Development, SANREM is focused on building the capacity of local people to make effective decisions about the environment (SANREM CRSP 2001).

SANREM developed a participatory research method for use in their research for development program. The method is Participatory Landscape/Lifescape Appraisal (PLLA) (Espaldon and Magsino 2001). It is derived from PRA, RRA, and farming systems research. PLLA is a rapid research method that helps one understand local knowledge, understandings, and perspectives of the landscape. The key difference between PRA and PLLA is the focus on the landscape rather than the farm. PLLA was used to help understand human-environment relationships within the landscape as well as understanding constraints for sustainable agriculture. A goal was to facilitate the community identification of the natural resources and their linkages in the landscape in which they lived. These serve as foundation for attempts to both understand the landscape and to help bring the whole range of local community members into the process. It is a way of producing participation. Along with this, PLLA helped begin the process of dialogue between the community and the SANREM researchers. Like PRA, PLLA is often thought to complement quantitative data. PLLA involves ground truthing of existing demographic or biophysical data. PLLAs have been done at all SANREM sites early in the project. Because they provide a "snapshot" of the landscape at a particular time, PLLAs are repeated annually to update understandings.

The problems with PLLA are similar to those associated with RRA/PRA. They can be incomplete and do not produce very precise information about frequency. In addition, because they make use of small group interaction to collect data and research conclusions, the biases of the person in the facilitator role can influence the outcome. Finally, the communities involved in the process can have raised expectations about the prospects of development.

SUMMARY

RRA and PRA are useful innovations in research method. These approaches have come into wide use in development settings. The initial motivation was the saving of time and money so as to allow the input of community members. Without RRA or PRA methods, project staff were subject to costly time delays associated with the use of both traditional survey approaches. Robert Chambers referred to this as the problem of "survey slavery" (Chambers 1983). Development projects that were designed to include research as part of initial planning faced long and costly delays because of the time it took to design the survey, implement it, and do the analysis. The development research community was quick to recognize the need to increase the level of community participation in the research process. This led to the emergence of PRA. One can argue that PRA and participation have emerged to a kind of social movement and that many PRA specialists are quite zealous. In any case all the participatory techniques share a great deal and resonate with each other.

FURTHER READING

Chambers, Robert. *Whose Reality Counts? Putting the First Last*. London: Intermediate Technology Publications, 1997. In this and other books Chambers describes the argument for participatory approaches.

Rhoades, Robert E. *Breaking New Ground: Agricultural Anthropology*. Lima, Peru: International Potato Center, 1984. Highly instructive case study of the use of anthropology in the development of new potato technology.

Chapter 9

Cultural Brokerage

Anthropologists often mediate between people of different cultures. Usually referred to as cultural brokerage, this takes a number of different forms. The most common is the situation where the anthropologist serves to mediate between health care providers and individuals or communities that are ethnically distinctive. In these settings anthropologists sometimes provide the service directly or support other staff through training, research, or the development of media. Other examples of cultural brokerage can be found in cultural resource management where the anthropologist links government agencies involved in the construction of a project and the community being impacted (Downum and Price 1999:233).

A more recently developed idea that is closely linked to cultural brokerage is cultural competency. A person who is culturally competent has increased understanding and appreciation of cultural differences and the capacity to provide culturally appropriate services. This view is most typical in situations in which the provision of culturally appropriate health care is the goal. Both concepts, cultural brokerage and competency, are aspects of the same process. The first focuses on role and the second on knowledge and practice. The idea of cultural brokerage developed within anthropology, while cultural competency developed in other disciplines. While the literature on these ideas tends to use one or the other, it is clear that an effective culture broker is necessarily culturally competent. In this chapter we discuss both perspectives. The treatment presented here of culture brokerage is based on the seminal work of the notable medical anthropologist, Hazel Weidman. Her treatment of the topic is conceptually rich and based on a well-designed research and service program which she and her colleagues carried out in Miami, Florida. The discussion of cultural competency is based on materials from a number of different U.S. government agencies and some of the work of anthropologist Jean Gilbert who was the Director of the Department for Cultural Competence for Kaiser Perma-nente, a very large health maintenance organization.

THE DEVELOPMENT OF A CULTURAL BROKERAGE MODEL

One model for cultural brokerage is that developed by Hazel Weidman (Lefley and Bestman 1984:120; Weidman 1973). She based her concept on the idea developed originally by Eric Wolf to account for those persons who served as links between two cultural systems (1956) but modified and extended it to serve socially useful purposes. Wolf's view of culture broker was conceptualized in the context of his research into the linkage between peasant communities and national life in Mexico. The broker provides the individual link between sociocultural units.

It is this concept of role that forms the basis of the cultural brokerage model. Cultural brokerage is an intervention strategy of research, training, and service that links persons of two or more sociocultural systems through an individual, with the primary goals of making community service pro-grams more open and responsive to the needs of the community, and of improving the community's access to resources. While other types of inter-vention affect the community in substantial ways, cultural brokerage sub-stantially affects the service providers. In other words the focus of change processes are the agencies themselves.

CONCEPTS IN CULTURAL BROKERAGE

There are five concepts that are essential to understanding the cultural brokerage approach (Weidman 1975:312). These concepts are culture, health culture, coculture, culture broker, and culture mediation. The con-ceptualization used for culture is "the learned patterns of thought and be-havior characteristic of a population or society—a society's repertory of behavioral, cognitive, and emotional patterns" (Marvin Harris, in Weid-man 1975:312). The concepts used in the project provided a means by which project personnel could think about the cultural complexity in the community without engaging in an evaluative comparison of the alternative systems. This represents an important conceptual innovation that is an es-sential aspect of Weidman's transcultural perspective. This perspective places the anthropologist at the margins of the cultures of both the health care providers and the community (Weidman 1982:203; 1979:86).

The project's conceptual structure is quite well developed and internally consistent, and rather more explicit than some of the other conceptual schemes discussed in this text. Importantly, the health care providers were able to respond well to these ideas because they made sense to them.

Coupled with the culture concept is the health culture concept which is defined as "all the phenomena associated with the maintenance of well-being and problems of sickness with which people cope in traditional ways within their own social networks" (Weidman 1975:313). Health culture encompasses both "the cognitive and social-system aspects of folk therapies" (Weidman 1975:313). Cognitively, this includes health values and beliefs, guides for health action, and the relevant folk theories of "health maintenance, disease etiology, prevention, diagnosis, treatment and cure" (Weidman 1975:313). The social component of the concept deals with the structural-functional aspects of health related social statuses and roles.

An essential aspect of cultural brokerage is the concept of *coculture*. Coculture is a conceptual substitute for "subculture," though it is different in very important ways. Most importantly it stresses parity. Cocultures are equal in value to their participants. As expressed by Weidman, the concept of subculture implies that one group is subordinate to another. The role of the culture broker is introduced to accommodate the link between cocultures. The role concept is appropriate to the "parity of cultures" notion. To quote Weidman, "The label seems applicable whenever there is need to recognize the existence of separate cultural or subcultural systems and to acknowledge a particular person's role in establishing useful links between them" (1975:313). The parity idea, and the responsiveness, respect, and support that it produces, contributes to the acceptance of the approach to community members. Parity does not mean that the cultures are the same. As Weidman states, use of the concept results in the juxtaposition of cultural systems that "provides the basis for comparison of congruent and non-congruent elements in them" (1982:210). This perspective is consistent with the comparative method of anthropology as a research science (Weidman 1982:210).

The concept, as noted above, developed out of research and teaching activities at the hospital and was ultimately expressed in project organization; that is, persons were hired as culture brokers. The culture broker's linkage activities occurred in two frameworks. The broker served to link the community health culture and the orthodox health care system so as to facilitate the provision of orthodox care that is "coculturally informed." The second arena for linkages is the community and the "broader social, economic, and political system" (Weidman 1975:314).

The process of linkage is labeled *culture mediation*. In practical terms this means the provision of culturally appropriate services. Effective mediation facilitates better interaction between representatives of the cocultures represented in a community. The basis for cultural mediation is the culture broker's knowledge of the involved cultures. This requires a strong commitment to synthesis of various health cultural traditions as well as various scientific disciplines. The process of mediation will be discussed below.

THE CULTURE BROKER ROLE

The culture broker is to be viewed as an important player in the interactions between two parts of a larger cultural system. In the scientific literature on brokerage, the broker links traditional and modern, national and local, or European and "native." Weidman stresses the buffering and mediation that serves to facilitate harmony and equality between cocultures, while they recognize that their approach restructures community services. The conception of the broker's role includes a purposive and intentional aspect that does not appear in the original conception (Weidman 1985).

The application of the cultural brokerage approach is motivated by the need to increase accessibility to basic medical care in the United States. There exists in every complex society a range of alternative health care systems that typically are in competition. Different viable health cultures are found throughout the world in isolated rural areas and in dense urban settlements. In one way or another, the therapeutic practices that are part of these health cultures are in competition with each other and modern medicine. The position of Western medicine in this competition is unique. As Weidman noted, "Since it emerged in the Western world, that social institution called 'scientific' or 'modern' medicine has been sanctioned internationally as being ultimately responsible for the health of national populations" (1979:85). In the total scope of human history this is a relatively recent event. Throughout the world much health maintenance behavior is based not on "scientific" medicine but on traditional health culture. According to Weidman, "Our field of inquiry is a culturally plural one. In every urban center in the world today we must recognize a 'pluriverse' of health cultures, one of which is our own or that of Western medicine, all of which are interacting or inhibiting from interacting on the basis of reciprocal images of each other" (Weidman 1973:8).

In these settings the culture broker links alternative systems that are equivalent. This, of course, relates to the discussion of coculture indicated above. The relationship between the systems is thought to be symmetrical. The parity concept is what distinguishes the culture broker from the more common outreach worker. This more typical role is consistent with the view that Western medicine is dominant and the cultural alternatives are to be aided, displaced, or changed because of their impotence. Typical outreach workers are usually agents for the dominant culture and often work in an inherently compromised political position.

Because the culture brokers are thought to operate between two systems at parity, the broker's function calls for substantial knowledge of the two systems involved. Therefore brokerage requires ongoing research.

THE PROCESS OF CULTURAL BROKERAGE

The process of cultural brokerage includes the establishment and maintenance of a system of interaction, mutual support, and communication between cocultures expressed through the culture broker's role. The process of mediation protects the cultural values of the involved ethnic groups. It is within this framework that change occurs. Change is toward increased cultural appropriateness, access to resources, better health, and more compliance with medical regimens (Weidman 1985). The potential for change goes much beyond health, social, and economic conditions and may also be positively influenced. The basic process can include a variety of strategies that benefit community members, including many of the strategies discussed in this section of the book, such as advocacy.

PHASES OF THE PROCESS

1. The compilation of research data on the health culture of all the cocultures in the community. This includes both the traditional and orthodox health systems.

2. The training of brokers in aspects of community life. Culture brokers are usually members of the ethnic group being related to, as well as being trained social scientists. The primary reference in the training is health culture. The training may involve participation in the initial research.

3. Early activation of the culture broker role usually involves collaboration with institutionally based health care personnel to assist in providing culturally more appropriate health care. In addition, the broker fosters referral relationships with traditional health practitioners and trains community people to assume broker roles. These activities are associated with continual involvement in research to increase the project's database and support community action projects.

4. The brokerage efforts cause change in both the community and the orthodox health care system. These include increased knowledge of the culture of the community on the part of the health care providers and improvements in the community's resource base. Overall improvements in mental health levels occur.

Prior to implementation of a culture broker program, interactions between community members and the health care facility are based largely on decisions of the individual community member. There are no outreach or other efforts at linkage. The institution does not possess any significant knowledge about the patient's way of life. This way of life is conceptualized in subcultural terms, that is, inevitably changing to the pattern of the institutional or dominant culture. The little information about patient subculture is obtained on a nonsystematic, ad hoc basis. Encounters between health care institutions and the community are almost always between therapist and "sick person." That is, the interactions are single-stranded.

In the early phase of implementation a new formal role is created, the culture broker, and the culture parity concept is asserted. The parity concept is an ideological commitment to be operationalized programmatically. Parity may not be manifested in the relationship between the two cocultures in the larger political realm. Later, the culture broker comes to be more throughly integrated into both cocultures, serving as a knowledge resource for both.

A CASE STUDY: THE MIAMI COMMUNITY MENTAL HEALTH PROGRAM

The Miami Community Mental Health Program was designed to serve the mental health needs of a large, ethnically diverse area of Miami (Lefley and Bestman 1984:122). The area was inhabited by five major ethnic groups: Bahamians, Cubans, Haitians, Puerto Ricans, and African Americans. Diverse ethnically, this population exhibited many of the stresses typical of low-income, inner-city populations. The area had higher rates of crime and unemployment and much substandard housing. Program designers felt that the standard "medical model" approach would be inadequate for achieving mental health improvements. It was felt that the traditional approach would not produce culturally appropriate health care. The diversity of causes of ill health and the cultural complexities of the community would not yield to the orthodox treatments available in the hospital.

The Miami model was built upon a thorough community research project. An important research finding was documentation of the distinctive differences in knowledge and behavior of the five ethnic groups vis-à-vis mental health. The diverse conditions under which they lived produced culturally patterned health conditions, including a number of culture-bound syndromes not recognized by the biomedically trained care providers. In the community "alternative healing modalities were widely used, often in conjunction with orthodox medical treatment" (Lefley and Bestman 1984: 121). "Differential perceptions of causation and remediation of illness" were identified (Lefley and Bestman 1984:121). The most fundamental and far-reaching conclusion from the research was that "culturally specific therapeutic interventions were needed to deal with ethnic variables in these diverse groups" (Lefley 1975:317).

Basing their approach on the existing mental health services of the hospital, the project attempted to develop a culturally appropriate approach. The county-owned hospital is a 1,250-bed general hospital serving an area of Dade County populated by 200,000 persons. This economically depressed area manifests significant numbers of mental health problems. Although the hospital seems in the middle of things, it is somewhat inaccessible to the residents of the catchment area. Public transportation is, for example, inadequate for getting patients to the clinic. The service is impersonal and culturally inappropriate. The diagnosis procedure is based on white middle-class conceptions of symptoms. Patients tended to come to the hospital only when they were desperate, when "They have been stabbed or shot or otherwise injured, when they are critically ill, or when they are so behaviorally deranged that the police deliver them to our doorstep" (Sussex and Weidman 1975:307).

The hospital's psychiatric service had operated as a disease-focused mental health service that viewed health in terms of the biomedical model. That is, care was based on

the assumption that a given *disease* should be treated in a certain generally accepted way because it always has the same cause, . . . and always responds (or should respond) to a particular type of treatment. So the standard nomenclature is used, the usual signs and symptoms of the mental-status examination are duly elicited and recorded, and the customary therapeutic procedures are prescribed. (Sussex and Weidman 1975:307)

The psychiatric service had a rather high case load largely derived from a busy emergency service. The goal of the service was behavior control, mostly through the use of drugs. Patients who did not respond were typically sent to a state hospital. Case management was made more difficult by limitations in after-care treatment.

As the project evolved, an action component was added. This effort emerged directly from the work of five field teams that were ethnically identical to the different communities. As is often the case with ethnographic field work, the teams developed good rapport with community members. Although not necessarily intended, the teams' efforts resulted in increased sensitivity to the possibilities for improved mental health services for the community. As an outgrowth of this, there was increased demand for appropriate services. The funding for action allowed the placement of the five ethnically specific teams. The five teams were ultimately supplemented with teams representing the substantial elderly Anglo-American and African-American populations. The efforts of each of the ethnically specific teams were coordinated by a community advisory board that assisted in defining program goals and team personnel recruitment. Each team was directed by a social scientist trained, in most cases, to the Ph.D. level. These directors were the culture brokers referred to as the key component of this approach.

One important role of the culture broker is to serve as a bridge between the community and the hospital. This effort included acting as liaison between community leaders and the hospital. There was to be a special effort at serving as a link between the different kinds of physicians and community members who face particular health problems. The broker was to serve as both a researcher and a teacher in the program. As teachers, the brokers were engaged in augmenting courses in various hospital training programs, instructing in community orientation classes for hospital staff, consulting on the health problems of individual patients, and assisting students on projects. Further, the culture brokers were to act as trainers of community representatives in various areas, as well as training various health professionals as culture brokers.

The other important aspect of the broker role developed in the community where they organized community groups with social action goals. These efforts often started with assessments of community needs that were used for community planning and proposal development. The brokers could be thought of as social change catalysts that acted primarily through their research. Research was done in support of many different goals that the community related to mental health problems. These included research in support of day care centers, hot lunch programs, and changes in housing policy. These community involvements also included acting as resource specialists to bring consumers together with service providers in Miami. This helped community members to act when agencies were lacking or inadequate (Lefley 1975:318).

Each ethnic community has its own pattern of program development, although each team provides "essential psychiatric services" (Lefley and Bestman 1984:127). Much of the content of program activities was based on advice given by community advisory boards. Some of the early efforts included research done on behalf of community groups (Lefley and Bestman 1984:127). It is important to remember that the teams functioned both in the hospital and community frameworks.

The Miami Project was based on the capacity of a group of anthropologists to effectively mediate between the cultures found in Miami and the culture of the care providers in a large public hospital. The precedents established in this project have been expressed in public-sector community mental health programming. For example, Dr. Evalina Bestman, one of the early culture brokers, continues to serve as the Director of the New Horizons Community Mental Health Center in Miami (Weidman 2001). This required skills and knowledge that subsequently came to be referred to as cultural competency. In the next section of this chapter, this emerging concept is discussed.

CULTURAL COMPETENCE

Cultural competence consists of the skills, knowledge, and policies that allow a person or organization to provide services effectively in a cross-cultural situation.[1] This idea has become an important concern in American medicine since the 1980s and was manifested in a number of ways. Professional associations such as the American Medical Association have published recommendations on how to offer culturally competent health care for specific types of clients (American Medical Association 2001). Federal agencies such as the Administration on Aging have developed guides for the provision of culturally competent services for older people (U.S. Administration on Aging 2001). The U.S. Public Health Service supported research toward the development of national standards for culturally and linguistically appropriate health care (Office of Minority Health, U.S. Public Health Service n.d.). The Medicaid Program, through its administrative agency, the Health Care Financing Administration (HCFA), has proposed regulations mandating that state Medicaid programs develop guidance for the provision of culturally competent care in Medicaid funded programs. Some large health care organizations, such as Kaiser Permanente, are addressing cultural diversity issues in service provision through training programs, education of staff, and publication of handbooks in order to achieve their quality of care and marketing goals. There are national associations that are serving as information clearing houses on these issues.

Concern for the impact of cultural differences on health care outcomes has drawn "the attention of regulatory and accrediting agencies" (Gilbert 1998:3). Some states have included specific cultural and linguistic conditions in their contract payments to organizations providing care for Medicaid recipients that come into effect when the population of a cultural group reaches a certain level (Gilbert 1998:3). Cultural training for health care professionals is now recommended by the Joint Commission for the Accreditation of Healthcare Organizations (Gilbert 1998).

The provision is achieved in many ways in health care organizations. Often discussed is support of the process of increasing cross-cultural knowledge and sensitivity resulting in respect for cultural diversity. In addition, the following activities are often included in cultural competency–enhancing programming: hiring members of the community to provide health care; offering patient education materials and signage in languages of the patients; developing a participatory relationship with the community; publication of handbooks that describe population characteristics for providers; including cultural competency content in continuing medical education; providing for and working effectively with translators; and assessing the organization's cultural competency.

The development of concern for cultural competency on the part of biomedicine is a corollary of increasing cultural diversity nationally. That is, there is increasing interest in these issues because of the changing nature of

1. This definition is based on a statement definition from the Child Development Center, Georgetown University (1989).

the American population through immigration resulting in many different ethnic communities in the United States and the changing political significance of ethnicity. These same forces also relate to the increased acceptance directed toward alternative or complementary medicine. Health care providers who are culturally competent will also tend to advocate certain kinds of alternative medicines. In addition, traditional healers may be incorporated in health care provider cultural competency training.

Concepts from anthropology are important in the cultural competency movement. Needless to say, the most important of these ideas is culture. The definition used in the U.S. Administration on Aging (AoA) publication, *Achieving Cultural Competence: A Guidebook for Providers of Services to Older Americans*, uses this definition of culture: "the shared values, traditions, norms, customs, arts, history, folklore, and institutions of a group of people" (2001:8). From the perspective of contemporary anthropology this definition appears inadequate and anachronistic because it assumes cultural homogeneity and does not recognize the creative impact of individual practices in cultural settings. It is likely that as the cultural competency literature expands, it will recapitulate many of the same conceptual developments in anthropological usage of the culture concept. The AoA Guidebook exemplifies this by noting that the "broad" ethnic and racial groupings that are often used such as African-American, Hispanic, and American Indian are "sometimes misleading" (2001:8). These categories reflect bureaucratic convenience and certainly mask tremendous significant diversity. Refinement of their use of the culture concept can be seen in their recognition of "factors that influence culture." The Administration on Aging's guidebook suggests that "the cultures of patients and providers may be affected by: educational level; income level; geographic residence; identification with community religious, professional, community service, political groups; individual experiences; place of birth; length of residency in the [United States], age" (2001:8).

While the goal of instilling cultural competency in health programs is good, it is not without potential negative consequences. The line between racial profiling and cultural competency is a fine one. There is a potential problem of ethnic stereotyping. Because of the problem of stereotyping, it is necessary to base the process upon which culturally competent care is provided on individual patient assessment rather than applying broad culturally specific guidelines about some ethnic group. Nevertheless, it is important for health care providers to have knowledge of the cultures of their clients in order to comprehend what is possible and what questions to ask. However much cultural knowledge is valued, it is important to recognize the individual. This means that interview practices that result in the identification of the client's circumstance are vitally important to providing culturally appropriate care. Also problematic is the potential that concern about cultural variables will mask the structural constraints that keep many ethnic minorities from having access to health care. These populations may also have limited income, no insurance, limited education, transportation problems, and substantial impairments. Poverty is not ethnicity.

KAISER PERMANENTE CULTURAL COMPETENCY PROGRAM: A CASE STUDY

Kaiser Permanente is the nation's largest not-for-profit health maintenance organization with over 8 million members in many states. The organization is interesting because of its role in pioneering the use of group practice prepayment for health services. This was done initially to provide health care for workers involved in Depression era public works construction in California and Washington and wartime ship construction in California. With the end of World War II, its membership was open to the public. Kaiser Permanente now provides health care in many states and is committed to addressing cultural issues (Kaiser Permanente 1996).

Kaiser Permanente's cultural competency programming is focused on training of staff and documentation of characteristics of the diverse populations represented among their members. Kaiser Permanente uses seminars to provide training in culturally appropriate clinical practice. The core of the training is scripted scenarios presented by an in-course acting group. These depict positive and negative clinical encounters between persons of different cultures and allow for discussion. Medical anthropologist, M. Jean Gilbert, at the time the Director of the Office of Cultural Competence for Kaiser Permanente, describes this training: "The use of acted scenarios provides an opportunity to bring up many subtle and not so subtle issues that may be barriers to good communication between patients and health professionals. Cultural misunderstandings are vividly portrayed. Preparation of the scripts requires the combined skills of the scriptwriter, physician and medical anthropologist" (Gilbert 1998).

In addition to training, Kaiser Permanente has developed a series of handbooks focused on the documentation of ethnic and cultural groups in its membership. These handbooks were prepared under the leadership of a Kaiser Permanente staff physician from the ethnic group. He or she works with a team of writers, researchers, and reviewer physicians. The documents include information about the demographics of the group, health beliefs, risk factors, and epidemiological data in an easy-to-use format.

SUMMARY

The ideas behind the cultural competency movement are parallel and consistent with cultural brokerage. The two approaches are similar in terms of purpose, values, and foundation concepts. The differences appear to be a matter of emphasis and perspective and disciplinary location. Cultural brokerage, focuses on a specific role. Being an effective culture broker in the sense discussed by Weidman involves cultural competency skills. The basic strategy of the cultural competency movement is to disseminate training that allows brokerage to occur within an organization.

The approaches presented in this chapter represent useful strategies for applying anthropological knowledge to a wide range of contexts. It, quite obviously, has had its utility demonstrated in health and medical programs. Its primary purpose is linking the culture of the agency with that of both individual users or communities, with the intent of increasing the cultural appropriateness of services and increasing the resource base of the community.

Cultural brokerage functions have long been a part of the applied anthropologist's role. What has come to be called cultural competency has always been part of the anthropological scheme of things, though unnamed. These approaches seem especially useful where there is a need to link a service-providing organization with an ethnic community, and where there is a commitment to cultural pluralism.

FURTHER READING

Kleinman, Arthur. *Patients and Healers in the Context of Culture.* Berkeley: University of California Press, 1980. This remains a classic statement on the issues associated with culture and health. It is frequently cited in the cultural competency literature.

MacArthur, John R., Sandra Dudley, and Holly Ann Williams. Approaches to Facilitating Health Care Acceptance: A Case Example from Karenni Refugees. In *Caring for Those in Crisis: Integrating Anthropology and Public Health in Complex Humanitarian Emergencies.* Holly Ann Williams, ed. NAPA Bulletin 21. Washington, D.C.: American Anthropological Association, 2001. This publication reports recent cultural brokerage work in a Thailand refugee camp.

Chapter 10

Social Marketing

Social marketing is a social change strategy that combines commercial marketing techniques with applied social science to promote voluntary behavior change that is socially beneficial. Although social marketing can be used for a wide variety of purposes, it has been most widely adopted by public health professionals (Ling, Franklin, Lindsteadt, and Searon 1992). Examples of healthy behaviors promoted using social marketing include condom use (Fishbein, Guenther-Grey, Johnson, Wolitski, and McAlister 1997; Smith and Middlestadt 1993), prevention of smoking (Hastings, MacFadyen, Mackintosh, and Lowry 1998), and contraceptive use (Rangun and Karim 1991).

Used in both the developed and developing countries (Manoff 1985: 221), social marketing represents a synthesis of "marketing, mass communication, instructional design, health education, behavioral analysis, anthropology, and related social sciences" (Academy for Educational Development 1987:67). Commercial marketing provides the conceptual framework and analytical techniques for segmenting market audiences, developing, pricing, testing, and distributing products.

This conceptual framework views the consumer at the center of an exchange process in which s/he is acting primarily out of self-interest—attempting to maximize their ability to satisfy wants and needs and minimize what they must sacrifice to obtain them (Kotler and Armstrong 1996). This framework includes five key concepts involved in the exchange process: the product (the health behavior being promoted) and its competition (the risk behavior currently practiced); the price (social, emotional, and monetary costs exchanged for the product's benefits); place (where the exchange takes place and/or the target behavior is practiced); and promotion (activities used to facilitate the exchange). (Coreil, Bryant, and Henderson 2001)

The bedrock of social marketing practice is "a commitment to understand consumer needs and to produce products, programs or practices to enable them to better solve their problems" (Bryant and Lindenberger 1992:1). Consistent with an anthropological perspective, social marketers study the sociocultural context in which change occurs and attempt to learn as much as possible about the people whose behavior they want to change.

Because the social marketing process requires skills and viewpoints that are part of being an anthropologist, we find anthropologists working in all stages of the social marketing process, especially those requiring research. Social marketing uses qualitative and quantitative research during its early planning phases and for careful testing of marketing strategies and promotional materials before an intervention is implemented. Social marketers also rely on careful monitoring and evaluation to make mid-course adjustments and assess program impact. Good ethnographers bring many useful skills to the process including the "creative interpretation of research into ingenious message design" (Manoff 1988:4). The attitudes of social marketers about research are highly consistent with those of ethnographers. Both have a strong commitment to the "native" viewpoint and an appreciation of respecting people's values, norms, and beliefs.

In this chapter social marketing is illustrated by a national breastfeeding promotion program developed by Best Start Social Marketing, Inc. This project began in the late 1980s as an effort to increase breastfeeding among low-income women in the southeastern United States. After conducting consumer research in the southeast, program materials were developed under the direction of anthropologists Carol Bryant and Jim Lindenberger, and the program was implemented in the early 1990s (see van Willigen 1993 for a description of the initial Best Start Project). More recently, a second phase of the program, called *Loving Support Makes Breastfeeding Work*, was funded by the U.S. Department of Agriculture's Food and Nutrition Service (FNS) and implemented nationally. This follow-up project is described later in this chapter.

While social marketing draws heavily from commercial marketing, there are differences (Academy for Educational Development 1987:70). First, the changes called for in commercial marketing are often less complex than those aspired to through social marketing. For example, it is less complicated to persuade people to switch cigarette brands than to stop smoking. Second, the new behavior or product may be more controversial. The promotion of safe-sex practices is made difficult because of public modesty standards. Third, the new products or practices advocated in social marketing may be less satisfying to people. In the case of smoking, for example, present gratification is exchanged for future health improvements. Fourth, often the intended audience of social marketing has fewer resources and cannot easily act on their new information. Many times the target population is poor. Fifth, the politics of social marketing often requires high levels of success. In the commercial realm a small increase in market share may justify substantial marketing investment, while in the public arena large, sustained increases are demanded.

DEVELOPMENT OF THE APPROACH

The use of the term *social marketing* dates from the late 1960s and grew out of discussions between Philip Kotler and Richard Manoff (Kotler 1975; Manoff 1985). Kotler was a professor of marketing from Northwestern University, and Manoff was director of a marketing firm that had begun to approach nutrition and health education as a marketing problem. The term social marketing was used to distinguish between marketing commercial products and marketing better health practices. The early 1970s saw the increased academic interest in the idea: there were more publications on it and, of course, considerable debate about the "but is it marketing?" question. In the last 15 years, social marketing has been adopted by a wide range of public health and social service organizations in the United States, including the National Cancer Institute, American Cancer Society, Centers for Disease Control and Prevention, U.S. Department of Agriculture, the Centers for Medicaid and Medicare, and the American Association of Retired Persons (AARP). Several textbooks have been published (Andreasen 1995; Kotler and Roberto 1989; Kotler and Lee in press; Siegel and Donner 1998), academic centers have been established at the University of South Florida and the University of Strathclyde, and a peer review journal, *The Social Marketing Quarterly*, has been published.

Key Concepts

There are a number of concepts that are fundamental to understanding the process. *Marketing* involves those activities that result in the movement of goods and services from producer to consumer in response to consumer demand, satisfying consumer needs, and achieving the goals of the producer. Increasingly marketing is seen as a process of meeting consumer demand rather than advertising or persuasion. The goal of commercial marketing is a profit or increase in market share. In social marketing the goal is societal improvement or social problem solving, a process that often involves creating demand for a socially beneficial product or developing products or programs to meet consumer needs. The people to whom social marketing efforts are directed are referred to as the *target audience*. The primary audience refers to the people whose behavior you wish to change. This group may be segmented in various ways: their current behavior, future intentions, the benefits they find most attractive, the price they are willing to pay, where they can be reached, their differential responsiveness to specific promotional tactics, or sociodemographic characteristics (Coreil et al. 2001). The secondary audience is comprised of people who influence the decision making of the primary audience. For example, the mothers and husbands of potentially breastfeeding women are a good example of a secondary audience. The tertiary audience is comprised of personnel and opinion leaders in the community who can serve as partners in bringing about the desired change. It may also include more distant influencers, such as the general public. Effective social marketing is often based on identification and targeting of a large number of audience segments. In a Brazilian breastfeeding promotion project eight distinctive target audiences were identified. These were doctors, health services, hospitals, infant food industry, industry in general, community, government officials and mothers (Manoff 1985:48).

Information or *communication channels* refers to the vehicles or means of communicating with the target audience. They include interpersonal channels (e.g., physicians), the media (television, radio, outdoor advertising), and non-traditional sources, such as libraries, retail outlets, or beauticians. Typically, mass media like radio and television are combined with print media and personal communication. An important task in social marketing is to identify the most effective channels for communicating each message. In general, mass media is used to transmit short, persuasive, or informational messages and create a climate conducive for change. Print material is used for more lengthy, instructional messages, and personal communication is used for the more complex information that requires interaction and social support.

Social marketing has various functions. *Demand creation* involves letting people know about the availability of a particular service or product. This requires more than simple publicity. The people need to know the relative advantage of a particular innovation and the community itself needs to be motivated to act on a particular situation.

THE SOCIAL MARKETING PROCESS

The social marketing process consists of a long-term program to produce sustainable changes in a clearly defined set of behaviors in a large population (Academy for Educational Development 1987:75). There are various conceptions of the process in the literature on social marketing (Andreasen 1995; Coreil et al. 2001; Fine 1981; Kotler and Roberto 1989; Manoff 1985). I based the discussion of process on the one developed in the Best Start project (Bryant and Lindenberger 1992).

The social marketing process has five phases according to Bryant and Lindenberger. These are audience analysis (initial planning and formative research), strategy formation, program development, program implementation, and program monitoring and revisions (1992). While there are five phases, in practice the different stages are repeated depending on the experience with the specific project. That is, if a part of the strategy is not working, the team will go through a phase of the process again. As they say, the process is iterative. You change what you do, based on what you learn.

Audience analysis starts with a review of recent literature on the problem and examination of existing programs that deal with the problem. Often staff of exemplary programs are interviewed and materials produced by their program reviewed. A team of program planners may make preliminary decisions about possible audience segments, behavioral recommendations, and the factors they may have to address to bring about change. Formative research is then conducted to obtain the information needed to segment the audience and to gain an understanding of how a segment perceives the product's benefits and costs, identify the most appropriate places to reach each segment, and determine the best promotional tactics for bringing about the desired change. Identification of program partners including collaborating agencies occurs in this phase. Research makes use of in-depth interviews, focus groups, and surveys of various types, creating a foundation for the project.

Formative research includes preliminary research on the community and agency context of the project. Social marketers need to know the nature of the organizations and persons with whom they will be working. These people need to achieve consensus on the nature of the problem. It is this consensus that makes things work. It is very important to identify the "real players" rather than the formal leadership as depicted in the organization chart. When the concerns of the cooperating professionals are not understood and addressed, projects fail.

Characteristically, formative research identifies the target population's perception of the problem and the nature of resistance points. When working in areas that have not been explored previously, marketing research typically has a very large qualitative component designed to identify the factors that motivate and deter people from adopting the target behavior. Formative research also requires the identification of the primary, secondary, and tertiary target audiences with the appropriate segmentations.

Staff identify media that are available for the project. Just what the target audience listens to, watches and reads are important questions. In developed countries this information is often readily available from media outlets. In less developed countries it may be necessary to research the question of media exposure. This information is necessary for the development of an effective media plan.

During this early phase the team carefully establishes network ties with organizations that may be interested in the project's problem. These can be private voluntary organizations, religious organizations, commercial organizations, and various governmental organizations. This collaboration will back up the media campaign. Organizational networking is done to multiply the impact of messages, to obtain feedback from stakeholders, and to decrease interagency competition. The second stage in the social marketing process, *strategy formation*, is done in planning sessions with staff and key advisors, who are often representative of stakeholders and program partners. The first step in strategy formation is to select specific audience segments to reach. Once the audience has been identified, the social marketing team determines the most appropriate behavioral recommendations or objectives for the project. These objectives are expressed in measurable action terms that relate to goals of the project. Objectives need to be measurable, expressed in terms of "required input, desired output, and a time frame" (Manoff 1985:106). Manoff warns that they can be "too broad, too vague, too unrealistic, or 'off-target'" (1985:106). It is important to have measurable objectives so that evaluation of performance is possible.

The strategy formation stage is concluded with identification of the product benefits to be promoted, the costs that must be lowered or made more acceptable, the best place to distribute products or information, and the "tactics and activities to facilitate change, e.g., legislative change, policy development and organizational change, professional training, peer counselor programs, curriculum development, consumer education, public relations, direct marketing, advertising, face-to-face communication, media advocacy, and grass roots advocacy"(Coreil et al. 2001). These decisions are summarized in a written social marketing plan. The third stage is *program development*, a stage often carried out with the help of an advertising agency or other creative team. Program development includes message design and materials development. The entire program development stage is directed by the social marketing plan. Media planning includes "preparation of draft or prototype materials; materials testing; final production and program inauguration" (Manoff 1985:111). The actual media can be developed "in-house" or they can be purchased from advertising agencies. Prototype versions of public service announcements, pamphlets, instructional tapes, advertisements, and other messages are prepared, carefully pretested, and revised. Pretesting is done to determine if the materials are comprehensible, culturally relevant, believable, persuasive, emotionally appealing, memorable, and free of annoying or offensive elements. Product development includes decisions about product names, packaging, price, and supportive promotion and sales materials. All this requires the technical skills of persons trained in media. The anthropologist will bring skills that will support the development of the product through research.

After pretesting, messages and materials enter final production. The team makes presentations of the project to public officials and community groups for approval and guidance. The presentation will include supporting research results that can guide their decisions about the effects of the materials.

Also part of the development stage is identification of "primary, secondary and tertiary audiences and their component segments" (Manoff 1988: 3). Persons and institutions that can advocate the desired change are identified, and if necessary, research is conducted to understand how to motivate them to participate in the program. The team looks for opinion leaders in the community or any person that would "enhance credibility" of the messages thus increasing the chances for change in behavior. The last component of the strategy development stage is the determination of the media use patterns of the population.

Channel analysis continues as part of the program development phase. In channel analysis researchers identify the pathways through which messages, products, and services can be delivered to a population (Lefebvre and Flora 1988:305) and how these pathways complement and compete. In the social marketing framework this can include everything from electronic and print media to social networks and opinion leaders. It is necessary to inventory all the places where a person encounters messages and these in turn become possible channels to use in the marketing process. Lefebvre and Flora speak of the identification of "life path points" that they exemplify from an American urban setting as laundromats, groceries, restaurants, and bus stops. In channel analysis the researcher not only knows what channels the population is exposed to but what are most influential and important. For example, for certain health behavior changes, mass media does not present credible information and personal networks do.

The fourth stage is *program implementation*. This phase includes implementation of policy changes, training of professionals, and distribution of educational materials. Also the public information program may be launched. Many social marketing projects require 6 to 18 months to reach the implementation phase, making social marketing incompatible with many planning cycles that expect funds to be spent and programs launched within a single fiscal year. Although coordination is important for any program, social marketing projects require managers to balance an unusually large number of staff, consultants, subcontractors, and other stakeholders simultaneously. Careful timing of multiple program components, such as legislative advocacy, service improvements, professional training, materials distribution, and communications activities is critical.

The last phase of the social marketing process is *program monitoring and revision*. This has two components, formative and summative. The formative evaluation determines strengths and weaknesses of project components so that the project can be improved. The team introduces improvements in process to increase effectiveness. Summative research finds out the actual impact of the project. Much of the summative research consists of studies to identify knowledge, attitudes, and practices of the project's products by potential consumers. These are repeated, with uniform measures and sampling, so that the results can be compared, wave after wave, to answer questions like, "What does the target audience know and do because of the project?" These may be supplemented with qualitative data collection to get at meanings that cannot be investigated with surveys.

SOCIAL MARKETING AND FOCUS GROUPS

A research technique often used in designing the social marketing plan is the focus group or group depth interview. Sociologist Robert K. Merton developed focus group technique, while doing research on German propaganda films done during World War II, to provide an interpretive framework for the quantitative data collected from propaganda film viewers to try to find out why they answered questions the way they did about their psychological responses to propaganda films (Merton and Kendall 1946; Merton 1990). Examples of the use of focus group research can be found in many areas, including social action programs (Schearer 1981), family planning (Folch-Lyon, Macorra, and Schearer 1981), vitamin supplement use (Pollard 1987), and educational evaluation (Hess 1991).

A focus group is a small group discussion guided by a moderator to develop understanding about the group participants' perceptions of a designated topic. While it can be argued that data collection efficiency is improved because you are increasing the number of interviewees being interviewed at one time, more important are the effects of the interaction of the participants being interviewed. Morgan states this clearly when he says, "The hallmark of focus groups is the explicit use of the group interaction to produce data and insights that would be less accessible without the interaction found in a group" (1988:12). While the interaction deals with the content specified by the moderator, the interaction should be informal and lively. Morgan describes it as being like a conversation between neighbors or friends.

The composition of focus groups is carefully planned to produce representative information about the population. The difficulty and cost of recruiting participants can vary considerably with the nature of the research problem. When a highly specialized population is being researched, it may be expensive to find qualified participants. The number of group participants is typically between six and eight, although sometimes the groups are larger (Morgan 1988).

Smaller groups involve more interviewee participation and are more susceptible to the impact of domineering persons. Larger groups require more moderator participation. Unless you are investigating the life of a small organization, it is unlikely that your research results will be statistically generalizable. It is best to over-recruit participants so that persons that are inappropriate can be easily replaced. The sessions usually do not last more than two hours. It is important to be very aware of the problem of bias in participant selection. It is also important to screen the participants carefully so that you are sure they do share the relevant attributes. As Morgan states it, "participants must feel able to talk to each other, and wide gaps in social background or life-style can defeat this" (1988:46). Gender, ethnicity, age, and class may influence willingness to discuss a topic. While participant similarity is important, it is better if the interviewees do not know each other.

The number of focus groups completed is an important consideration methodologically and practically. The increase in the number of types of participants, of course, will lead to an increase in the number of groups. For example, if urban and rural differences are important, you will need groups for each type.

An important part of quality data collection is the creation of a permissive, nonthreatening atmosphere, conducive to revelation and disclosure (Bryant, Lazarov, Light, Bailey, Coreil, and D'Angelo 1989:19). Moderator skill and group homogeneity are important factors in establishing these conditions. Moderator involvement varies with the purpose of the research. As Morgan states it, "If the goal is to learn something new from participants, then it is best to let them speak for themselves" (1988:49). High involvement may be called for when it is necessary to get the discussion back on the topic, when the group loses energy, when minority positions are stifled, when domineering individuals need to be shut down, and when some participants need to be encouraged (Morgan 1988:51). Morgan encourages low involvement through a process he calls group "self-management." To a large extent this involves simply giving the focus group participants expectations of their own behavior through instruction that will lead them in the desired direction. For example, you might tell them to expect that if they get off track a member of the group will pull them back. Other practitioners of the technique may more directly intervene. It is also possible to intervene more at the end of the session to help make sure that the ground is covered. In any case, the interviewer "must develop the practice of continuously assessing the interview as it is in process" (Merton, Fiske, and Kendall 1990:11).

Like other techniques, focus group interviewing has both strengths and weaknesses. The technique is practical because it can be done quickly and easily. Morgan says, "when time and/or money are essential considerations, it is often possible to design focus group research when other methods would be prohibitive" (1988:20). A focus group–based research project does not require large teams of interviewers. Kumar estimates that a project based on 10 to 15 interview sessions can be carried out within six weeks under normal conditions (1987:6).

Focus groups are most useful for the initial discovery of factors that must be addressed in social marketing projects, such as perceived benefits and costs. They are not appropriate, however, for collecting quantitative data needed to determine which factors have a statistically significant impact on behavior. Unfortunately, some social marketing researchers have relied too extensively on focus groups and attempted to quantify results, and as a result, their findings have been misleading. Focus group research also requires careful planning, facilitation skills, and interpretation. The approach may not work well on topics that are highly private, and it is sometimes difficult to get all persons in the group to participate equally. It is imperative to note that an important principle in ethical research practice is that the researcher does not share information obtained from one informant with another. While this is the essential feature of the focus group approach, people can choose not to talk. While this goes far to solve the ethical problem, it raises considerable methodological issues. Privacy and confidentiality may go far to encourage talk.

BEST START: A BREASTFEEDING PROMOTION PROJECT— A CASE STUDY

Best Start Social Marketing is a nonprofit social marketing firm that began as a clearinghouse for materials related to Bryant and Lindenberger's first breastfeeding promotion project in the southeastern United States. The company soon expanded into a social marketing firm, specializing in public health program design and materials development. Its most recent breastfeeding promotion project, called *Loving Support Makes Breastfeeding Work*, is a comprehensive, national program for promoting breastfeeding initiation and duration among women participating in the Supplemental Food and Nutrition Program for Women, Infants, and Children (WIC) and other economically disadvantaged families in the United States. Breastfeeding offers considerable advantages over bottlefeeding. Mothers benefit because it offers a quicker recovery from childbirth, stronger bonding with the infant, and an emotionally satisfying activity. The infants are better off because it offers the best nutrition for normal growth and development, protection against disease, especially ear infections and gastrointestinal illness, and decreased risk of allergies. There are significant societal benefits. Breastfeeding results in stronger family bonds, increased self-esteem of women, decreased cost of infant formula in food subsidy programs and decreased health care costs for infants (Bryant et al. 1989:11). Because of these advantages the U.S. Department of Health and Human Services' national health objectives include the goal of increasing breastfeeding initiation to 75 percent of mothers at hospital discharge and 50 percent at six months (http://www.cdc.gov/breastfeeding/policy-hp2010.htm). That is, increasing breastfeeding is a matter of national policy in the United States.

In spite of the advantages of breastfeeding and considerable investment in public health education programs, the rate of breastfeeding among economically disadvantaged women enrolled in WIC remained low. When this project was initiated in 1995, 59.7 percent of infants in the United

States were breastfed in the hospital and 21.6 percent at six months post-partum, in contrast to only 46.6 percent and 12.7 percent respectively of infants enrolled in the WIC (Ryan 1997).

Aware of the potential to reach millions of pregnant women enrolled in WIC, Best Start Social Marketing presented a proposal to the U.S. Department of Agriculture, Food and Nutrition Service (FNS) in September 1995 requesting support to develop a national breastfeeding promotion project. Specific goals for the project were to increase breastfeeding initiation rates, increase breastfeeding duration rates among WIC participants, increase referrals to WIC for breastfeeding support, and increase general public support for breastfeeding.

Social marketing was used because it had already proven effective in Best Start's earlier work in the southeastern region while more traditional, clinic-based approaches had relatively poor results.

Audience Analysis

During the audience analysis phase, Best Start staff met with FNS representatives and members of their Breastfeeding Promotion Consortium to finalize program objectives, select states to serve as pilot sites for the project, and gain a better understanding of current breastfeeding promotion activities and challenges within the WIC program (Lindenberger and Bryant 2000). The primary target audience for the program was comprised of pregnant Anglo-American, African-American, and Hispanic-American women who were enrolled in the WIC program and those income-eligible to participate (i.e., income below 185 percent of the U.S. poverty guidelines). Secondary audiences, people who influence the primary target population, included pregnant women's mothers and husbands or boyfriends, WIC nutritionists and clerical staff, and prenatal health care providers. The general public was also designated as an influential tertiary audience because social norms related to breastfeeding, especially in public settings, are known to influence women's infant feeding decisions. Ten states were selected to serve as research and demonstration sites for the project. These states provided the research team with access to a representative sample of research subjects.

Because social marketing demands a thorough understanding of consumers and the people who influence their decisions, the formative research phase requires a far more in-depth analysis of consumers' beliefs, values, and behavior than is typically accomplished in program needs assessments. Research objectives were to:

- identify WIC participants' perceptions of breastfeeding and bottlefeeding;
- identify the factors that influence WIC participants' infant feeding decisions;

- identify effective information channels and spokespersons for promoting breast-feeding among WIC participants;
- identify secondary audience's (WIC employees, WIC participants' mothers and husbands/boyfriends and other prenatal health care providers) perceptions of breastfeeding;
- identify the factors that motivate and deter secondary audiences from encouraging women to breastfeed.

A review of published literature, program reports, previous research conducted by Best Start Social Marketing researchers and other existing data sources provided the research team with an understanding of factors shown to influence infant feeding decisions among economically disadvantaged, minority, and other special populations similar to the target audiences. As a result researchers decided to focus their research efforts on the women's perceptions of breastfeeding's benefits and costs, self-efficacy as breastfeeders, and the impact of kin and health professionals on infant feeding choice. The need to gain a better understanding of WIC nutritionists' and clerical staff members' perceptions of breastfeeding promotion was also identified.

Formative research relied on a mix of qualitative and quantitative methods to collect data from WIC participants, their family members, WIC employees, and other health care providers. Participant observation was conducted in a variety of urban and rural clinics in five states. Approximately 200 in-depth interviews and 13 focus group interviews were conducted with WIC participants, and telephone interviews were conducted with fathers and grandmothers of the WIC babies. Interviews were conducted in health departments and other places where the women usually received health or social services. Interviews involved from five to nine people plus a moderator and assistant. The moderator introduced topics, asked questions, and guided the discussion, while the assistant monitored audio recording equipment, took notes, and assisted with logistical concerns. Focus group interviews lasted from one to three hours; individual interviews were usually much shorter. Often participants expressed satisfaction about participating in the process because of the opportunity to help develop a national program and learn from their peers.

Qualitative data analysis emulated Krueger's "chronological sequence of analysis" and made use of ideas expressed by various other researchers (Glaser and Straus 1967; Krueger 1988; Miles and Huberman 1984). After each session the moderators prepared short summary statements on various topics. They also identified themes concerning breastfeeding constraints and motivational factors that might stimulate change. Differences between participants were noted. Researchers considered the way these women spoke about the topic. This information often influenced the questioning process in subsequent sessions. The moderator's techniques and the interview success were evaluated.

Researchers processed each interview with the help of a qualitative data analysis computer program. This program allows the coding, indexing, and subsequent retrieval of portions of the interview transcript. The program was used to sort transcripts by coded topics. All material filed by each topic was read by at least two researchers. Recurring themes and the range of diversity in responses were identified, summary and interpretive statements were developed, and passages worthy of quotation were flagged. When computers are mentioned, some might assume that the analysis is a mechanical exercise. This software serves only as a more efficient and complete means for shuffling through and reading all the field notes. It is still necessary to think it through and interpret the meaning.

Qualitative research results were used to identify areas that merited further exploration and develop a 53-item survey instrument administered to 292 WIC participants in 12 WIC or prenatal clinics selected to represent urban, suburban, and rural communities in one state.

Major Research Findings

Research results showed that most WIC participants knew and believed breastfeeding offered important benefits to them and their babies. Breast-feeding was viewed as a way to realize families' goals to have healthy babies and enjoy a special time with their newborns. Compared with infant formula, breast milk was considered by most to provide optimal health benefits and a closer maternal-infant bond. For many women, the enjoyment they expected to experience and the special time they associated with breastfeeding were breastfeeding's most important benefits.

Consistent with their earlier findings, Bryant et al. (1989) found that teenagers viewed motherhood as an opportunity to come of age, to gain positive attention from friends and family, and to establish a long-term relationship with their child. They also thought that breastfeeding was a sign of maturity and responsibility and a certain adventurousness that can set one apart from her peers. These mothers were also concerned about their children becoming too attached to the others that often provide child care. They felt that breastfeeding can help prevent the child from becoming too attached to these other people.

Despite being attracted to breastfeeding's emotional and other benefits, many women were deterred by the sacrifices they would have to make if they breastfed.

They worried that breastfeeding would create many embarrassing moments in public situations or open them to criticism from friends or relatives who viewed breast-feeding in a sexual light. Some women worried that breastfeeding would conflict with work, school, or social life; and some women worried that their close social network would feel "left out" of the feeding experience and fail to bond to their baby. Other "costs" associated with breastfeeding were pain, changes in dietary and health practices, and anxiety about their ability to produce the required quality and quantity of breast milk. In addition to the unfavorable ratio between benefits and costs, women's infant-feeding decisions reflected their lack of self-confidence as potential breastfeeders and a lack of support from relatives, friends, and some health providers. (Bryant and Lindenberger in press)

Research also identified the babies' fathers and grandmothers as important secondary audiences and health professionals as powerful information channels for reaching them during the prenatal period. Many women reported learning about breastfeeding from WIC employees but were confused by the lack of information provided by their obstetrical providers. Many women also reported having difficulty initiating breastfeeding in the hospital, and many said they stopped lactating before they had planned because they had little or no support once they returned home from the hospital.

Finally, in contrast to the late 1980s, most WIC nutritionists and many clerical staff were supportive of breastfeeding promotion. Because of their commitment to "make a difference" in the lives of their clients, they were frustrated when their clients did not breastfeed. Many WIC employees said they would welcome more effective promotional strategies and materials.

STRATEGY DEVELOPMENT

Drawing on these findings, Best Start Social Marketing and FNS staff developed a social marketing plan organized around marketing's 4 Ps (product, price, place, and promotion). The product strategy focused on the close, loving bond and special joy that breastfeeding mothers share with their babies. Although breastfeeding's health advantages were mentioned in program materials, the emotional benefits were emphasized because they most clearly distinguished the product from its competition—bottle-feeding. Breastfeeding was defined as a way families can realize their dreams of establishing a special relationship with their children, and the campaign brand symbol—"*Loving Support Makes Breastfeeding Work*"— and program materials emphasized the role the support network of family members, friends, and the general public play in a mother's ability to breastfeed. This strategy is consistent with Best Start's earlier work and represents an important departure from traditional public health approaches in which breastfeeding has been promoted as a medical choice rooted in health benefits.

The pricing strategy was especially important in the *Loving Support* project. As noted above, many women were unwilling to pay the price for breastfeeding benefits. Therefore, a major goal of the project was to lower the price of breastfeeding by teaching health providers to use a three-step counseling strategy to quickly identify the perceived costs and help mothers develop their own ways to overcome the problems they anticipated. Public information and consumer education materials were recommended to change the public's attitudes about breastfeeding in public and counter misperceptions about the sacrifices required to breastfeed.

The placement strategy delineated a variety of settings in which women and their social network members seek information about infant feeding. The plan outlined strategies for reaching women within and outside the WIC setting. For example, Best Start staff began working closely with the Baby Friendly Hospital Initiative to advocate for improved support in the hospital and advocate changes in regulations restricting breastfeeding in public and work places. The project theme—*"Loving Support Makes Breastfeeding Work"*—and mass media materials were designed to elicit support from family, friends, and the public at large for women who breastfeed.

The promotional strategy described the specific tactics and activities recommended to facilitate change (e.g., legislative change, policy development and organizational change, professional training, peer counselor programs, curriculum development, consumer education, public relations, direct marketing, advertising, face-to-face communication, media advocacy, and grassroots advocacy). Message design guidelines were prepared to assist an advertising agency in developing television, radio, outdoor, and print materials. These guidelines recommended an emotional appeal with an upbeat, congratulatory tone, a vignette manner of presentation, and the use of families as spokespersons.

PROGRAM DEVELOPMENT AND STRUCTURING

Best Start contracted with an advertising agency to design and develop campaign materials. An instructional designer was hired to assist with the redesign of the 3-Step Counseling Program originally developed in the late 1980s. Using these guidelines, the advertising agency developed five campaign concepts, each with a distinct "look," tone, general messages, color palette, typestyles, and photographs. One concept was eliminated in staff review because it was not consistent with the marketing strategy and the other four were pretested with WIC participants and staff members. Individual interviews, rather than focus groups, were used to avoid "group think" and encourage frank appraisals of the materials. Based on this initial round of pretesting, two concepts were eliminated and revised for further testing. A second round of pretesting in five of the pilot states and Florida was conducted until it became clear which worked most effectively in all regions.

The final concept was then used to create the following campaign materials:

- three 30-second television commercials in English and one spot in Spanish;
- three 60-second radio commercials, two in English and one in Spanish;
- outdoor advertising boards, in English and Spanish;
- nine posters, targeting the primary ethnic groups in WIC (English and Spanish);
- nine educational pamphlets, targeting the primary ethnic groups in WIC (English and Spanish);
- a motivational/information booklet for WIC staff;
- a Breastfeeding Resource Guide;
- a Breastfeeding Promotion Guide;
- a WIC Staff Support Kit pocket folder to hold Breastfeeding Resource Guide, Breastfeeding Promotion Guide and motivational booklet for WIC staff;
- pamphlets for native American families; and
- *The Physicians and Health Care Providers Breastfeeding Promotion Kit, a* comprehensive kit of promotional materials to assist health providers in promoting breastfeeding.

For the television commercials and photographs used in the print media, talent was cast to represent the three major ethnic groups targeted for this campaign (Anglo Americans, African Americans, and Hispanic Americans). Whenever possible, WIC participants were cast as the talent for the print and electronic materials produced.

PROGRAM IMPLEMENTATION

Critical to the program's success was careful training of WIC staff members who would implement the program at the state and local level. A training conference was held for teams from 30 states. The conference included

- research results for the WIC National Breastfeeding Promotion Project;
- a review of the media package, *Loving Support Makes Breastfeeding Work*;
- working with the media;
- utilizing nontraditional communication channels;
- orchestrating community-building for breastfeeding promotion;
- a fresh, new approach to breastfeeding promotion and team-building; and
- preparing for project implementation.

Special skills breakout sessions and team planning sessions were held to allow state WIC to develop work plans for their states. When attendees concluded the conference, they left with an outline of a state plan for implementation. The program was launched during World Breastfeeding

Week (August 1–7, 1997) with a national press conference in Washington, D.C. Best Start Social Marketing has provided technical assistance to the pilot states and many other state, local, and territorial WIC programs that have implemented parts or all components of the campaign. And, in an effort to institutionalize many of the marketing plan's policy recommendations, Best Start's Executive Director, Jim Lindenberger, is serving on the U.S. Breastfeeding Committee and board of directors for the Baby Friendly Hospital Initiative.

MONITORING AND EVALUATION

Although program materials or activities have been implemented in all 50 states and many U.S. territories, only one state received funds for a thorough evaluation of the *Loving Support Makes Breastfeeding Work* program. In Mississippi, a quasi-experimental design, including 13 intervention and 13 matched comparison clinics, was used to evaluate the program. In the intervention sites, *Loving Support* was implemented in a comprehensive fashion that included patient and family education, a public awareness campaign, health professional outreach, and partnerships with the community (Khoury, Mitra, Hinton, and Moazzen 2001:5). In the comparison sites, families were exposed to only limited aspects of the program. Although similar before program implementation, afterward, intervention sites had significantly better composite scores than control sites for women's perceptions of breastfeeding's benefits and barriers and their perceptions of support from health providers and relatives; WIC staff members' knowledge about breastfeeding and self-efficacy in breastfeeding promotion; and aspects of clinic environments that facilitate breastfeeding. Most importantly, however, was the program's impact on breastfeeding rates. After program implementation, breastfeeding rates in the intervention sites (44.8 percent at hospital discharge and 30.8 percent at four months postpartum) were significantly higher than in control sites (30.9 percent at hospital discharge and 18.9 percent at four months postpartum) (Khoury et al. 2001). Moreover, breastfeeding at hospital discharge increased from 37 percent to 48 percent and breastfeeding at six months postpartum climbed from 10 percent to 19 percent, compared to much smaller increments in Louisiana and Alabama where the program had been implemented less comprehensively.

The *Loving Support* marketing program illustrates how social marketing can be used to design a social change strategy for bringing about beneficial voluntary behavior change. It also highlights the role anthropologists can play in the social marketing process.

At the heart of the social marketing approach is the assumption that an understanding of consumers' values and aspirations is needed to develop programs people truly want and will use. Anthropologists play an important role in both conducting the formative research upon which culturally appropriate program strategies can be built and recommending effective culture change strategies. Social marketing organizations turn to anthropologists because of the discipline's holistic approach, mastery of qualitative research methods and understanding of culture change" (Bryant et al. 2001:244).

SUMMARY

Social marketing applies the concepts of marketing and marketing research to the task of cultural change. It is mostly used in the public health arena. It is quite different from the other approaches presented in this volume in that it almost always starts with some sort of expert evaluation concerning a particular issue. That is, someone decides that smoking is bad and seat belts are good. The task of the social marketer is to figure out how to reach people with carefully designed messages so that they change their behavior. The anthropologist's strength in this process is her or his capacity to tap the meanings associated with a particular useful behavior and to collaborate with "message designers" to produce useful ads, public service announcements, brochures, and other kinds of promotional content to achieve the goal.

FURTHER READING

Bryant, Carol A. and Doraine F. C. Bailey. The Use of Focus Group Research in Program Development. In *Soundings: Rapid and Reliable Research Methods for Practicing Anthropologists*. NAPA Bulletin 10. John van Willigen and Timothy J. Finan, eds. Washington, D.C.: American Anthropological Association, 1991. This is a detailed and concrete discussion of the formative research process in the Best Start project. It shows in remarkably clear terms how this process works.

Bryant, Carol A., James Lindenberger, Chris Brown, Ellen Kent, Janet Mogg Schreibert, Marta Bustillo, and Marsha Walker Canright. A Social Marketing Approach to Increasing Enrollment in a Public Health Program: A Case Study of the Texas WIC Program. *Human Organization* 60(3):234–245, 2000. This article expands the description of the social marketing process described in this chapter.

Kotler, Philip and Eduardo L. Roberto. *Social Marketing: Strategies for Changing Public Behavior*. New York: Free Press, 1989. This comprehensive and straightforward guide shows how organizations can be more efficient using a social marketing approach.

Part III

Policy Research in Anthropology

Chapter 11

Anthropology as Policy Research

The purpose of policy research is to provide information to decision makers in support of the rational formulation, implementation, and evaluation of policy. Policies can be thought of as strategies of action and choice used to achieve desired goals. Mostly we think of policy in the context of various kinds of formal organizations like social agencies, educational institutions, business firms, and governments at all levels. There are many different kinds of policy. We use terms like public policy, social policy, food policy, employment policy, industrial policy, foreign policy, and others to designate the strategies of action and choice used by governments and other organizations in various aspects of life in complex societies. These terms reflect rather different situations in content and scope, yet all relate to the same set of basic issues. That is, all policy is concerned with values. Policy formulation involves specifying behavior which is to result in achieving a valued condition. In a sense, a policy is a hypothesis about the relationship between behavior and values. It takes the form: if we want to be a certain way, we need to act *this* way. At a basic level, policies involve allocation decisions—decisions to spend money and time to achieve something. The "something" can be quite diverse, including increases in gross national product, decreases in unemployment, decreases in the relative cost of food staples in urban areas, decreases in the number of teenage pregnancies, or increases in fairness in the allocation of housing. These large-scale national concerns can be matched with smaller-scale, local concerns, like increases in public input in the planning of the construction of a dam, the determination of the usefulness of a particular development project, or the identification of local needs for a certain kind of educational program. Policy research can occur on both sides of a policy issue and can be adversarial.

Community groups can carry out policy research as a political counterpoint to research done by the government.

POLICY PROCESS

Policy should be thought of in terms of a process. The policy process is very complex. Stating the process in the simplest possible terms, we can say that the process consists of the following stages:

1. Awareness of need
2. Formulation of alternative solutions
3. Evaluation of alternative solutions
4. Formulation of policy
5. Implementation of policy
6. Evaluation of implementations

This process is carried out in the political arena in which there is much competition for resources. Thus what would appear in a schematic diagram as neatly rational and orderly in reality may be determined by compromise, hidden motives, and blunt applications of political power. The basic problem is that everything can not be done at once. Competition forces more careful allocation decisions. The complexity of the competition creates opportunities for policy researchers.

Policy research includes a large variety of activities which in one way or another support the process by which needs are identified and policies are formed, implemented, and evaluated. Each stage in the policy process is associated with research needs and opportunities.

Much (probably most) policy is formed without the aid of specific research efforts. Then again, social science tends to generally inform participants in the policy arena so that it is continually brought to bear on policy problems without actually being commissioned for a specific policy formation purpose. In these cases we can speak of policy-relevant research. There are many different points in the policy process where research done by cultural anthropologists can be used. Most research done by anthropologists in this arena involves research that is done because of a policy rather than to determine what policy should be. Program evaluation, a type of research commonly done by anthropologists, is a good example of this. Some may want to contrast policy research with program research.

In any case, this is not new ground for anthropologists. In fact, one could argue that policy research needs accelerated the development of anthropology as a discipline in the nineteenth century. This view is argued in Chapter 2 on the history of the development of applied anthropology. Anthropology as an organized discipline in many national traditions is a function of policy research needs associated with colonial administration, both internal or external. At the beginning, this took the form of doing basic ethnography in unknown areas or doing troubleshooting concerning inter-cultural relationships.

As early as 1895, James Mooney carried out research which had as its goal the determination of what the U.S. Department of War should do in response to the Ghost Dance as practiced among certain Plains Indians (Wallace 1976).

The appointment of the early faculty of anthropology at the great English universities was based on the need to train colonial administrators.

In spite of this time depth, anthropology's experience as a policy science is quite limited. It was not until the 1970s that anthropologists became involved more extensively in policy research efforts. As stated in Chapter 2, this involvement relates to both push and pull factors. The push factor is the collapse of the academic job market. The pull factor is the increase in policy research efforts because of federal legislation. This last factor, of course, is most important in the United States.

As a corollary to the policy research function, anthropologists have, to some extent, become policy makers. This function is rare and very poorly documented. One interesting example is the work of anthropologist Robert Textor in the Peace Corps. Textor participated in the development of the so-called in-up-and-out personnel policy of the Peace Corps which re-stricted the length of employment in the Peace Corps so as to maintain a higher rate of innovation and what might be called "organizational youth" (Textor 1966). My own experiences in development administration in-volved small-scale policy formulation in response to a community devel-opment effort done for a Native American tribal government. One cannot overlook the cases where anthropologists have assumed high-level admin-istrative positions in federal and state government. Some noteworthy ex-amples are Philleo Nash who served both as Commissioner of Indian Affairs in the U.S. Department of the Interior, and Lieutenant Governor of the state of Wisconsin (Landman and Halpern 1989); Aguirre Beltran who served as Director of the National Indian Institute of Mexico; Jomo Ken-yatta who was the first Prime Minister of Kenya; and Nirmal Kumar Bose who was appointed Commissioner for Scheduled Castes and Scheduled Tribes for India (Sinha 1986). In all cases these people were intimately involved in policy formation. There are, of course, a number of knowl-edgeable applied anthropologists who have very eloquently argued against such involvement. A good example is Homer G. Barnett who did extensive applied work in the Pacific following World War II. He argued that our effectiveness as applied anthropologists would be reduced if we took over administrative functions.

In any case, most involvement of anthropologists in the policy arena is as researchers. In this framework they are said to be most effective at the local level (Chambers 1977); or, when they work at the level of national policy formation, they function best in large multidisciplinary research teams (Trend 1976). Both Chambers and Trend seem to be arguing from the same ground, which is that the traditional, holistic, participant-observation based research methodology works best in smaller scale contexts. While this is probably true, there are ways of escaping the effects of the constraint. One is to learn other research techniques.

Policy research is not a monolith. There are many different types. For example, each stage in the policy process is associated with different research needs. There are many different types of current policy research practice that see anthropological involvement. Anthropologists do evaluation research, needs assessment, social impact assessment, social soundness analysis, cultural resource assessment, as well as various other kinds of policy research. In addition to the research carried out in support of the development, implementation, and evaluation of specific policies, there is also research that is referenced to general areas of social concern. This can be referred to as policy relevant research. In regard to this distinction, it is possible to speak of anthropology *in* policy, and anthropology *of* policy. This follows a contrast originally made by the medical sociologist Robert Straus (1957), who spoke of researchers serving in support of medical care as opposed to researchers who study medical care. The first was referred to as sociology *in* medicine, and the second is the sociology *of* medicine. DeWalt applied this distinction to his analysis of agricultural anthropology (1985). Both are very important. It is, however, important to recognize the distinctions between the two kinds of work. All the policy anthropology that we refer to here is of the "anthropology in policy" type.

All the different types of policy anthropology represent important kinds of research activity for anthropologists in many different employment situations. Further, if one considers all the different purposes and funding mechanisms for research done by anthropologists, one finds that the contrast between applied and basic research becomes reduced. We have, on the one hand, research that is specified, bought and paid for by clients to meet some practical need, and, on the other hand, research planned and carried out by researchers referenced only to their curiosity and sense of the direction of the discipline. What exists between these polar types is a product of a mix of personal inclination and many different incentives. For example, many programs that fund basic research will fund that basic research in terms of a set of priorities that are derived from general policy questions. These specific economic incentives come to be converted to "hot topics" and short-run tendencies in research topic selection. Under certain circumstances research produced for specific applied purposes can begin to appear in print as if it were basic research. This then influences research topic selection in yet another way. The point is that the contrast between *applied* and *basic* is rather weak. Further, there is a great deal of flow between the two realms.

SOME CURRENT TYPES OF POLICY RESEARCH PRACTICE

The types of policy research discussed here range from standardized research methods geared to specific policy issues, to large and generalized research orientations applicable in a wide variety of situations. The contribution of anthropologists to the development of the methods and techniques used varies from a great deal to very little. Except for a few cases, the anthropologist involved in the use of these practices needs to know general social science research methods in addition to those more traditionally associated with anthropology. As is mentioned in Chapter 13 on evaluation, one needs an integrated research methodology in which the researcher is capable of drawing on a variety of different techniques depending on the problem at hand. To give you a glimpse at the various types of policy research, a listing is provided below. As suggested above, some of these types have specific technical meanings, other categories are general and include a wide variety of research functions.

Evaluation

In evaluation, research is done with the goal of determining the worth of something, such as a project, program, or set of training materials. The process can involve a wide variety of research designs from highly structured experiments with control groups to descriptive ethnographies. Evaluation can serve many purposes. Many evalutions are done to determine the effects of a specific project or program. Evaluation can also be done to see if some activity is working as expected, with the goal of improving it. Evaluators can use a wide variety of data collection techniques. Evaluation can be used to test the feasibility of wider application of innovations. Research can be used to evaluate alternatives in the design process. Evaluation is one of the most important types of policy research done by the applied anthropologist.

There is currently more interest in the use of ethnography in evaluation. Using this approach, the task becomes one of finding out what is going on in a specific situation rather than technical determination of effects. The chapter on evaluation includes case studies of evaluations which involved anthropologists. Anthropologists working in evaluation often use case study methodologies. In some cases they serve as ethnographers studying large-scale projects as part of multidisciplinary teams.

Social Impact Assessment

In social impact assessment, research is done which is geared toward predicting the social effects of various kinds of projects. Usually the process involves the examination of unplanned effects of major construction projects on families and communities before the project is built. In this limited sense, social impact assessment is a kind of effect study. Social impact assessment is especially important in the design process. Usually the process involves the consideration of the effects of various design alternatives. Social impact assessment often involves the use of secondary data. This is an important kind of policy research for cultural anthropologists. An entire chapter is given to social impact assessment in this text. It is worth noting here that often the research methodologies used in social impact assessment are mandated by the contracting agency. In the United States, various kinds of impact assessment research is done in compliance with a number of different federal laws, including those which are concerned with protecting the environment.

Chapter 11 contains an expanded discussion of social impact assessment with a case study of a specific assessment project. You will find that social impact assessment, in part, resembles the traditional anthropological/sociological community study, except that it places emphasis on the use of secondary data. The use of secondary data is encouraged because of the need for speed and standardization between different project assessments. While social impact assessment can be done in many different settings, it is specifically geared to use in conjunction with the planning of projects in the domestic United States. It is used in a wide variety of settings involving the projection of the effects of everything from dam construction to fisheries management policies. This kind of research is done to evaluate design alternatives prior to implementation.

Needs Assessment

In needs assessment, research is done which determines deficiencies that can be treated through policies, projects, and programs. It is done as part of the planning process and is sometimes thought of as a kind of evaluation. Sometimes, needs assessment takes the form of large-scale survey research projects which serve to identify and rank preferences for certain developments. Such surveys usually require two waves of standardized data collection, one to identify and one to rank. Needs assessments can also be based on existing census data used as social indicators. Many factors that are targeted by policy can be measured this way, such as education and income levels, number of violent deaths, and disease rates. Working in smaller scale contexts, the needs assessment process may involve the use of community meetings of various kinds. Obviously, needs assessment occurs early in the policy process and can set the scene for a variety of different kinds of policy research procedures. The operation of many intervention strategies may involve needs assessments of various kinds. The identified needs often were used in program monitoring and evaluation at subsequent stages.

Social Soundness Analysis

Social soundness analysis is used to determine the cultural feasibility of development projects. This generalized approach to project assessment came to be used by researchers working for the U.S. Agency for International Development starting in the mid-1970s. The approach, in large part, was developed by the anthropologist Glynn Cochrane (1979). Cochrane had done assessment work for various development agencies, including the World Bank and the British Ministry of Overseas Development.

An important element in social soundness analysis is the identification of the different beneficiary groups associated with the effects of a specific project or other activity. This is important because of the policy framework of American international development efforts which, since the amendments made to the Foreign Assistance Act in 1973, had a mandate to direct their attention to the needs of the "poorest of the poor." This required a commitment to what Cochrane called social mapping. Social mapping is basically a process of ethnography which requires the collection of data on ethnicity, social organization, belief systems, wealth forms, patterns of mobility, and access to basic human needs. The approach is currently used in the U.S. Agency for International Development project planning process in conjunction with other research approaches.

Technology Development Research

In an effort to help assure the appropriateness of technology developed for use in less developed countries, a number of agencies have become committed to the use of social science to inform the technology development process. This is well developed in farming systems research and extension (DeWalt 1989; Hildebrand 1976; McCorkle 1989). Farming systems research is geared toward linking farmers with those who do the development of agronomic technology. Part of this linkage is the provision of comprehensive accounts of the farming system. The concept of farming system is focused on the analysis of the production and consumption decisions of farm households. In this research, attention is paid to the identification of development constraints and opportunities. One way that technology development research can operate in the agronomic context is through the on-farm research. This involves the actual implementation of agronomic research on the farms rather than in the experiment stations. In this setting the social scientist can serve as a broker for the experimentation program.

Cultural Resource Assessment

Starting in the early 1970s, a great deal of archaeological research in the United States has been carried out in response to legislative mandates. This led to the emergence of cultural resources management (CRM). CRM is concerned with identifying the impact of federal and other kinds of development on archaeological sites, historic buildings, and like things, and then managing the impact in various ways. Management usually involves identification and documentation, but may include mitigation and protection. Mitigation may include thorough research and documentation of the resource. Protection may include physical stabilization and the establishment of zones of protection. Large numbers of archaeologists, architectural historians, and other researchers have been active in CRM. Recently this assessment process has begun to be directed toward contemporary communities as cultural resources. The emphasis in this research is toward the documentation of the folk knowledge of communities that are displaced by development projects.

Of course, there are other types of policy research besides those mentioned here. Nevertheless, these are important because of the numbers of anthropologists involved in them. Clearly, the most important are social impact assessment and evaluation research. In addition to the types of research described to this point, anthropologists have also been involved in the development of these research methodologies. This is especially apparent in the area of social impact assessment methodology for the Army Corps of Engineers. Also, anthropologists have served as evaluators of the products of social impact assessment and evaluation research. The point is that there are many different ways of participating in policy research endeavors.

A FRAMEWORK FOR INCREASING THE USE OF POLICY RESEARCH

The crucial question facing the applied or policy researcher is "How can I get my research used?" The literature on the different types of policy research in all cases contains references to the problem of underuse of research results. It is clear that this is a consistent problem in the policy research realm. It is a problem that stimulates its own research. This section of this chapter is intended to give practical advice on how knowledge utilization can be increased. This advice is organized around a series of principles that when followed will increase the probability of the use of knowledge. The advice is intended to be general enough to cut across the various research types.

In dealing with the question of utilization it is important to be neither naive nor cynical. It is necessary to recognize that our research, however sound, may not affect the situation. Also, in many situations decision makers may be poised to act on the basis of the knowledge provided them through policy research.

FRAMEWORK FOR PUTTING KNOWLEDGE TO USE[1]

Getting our research used may be the most important issue facing applied and practicing anthropologists. Sometimes research just happens, but usually applied researchers have to work hard at it. The framework presented here, developed by Barbara Rylko-Bauer and me, has ideas that are useful for increasing the impact of anthropological research. You could think of it as a theory of research effectiveness.

Before discussing the framework, some basics need to be established. First, because we can control our own actions, we need to think primarily about what we do rather than what others do. I say this because often researchers blame the agency for not making use of the research. While this may be true to some extent, it is more productive to focus on what we can do to improve the potential for getting research used. Second, we need to treat knowledge use as something that needs to be planned into the design of projects. Research designs guide research projects. Applied research should include a knowledge utilization design or plan. The framework suggests elements that can be included in such a plan. Third, we need to think realistically about our goals and look at utilization broadly. Researchers in this area point out that a narrow conception of utilization overlooks the complexity of policymaking and fails to recognize that reducing uncertainty, clarifying issues, and providing new understanding of how programs work are also real effects (Beyer and Trice 1982; Caplan 1977; Patton 1986; Weiss 1977, 1981). More significantly, research "can gradually cause major shifts in awareness and reorientation of basic perspectives" without seeming to be directly and immediately applied (Weiss 1981:23).

Knowledge Utilization Factors

The framework includes factors to be considered in developing a utilization design. The context of a research situation will determine which knowledge utilization factors have more relevance.

1. This section was written by Barbara Rylko-Bauer and John van Willigen. It is derived from "A Framework for Conducting Utilization-Focused Policy Research in Anthropology," a chapter included in *Speaking the Language of Power: Communication, Collaboration and Advocacy*, compiled by David M. Fetterman.

Collaboration Factors

The most significant factor in getting research findings used is collaboration between researcher and clients (Alkin 1985; Glaser, Abelson, and Garrison 1983; Leviton and Hughes 1981; Patton 1986; Rothman 1980). Collaboration means involving decision makers and other potential stakeholders (e.g., community members) in the research process. Carefully working with people to identify their information needs and ways they can use the research will increase their commitment to the application of the research. It is important to foster an identifiable individual who personally cares about the project and the information it generates. Patton refers to this as the "personal factor" (1986).

Because of the value of the idea of stakeholder, it is useful to review the idea here. The concept was developed by evaluator Michael Quinn Patton (Practical Evaluation 1982:55). The stakeholders associated with a project consist of the individuals, groups, or organizations that perceive that their interests will be affected in some way by the project. The category includes project beneficiaries, the funding agency, and all the others who are impacted by it. It is useful to do a stakeholder analysis prior to project implementation as part of the planning process.

We will see later that federal law in the context of social impact assessment and cultural resource management requires a consultation with what are, in effect, stakeholders.

User participation also presents some potential ethical dilemmas. Frequently noted is cooptation of the researcher, which may occur if decision makers shape the research to provide results that support preferred or already existing policies and actions, and that do not challenge their role within the organization (Ballard and James 1983; Beyer and Trice 1982; Dawson and D'Amico 1985). Selecting stakeholders involves a judgment about whose questions will guide the research (Mark and Shotland 1985) creating potential for a different sort of cooptation, the preempting of criticism of the project by the inclusion of stakeholders who might have been likely to do so. Finally, if the researcher does not provide stakeholders with the necessary information for effective and knowledgeable collaboration, then user participation can become a form of "pseudoempowerment" (Mark and Shotland 1985:143–144).

Models of collaborative research are well developed in anthropology (e.g., Stull and Schensul 1987) and evolved from a value orientation that recognizes the validity of self-determination as a major force in sociocultural change. Recently the idea of user participation has been explicitly suggested as a strategy for increasing the use of anthropological knowledge (Davidson 1987; Schensul 1987; Stern 1985; Whiteford 1987).

Communication Factors

Communication of research findings is often limited to the writing of a final report; yet this is not a very effective way of passing on information and often results in too much, too late. Perhaps the most important strategy is to discuss preliminary findings throughout the research process and maintain an ongoing dialogue with feedback between researcher and information users (Glaser, Abelson and Garrison 1983; Rich 1975). This is much easier to do if decision makers are collaborating in the research process (Dawson and D'Amico 1985; Patton 1986).

Other communication strategies include using multifaceted and appropriate means of communication, such as workshops, conferences, publication in trade magazines, in journals from other disciplines, and widespread distribution of short draft reports (Ballard and James 1983; Beyer and Trice 1982; O'Reilly and Dalmat 1987; Patton 1986; Schensul 1987).

Presenting findings in the language and style of users is supported by our common sense, yet all social scientists have great difficulty avoiding using their jargon, keeping reports brief, and presenting findings and recommendations in a manner familiar to potential users (Ballard and James 1983; Rothman 1980).

It is important to communicate findings directly to relevant decision makers. Practitioners need to provide concrete, specific recommendations about what is to be done, by whom, and when (Patton 1986; Rothman 1980). Policy makers do not usually expect primary data and research reports; they want recommendations on what to do (Cernea 1991b).

Agency Factors

Collaborative research is more likely to succeed if one understands the the client agency, community, or group and the political context within which the research and knowledge use is to occur. Do an ethnography of the research situation. Becoming informed about the ways in which communities and groups may be affected by the research, and about the client group and its decision making process, gives the researcher some understanding of the relationships among relevant groups, who the key decision makers and community leaders are, and the potential areas of conflict and possible forums for resolving them.

In studying the nature of the client group, one can focus on questions such as who are relevant decision makers and potential users of the information, how are decisions made within the organization, what are the usual channels of communication, and what are the constraints and/or incentives to use of the information within the agency?

Community and Political Factors

Always be aware of the potential impact of research findings, and endeavor to understand the relationship that exists between the client agency and those individuals, groups, or communities that may be affected. Often, the client may be in a position of relative power vis-à-vis the community, and the agency's values and bureaucratic needs may conflict with those of community members (van Willigen 1986). Recommendations perceived as threatening by those outside the agency may enable a community to mobilize public support to defeat such action. Conversely, the agency may decide not to act on recommendations perceived as going against its best interest, even if they are beneficial to the community that it serves. Research based in an established community institution with political clout has greater likelihood of having an impact and bringing about desired social change (J. Schensul 1987).

Research Process Factors

Research needs to be designed, from the onset, with utilization in mind (Patton 1986). There are three features of research that increase the potential for use.

Diversity of research methods, in particular the creative combination of quantitative and qualitative methods and analysis, can provide an insightful, valid, and convincing representation of social reality, while meeting time constraints, as well as criteria of reliability and generalizability that policy makers often expect (Beyer and Trice 1982; Fetterman 1989; J. Schensul 1987; Trotter 1987).

Use is directly related to the credibility of the research process (Caplan 1977; O'Reilly and Dalmat 1987; Weiss and Bucuvalas 1980; Whiteford 1987). This includes perceived accuracy, fairness, understandability and validity of research design, and methods (Patton 1986). Research quality issues become more important in situations of political debate, where the policy maker cannot afford to have the research discounted due to uncertain methodology (Weiss and Bucuvalas 1980).

The potential for use also increases if the research focuses on variables that can be acted upon, that are accessible to control (Gouldner 1957). We call this applicability. Several studies suggest that decision makers are more likely to use findings if recommendations are feasible and the results conform to users' expectations or existing knowledge (Caplan 1977; Leviton and Hughes 1981; Weiss and Bucuvalas 1980).

Time Factors

Policy research often has a short time frame, and recognition of this has led to many developments by anthropologists doing policy research (van

Willigen and DeWalt 1985). Perhaps most notable is the development of problem-focused, short-term research techniques such as focus groups and rapid appraisal (van Willigen and Finan 1991). One example is the informal or reconnaissance surveys done in farming systems research. In these efforts there is a heavy reliance on key informant interviewing, judgmental sampling, use of secondary data, and on-site observation. Another example is "rapid assessment procedures," such as those developed for evaluating and improving primary health services (Scrimshaw and Hurtado 1987).

ADVOCACY FOR RESEARCH FINDINGS

Promoting one's research findings and recommendations also can improve the prospects for use (Barber 1987; Jones 1976; Rothman 1980; Siegel and Tuckel 1985). Advocacy works best from inside the system. One way of personally ensuring that research is used is to become one of the decision makers. It is much harder to influence the policy process from the outside, and increasingly anthropologists encourage direct involvement in program management and policy making (Cernea 1991b). In whatever role, you have to be committed to change.

Clearly there are many variables that influence whether or not research is used. It is important to once again emphasize that the policy researcher include in his or her research a knowledge utilization design that reflects actions that will increase the probability that research be used (Rylko-Bauer and van Willigen 1993).

SUMMARY

Anthropologists provide a wide variety of research services in response to various needs associated with the process of policy formation, implementation, and evaluation. More detailed charting of the policy process would no doubt produce more different types of applied or policy research. While anthropologists bring certain methodological and conceptual tendencies to these research efforts, the content of these approaches is defined in reference to the policy process itself as well as other disciplines. The major types of applied research done in reference to the policy process are evaluation, social impact assessment, needs assessment, social soundness analysis, technology development research, and cultural resources assessment. Certainly other specific types will emerge in the future. The differences between these research methods are not so much based on technique and design but purpose and intent. Further, in some settings the research technique used is really geared toward being appropriate to specific administrative requirements. It is clear that preparation for involvement in policy research calls for broad preparation in social science as well as preparation in the traditions of ethnographic research.

FURTHER READING

van Willigen, John, Barbara Rylko-Bauer, and Ann McElroy, eds. *Making Our Research Useful: Case Studies in the Utilization of Anthropological Knowledge.* Boulder, Colo.: Westview Press, 1989. Presents a variety of case examples of anthropologists having an impact through their research.

Chapter 12

Social Impact Assessment

Social impact assessment (SIA) is a kind of policy research frequently done by cultural anthropologists. While the term is applied to a variety of policy research activities, it usually entails the collection of sociocultural data about a community for use by planners of development projects. The data are usually intended to help project planners understand project impacts and to help them decide whether a particular project should be built or how it should be modified so as to mitigate negative impacts. Considered in its most narrow context, SIA is done as part of the environmental impact assessment process carried out under the mandate of the National Environmental Policy Act and other federal statutes in the United States.

SOCIAL IMPACT DEFINED

A useful general definition of social impact is provided by a committee organized by the U.S. National Marine Fisheries Service. The committee defined social impact as

the consequences to human populations of any public or private actions that alter the ways in which people live, work, play, relate to one another, organize to meet their needs and generally cope as members of society. The term also includes cultural impacts involving changes to the norms, values, and beliefs that guide and rationalize their cognition of themselves and their society. (Interorganizational Committee 1994:1)

This definition covers a range which includes the highly structured research mandated by federal statute and regulation, to generalized futures research.

SIA can be done in reference to a variety of potential actions and in many different settings. Actions consist of both physical project construction and policy implementations. Examples of projects that may require an SIA may involve mining; oil and gas drilling; hazardous waste disposal; construction of power plants, reservoirs, airports, highways, pipelines, sewers, waterways; and building construction (Burdge 1994:107). An example of a policy action for which an SIA is appropriate would be a change in a policy for the management of ocean fish stocks. This could have major consequences on communities whose economy is based on fishing. Other policies are changes in land use designations and designations of sacred sites.

SIAs can serve many different purposes. The most appropriate to our interests here is the use of SIA in conjunction with the planning of major governmental projects. In this setting the social impact assessor is called upon to provide projections about future effects which inform all the parties involved in the project, including planners, designers, political leaders, and the public. Often this involves assessing a number of different project options. For example, an interstate highway could be routed in a variety of ways, have interchanges in various locations, and vary in other features of design. Usually one design alternative considered is "no project." This type of SIA project will often require a number of determinations of impact as the project becomes redefined. In addition to the data collection effort, the social impact assessor may also be involved in the process of informing the public about the project and the findings of the research.

Work by anthropologists in social impact assessment can take other forms. Some have worked in research and development leading to new SIA methods. These may be expressed in the form of agency regulations and guidelines as well as in general field research manuals.

NATIONAL ENVIRONMENTAL POLICY ACT (NEPA)

NEPA was signed into law by President Richard Nixon in 1969. The law required that projects that involved federal land, money, or jurisdictions had to be evaluated in terms of their impact on the environment and reported in an environmental impact statement (EIS). In addition to impact analysis, the law also mandated mitigation of impacts and subsequent monitoring (Burdge 1995). In addition, NEPA also serves as an important foundation for cultural resource assessment (King 1998).

The most practical component of NEPA for anthropologists and other social scientists is paragraph (c) of section 102. This paragraph enjoins all agencies of the federal government to

include in every recommendation or report on proposals for legislation and other major federal actions significantly affecting the quality of the human environment, a detailed statement by the responsible official on (I) the environmental impact of the proposed action, (II) any adverse environmental effects which cannot be avoided should the proposal be implemented, (III) alternatives to the proposed action, (IV) the relationship between local short-term uses of man's environment and maintenance and enhancement of long-term productivity, and (V) any reversible and irretrievable commitments of resources which would be involved in the proposed action should it be implemented. (U.S. Congress 1971:853)

This portion of NEPA has led to the emergence of environmental impact assessment practice and a new form in the literature of science, the environmental impact statement (Burchell and Listokin 1975:1). Social impact assessment is often an aspect of environmental impact assessment.

As is typical with federal law of this significance, NEPA stimulated a tremendous quantity of interpretative literature around it. This included general federal administrative guidelines, case law, specific agency guidelines, various commentaries from the academic community, as well as the EISs themselves. In addition, the law served as a progenitor for substantial parallel legislation at the state and county level. Following the development of this practice in the United States, environmental impact assessment has become important in domestic policy of other countries (Carley and Bustelo 1984:2) and in international development work (Derman and Whiteford 1985). The U.S. Agency for International Development developed social soundness analysis which is a kind of SIA (Burdge 1994). Conceptually related activities are done at the World Bank and the World Health Organization.

Although it is clear that section 102 (c) of NEPA requires the EIS on "major federal actions significantly affecting the quality of the human environment" (U.S. Congress 1971:853), it is not always possible to determine where an EIS is required.

In addition, it is not apparent from NEPA what constitutes an appropriate method for determining impact, nor is the relative importance of social impact as opposed to environmental impact indicated. Further, there is a great deal of variation in methodologies used in social impact analysis. The extent to which the social dimension is considered is often limited, although social impact assessment would seem to be part of the requirement of an adequate environmental impact assessment. The inclusion of SIA in EIA emerged through the years as a product of political process, case law, and changing regulation. SIA was not clearly present when the NEPA was implemented in 1970.

THE ENVIRONMENTAL IMPACT STATEMENT

According to federal regulation, agencies of the federal government are subject to the EIS provisions of section 102 (2) (c) of NEPA. Each agency was to view the act as supplementary to its own authorization. A wide range of "actions" are included under the provisions of the act. These include all "new or continuing projects and program activities: directly undertaken by federal agencies; or supported in whole or in part through federal contracts, grants, subsidies, loans, or other forms of funding assistance . . . or involving a federal lease, permit, license certificate or other entitlement for use" (Council on Environmental Quality 1973:20551).

In order to be reviewed, projects of the types indicated above must be "major" and be capable of "significantly affecting the quality of the human environment." The responsibility for making the determination is in the hands of the specific agency that must consider the "overall, cumulative impact." A number of related small-scale projects may be subjected to this analysis if the projects taken as a whole have significant impact. The significance of a project may relate as much to the location as project design. That is, "the significance of a proposed action may also vary with the setting, with the result that an action that would have little impact in an urban area may be significant in a rural setting or vice versa" (Council on Environmental Quality 1973:20551). The agencies were instructed to determine guidelines which would in some way define "significance."

NEPA and its related regulations require that individual agencies develop their own guidelines in carrying out their charge. This means that EIS's done for individual federal agencies should follow specific defined sets of practice, many of which are derived from the more general NEPA expectations. In addition, certain agencies, such as the Army Corps of Engineers, are subject to the requirements of their own "NEPAs." In the case of the corps, there is section 122 of the River and Harbor and Flood Control Act of 1970 (Public Law 91–611), which provided for economic, environmental, and social assessments. This law requires that "the Chief of Engineers . . . shall . . . promulgate guidelines designed to insure that possible adverse economic, social and environmental effects relating to any proposed project have been fully considered in developing such projects" (U.S. Congress 1972:1823). Section 122 of the law goes on to specify a number of adverse effects which must be assessed. These include (1) air, noise, and water pollution; (2) destruction or disruption of man-made and natural resources, esthetic values, community cohesion, and the availability of public facilities and services; (3) adverse employment effects, and tax and property value losses; (4) injurious displacement of people, business, and farms; and (5) disruption of desirable community and regional growth. The River and Harbor and Flood Control Act is especially noteworthy because of its explicit treatment of social variables. Other legislation includes the Housing and Community Development Act of 1974; the Magnuson Fishery Conservation and Management Act of 1976; Nuclear Waste Policy Act of 1982; and the Superfund Amendments and Reauthorization Act of 1986, among others. All these laws provide for social impact analysis.

It must be made clear that environmental impact assessment (EIA) and social impact assessment are not the same thing. The original Council on Environmental Quality (CEQ) guidelines that respond to NEPA do not single out and stress the social component of the total impact of a project. The orientation, although at times vague, is more holistic. Social impacts are part of the total "package" of effects to be reviewed. In this context we might think of social impact assessment as a term which is applicable to a portion of the entire EIA process. Even a cursory reading of the CEQ guidelines indicates the importance of the social component in total impact determination. This orientation is made even more explicit in many of the developed agency guidelines. For example, the Army Corps of Engineers has funded a number of projects that have led to the publication of various guidance documents for preparing and contracting for what are explicitly labeled social impact assessments. Thus in the context of certain agencies, SIA is an official concept.

Although the EIA procedure originally seemed to be oriented toward biophysical data, it is quite apparent that the role of the social scientist in the EIA process has developed in a significant way.

METHODS AND TECHNIQUES

The discussion of method and technique will be primarily based on *Guidelines and Principles for Social Impact Assessment* (Interorganizational Committee 1994) and Rabel J. Burdge's *A Conceptual Approach to Social Impact Assessment* (1994). It is very important to note that social impact assessment methodology is highly variable. The social component review of any project will vary in importance because of the lack of uniform criteria for evaluating SIAs.

There are a number of different factors which influence the content and importance of a specific social impact assessment. Of course, the nature of the project itself has a lot to do with the design of the SIA. The type, scale, and use of the project influences the structure of the SIA. The political situation associated with the project will influence how the SIA is handled. When a project is controversial, more elaborate assessment often is done. Projects that are resisted in a systematic way are assessed differently. The nature of the community impacted also is relevant. Community factors include population density, culture and cultural diversity, residential stability and community cohesion, uniformity of impact throughout the community, and knowledge of project that exists in the community. There are a number of administrative factors. An important factor is the identity of the lead agency. Different lead agencies may have different guidelines for doing SIA. Other factors that are relevant are the quality and availability of secondary data.

Unfortunately, much of the methodology that we learn as anthropologists that focuses on culture change is retrospective in nature. Yet we must predict the future in SIA. Even standard trend analysis is difficult to apply because the "treatment" that we are trying to assess hasn't yet happened. The most basic studies of culture change attempt to identify baseline data with which to compare postchange data so as to determine the extent of change.

The primary task of the preliminary phases of SIA is the identification of the relevant populations and the assimilation of as much information as is possible concerning the group. Details as to the scope of the area of impact can often be determined from an analysis of the technical specification of the project.

Following an initial assessment of the project and project area, the researcher must develop some notion of who he or she will be attempting to draw into the research activities. In certain kinds of projects, it is necessary to supplement the research team with special expertise. Special experts may include other social scientists, community members, and "lead" agency personnel who might have special knowledge of the design of the project. Some agencies require multidisciplinary teams. As understanding of the project develops, it is necessary to comprehend how the particular project is justified in legislation. For the social scientist the important factors are the specific laws and regulations that govern social impact assessment. This knowledge will strongly affect the methodology selected.

It is beyond the scope of this work to delineate the complexities of the methodology selection process, but it is necessary to assert that there is not a "right" methodology for this type of analysis. As indicated above, the process is influenced by many factors.

The selected research design may be continually refined. This recognizes the impact of the research on the researcher who will redefine approaches as an understanding emerges. This indeterminate discovery process is important because it will increase the chances of understanding the diversity of the project and its potentially changing nature.

Projects can be thought of as having stages. Different stages will have different impacts. It is important to distinguish stages in doing SIA and discuss impacts differentially in terms of the different stages. The project stages or steps used in *Guidelines* are (1) Planning/Policy Development, (2) Construction/Implementation, (3) Operation/Maintenance, and (4) Abandonment/Decommissioning.

Planning/Policy Development

This stage refers to the activities that occur between project conception and implementation. The period of talk and planning is nowhere near benign. As soon as a project is proposed, change occurs. Take for example a proposal to build a reservoir. People almost immediately incorporate the project in their market decisions. Land speculators may buy land so that they can benefit from a major construction project. The value of business enterprises that would appear to benefit from the project may increase. If relocation is involved, people may defer maintenance on their homes. Political alignments of those in favor or against a project may occur.

Construction/Implementation

This stage starts once the decision is made to proceed with the project. The process may start with land-clearing and the building of access roads. Often, projects result in in-migration of construction labor. Suddenly the community is forced to deal with the needs of a new population of "outsiders" who may have different values and different stakes in the community. It can be quite a problem resulting in "newcomer" and "long-term resident" conflict and resentment. Construction may require relocation. Relocation is a stress producer for individuals. At the community level it can result in loss of needed leadership and skills.

Operation/Maintenance

Once the project is constructed or implemented, new kinds of impacts may occur. The in-migrant population associated with construction shrinks. In this phase the community may be able to adapt to the changes that have been caused by the project.

Abandonment/Decommissioning

Projects come to an end and this also will have a social impact. This process may start with the mere announcement of closure. In the case of U.S. government "projects" like military bases, there may be considerable local and state resistance to closure. There are, in fact, special guidelines for assessing the impact of base closure. Loss of an economic base is a big problem.

When doing an SIA, it is important to be aware of the differential impacts associated with the stages and focus on those particular stages where the impact is most critical.

STEPS IN THE SOCIAL IMPACT ASSESSMENT PROCESS[1]

SIA involves 10 logically sequenced, sometimes overlapping steps. These steps are:

1. The foundation for this discussion is the Interorganizational Committee's *Guidelines and Principles for Social Impact Assessment* (1994). See http://www.gsa.gov/pbs/pt/call-in/sia-gide.htm. The steps used here are from these guidelines. These were derived from Council on Environmental Quality guidelines.

1. Public Involvement—Develop an Effective Public Plan to Involve All Potentially Affected Publics

SIA requires the team to identify and work with all the different kinds of people affected by the project. Those affected by the project may include persons who live near the project, especially those who may be forced to relocate. In addition, there will be persons interested in the project who live elsewhere. These people are also one of the "publics" that needs to be consulted. Because projects often require new community-financed infrastructure to be built, taxpayers are also one of the affected groups. Persons impacted by the influx of construction labor and the new users of the project need to be consulted. This step in the SIA process can benefit from key-informant interviewing, public meetings, and sample surveys. Every SIA involves an on-going program to achieve public involvement. Some anthropologists have become public involvement specialists.

2. Identification of Alternatives—Describe the Proposed Action or Policy Change and Reasonable Alternatives

It is essential to describe the project in all its alternative forms in order to design the SIA data collection process. A minimal checklist of aspects to be described is provided in *Guidelines* and includes locations of facilities, land requirements, needs for ancillary facilities (roads, transmission lines, sewer and water lines), construction schedule, size of work force (construction and operation, by year or month), facility size and shape, need for a local work force, and institutional resources (1994:13). This sets the scene for data collection. While the variables for collected data differ somewhat from project to project, the discussion provided in *Guidelines* represents a well-thought-out foundation point.

Population Characteristics. The starting point in the development of a baseline is the present demographic data on the population. There is no question that demographic data is very important and that the SIA process requires being able to deal with secondary population data. Understanding population trends is also important; therefore, there needs to be some historic depth to the demographic inquiry. The available demographic data needs to be disaggregated in various ways. You will need to know the age, gender, ethnic, occupational, and wealth composition of the community. Seasonal population is also part of the scheme. The demographic component has a stakeholder analysis aspect to it. Ask yourself: Who is impacted by the project, and how?

Community and Institutional Structures. A good starting point is the determination of the structure and size of the various levels of local government. Their linkages both in and out of the community are important to understand. Nongovernmental community organizations such as religious organizations, voluntary associations, and various kinds of interest groups need to be understood. The local economic system needs to be understood. This means employment and income levels and industrial, agricultural, and commercial diversity need to be described. Planning and zoning activity are important parts of this.

Political and Social Resources. It is in this framework that identification of stakeholders and their interests occurs. It is important to understand who the different publics are, what their interests are, and how power and authority is distributed. The nature and extent of leadership capability needs to be understood.

Individual and Family Changes. Projects affect individuals and families. The baseline should include a description of the society being impacted. Residential stability and the nature of relationships are important to understand. What are the attitudes, perceptions, and knowledge that community members have about the project? How do they see project-related risk, health, and safety issues? What are their concerns about possible displacement and relocation?

Community Resources. Resources include both natural resources, such as land and water, and human-produced resources, such as housing, health, police, fire protection, and sanitation. What kinds of changes will the project cause in terms of community infrastructure? What are the effects on cultural, historical, and archaeological resources? These are important aspects of the continuity of the community.

3. Baseline Conditions—Describe the Relevant Human Environment/Area of Influence and Baseline Conditions

An important part of the SIA process is doing a baseline study of the area and people impacted by the action. This study is not just a time slice but also accounts for historic process. It's important to know what the trends are in the community in order to factor out what is a product of the project and what is history unfolding.

The amount of effort in preparing the baseline relates to size, cost, and expected impacts of the project.

The anthropologist must contact individuals who reflect a variety of life experiences. Besides the usual categories of concern such as gender, socio-economic strata, age, and occupation, there must be an attempt to identify and interview those who are supporters or opponents of a specific project as well as those who are neutral. Other stratification can be made based on levels of knowledge of the project. One way to monitor this use is to establish a representation grid in which persons in the various significant categories of representation are tallied as compared to the appropriately proportioned ideal. It is assumed that given time constraints and the difficulties in establishing an adequate sampling frame, the individuals in various categories will be somewhat disproportionate and selected purposively.

4. Scoping—After Obtaining a Technical Understanding of the Proposal, Identify the Full Range of Probable Social Impacts

The basic question in scoping is: How big a problem is it? (Wolf 1983: 13). Scoping is a preliminary informed estimate of impacts. After developing an informed understanding of the consequences of the project, the SIA team selects variables linked to predicted impacts for further assessment. In doing this it is necessary to deal with perceptions of impacts from both the involved agency and the affected groups and community. It is very important to understand the affected persons' perceptions of impact and incorporate these concerns into the on-going assessment process. SIA is iterative.

5. Projection of Estimated Effects—Investigate the Probable Impacts

Projection involves estimated effects based on "data from project proponents; records of previous experience with similar actions [as documented in the literature]; census and vital statistics; documents and secondary sources; field research, including informant interviews, hearings, group meetings, and surveys of the general population" (1994:15).

A component of the projection process is that of "forecasting," that is, to actually predict the future. It is essential in the SIA process to make predictions concerning the future. However, because of the state of the art, this tends to be a "black box" affair. That is, specific data is collected in explicit ways and somehow forecasts are made. There are many ways of doing this; however, many of the techniques are largely intuitive.

Flow Chart and Diagram Construction. Some techniques cited are simply means for displaying the relevant data. Flow charts and other graphic displays of this type can be used to depict the directions of change and, more importantly, the interaction between various components of the project and the "human community." These approaches can vary significantly in terms of sophistication.

Metaphors, Analogies, and Comparison. Project effects can be determined by comparing the unimplemented project with those that are similar. The applicability of this approach is limited by the shortage of comparative data, the lack of bibliographic control, and access to relevant case studies. The diversity of each completed project makes it difficult to carry out controlled comparisons.

Delphi Technique. Delphi technique was developed at the Rand Corporation in the late 1940s (Sackman 1975:xi).

Delphi is an attempt to elicit expert opinion in a systematic manner for useful results. It usually involves iterative questionnaires administered to individual experts in a manner protecting the anonymity of their responses. Feedback of results accompanies each iteration of the questionnaire, which continues until convergence of opinion or a point of diminishing returns is reached. The end product is the consensus of experts, including their commentary, on each of the questionnaire items, usually organized as a written report by the Delphi investigator (Sackman 1975:xi).

Trend Extrapolation. This technique assumes some constancy in existing processes of directional change. That is, trends will relate to conditions at some future point. There are various types of trend extrapolation.

Scenarios. Scenarios are "future histories" or "narrative descriptions of potential courses of developments" (Vlachos et al. 1975:63). Scenario writing draws, in an intuitive way, from the profile narrative. Scenarios may make use of the existing case literature and can be done using an expert panel (Burge 1994:115). Scenarios are very useful for presenting the nature of the project and its effects to a lay audience. The scenario should reflect various alternative courses of the project. Scenarios are usually developed "with the project" and "without the project." It is important to consider the opportunity costs associated with specific project scenarios.

6. Predicting Responses to Impacts—Determine the Significance to the Identified Social Impacts

This is a difficult step in the process. It is basically a projection of the response of the different interest groups in the community to the impacts themselves. Things change, and people adapt. This addresses the adaptation. Previous assessments are especially important in this.

7. Indirect and Cumulative Impacts—Estimate Subsequent Impacts and Cumulative Impacts

It is useful to think through causal sequences of impacts. Direct impacts have subsequent impacts. Projects may result in additional projects or projects that are made possible by the initial project.

8. Changes in Alternatives—Recommend New or Changed Alternatives and Estimate or Project Their Consequences

Impact assessment along with ongoing political processes may result in the project being redesigned. The SIA process treats these as iterations of the basic process. Scenario development is a useful tool because it anticipates changes and alternatives.

9. Mitigation—Develop a Mitigation Plan

The SIA process should identify ways of reducing, rectifying, or avoiding negative impacts. This can occur through project redesign or compensation in the form of facilities, resources, and opportunities.

10. Monitoring—Develop a Monitoring Program

Projects need to be monitored to identify unanticipated impacts and deviations from the basic plan. The SIA should include a monitoring plan. The plan should "spell out the nature and extent of additional steps that should be take place when unanticipated impacts larger than the projections occur" (1994:18).

MICHIGAN PLANS FOR SUPERCONDUCTING SUPER COLLIDER ASSESSED: A CASE STUDY

In the 1980s the U.S. Department of Energy proposed the construction somewhere in America of a particle accelerator of a scale heretofore unknown. Think of it as a colossally large piece of physics laboratory equipment. The device accelerates atomic particles through an oval underground tunnel 52 miles in circumference and then collides them, breaking them into their component parts, providing research data on the physical properties of matter and energy. The project resembles the Fermi National Accelerator Laboratory located in Illinois built in the late 1960s. The project was spatially one of the largest and most expensive federal actions ever contemplated. The project was seen to have limited environmental consequences but many large social and economic impacts. Thought to take at least seven years to construct, the project would have brought thousands of workers and billions of dollars to the state that is the selected site. Further, it would result in an influx of "world-class" scientists to the region of the site and the development of many high technology spin-offs. A number of states proposed that the super-colliding, superconductor (SSC) be located in their states. As part of this, states were to provide various kinds of information about their sites. The Michigan proposal included a social impact assessment of the SSC done by a team led by anthropologist Richard W. Stoffle, then at the Institute of Social Research of the University of Michigan.

Stoffle and his ISR colleagues produced what is termed a "class one scoping report" based on research carried out very early in the planning process so as to contribute to the information that the designers have available for consideration. The information in the scoping report is normally used along with many other kinds of information to structure project alternatives. The data upon which the scoping was done included interviews and other contacts with hundreds of persons and a review of the literature. Local farmers and townspeople as well as state-level experts were interviewed in some cases in groups. The scoping report contains documentation of local concerns about the impacts of the accelerator ring itself and the campus of the facility.

Stoffle and associates also included a discussion of local and national analogues and an assessment of public reactions. Documentation of local concerns was an important part of the state of Michigan's proposal to the Department of Energy (Stoffle, Traugott, Jensen, and Copeland 1987b). The SIA research results became part of the public discourse over the multiyear period that the team was engaged in the research. Research findings stimulated the state of Michigan to "seek solutions to potential adverse impacts" (Stoffle et al. 1987b). The research identified public concerns with the project. Mitigation of concerns identified by the research was incorporated into the project. This in term led to increases in the amount of community support for the project. This interaction is a classic component of effective contemporary SIA. Anthropologists in SIA often are involved in this public discourse. That said, the project was never built. Nevertheless the documentation provided by Stoffle's team was used extensively by state officials. The utility of the impact assessment was high.

SUMMARY

Social impact assessment in the final analysis is not a scientific practice as much as a political one; which is to say, SIA produces documents that assist the process of decision making. This decision making is based on the evaluations presented in the report and the politicians' interpretation of them. The decision takes the form of a selection from among the alternatives. The analyst does not evaluate in the final accounting. That is the task of the politicians and/or the public. This step of the process is often made more public than earlier stages.

Because evaluation is a political process, it is difficult and unpredictable. Its difficulty is caused by the confrontation of local community and development agency values. The focal point may in fact be the impact statement itself. The stress generated by this can be mitigated by openness in executing the impact assessment. The amount of stress relates to the amount of controversy concerning the project. More controversial projects should be more public, and the openness should occur right from the very beginning.

Social impact assessment is a type of policy research frequently done by anthropologists. In many ways it is very similar to the community study method used by both anthropologists and sociologists for many years. The process of social impact assessment can be highly structured by agency requirements. As this field has developed, the number of regulations and guidelines that structure the work has increased dramatically. A person engaged in social impact assessment practice must carefully keep up with agency procedures. Just as agency guidelines change and develop so does the market for such services. An important factor in shaping the market is the amount of federal spending in construction. Decreases in spending on such construction, recently coupled with changes in federal policy toward the whole environmental impact assessment process, have decreased the amount of this kind of work that is done.

An interesting quality of social impact assessment is that learning its techniques can be very useful for most cultural anthropologists. This is true because there is great utility in learning how to acquire secondary data and treat it in the context of change. An emerging adjunct to the social impact assessment process is the field of public participation coordination.

FURTHER READING

Burdge, Rabel J. *A Conceptual Approach to Social Impact Assessment*. Middleton, Wis.: Social Ecology Press, 1994. A collection of useful chapters by a sociologist experienced in SIA.

Derman, William and Scott Whiteford, eds. *Social Impact Analysis and Development Planning in the Third World*. Boulder, Colo.: Westview Press, 1985. Contains good case material and overview discussions.

Goldman, Laurence R., ed. *Social Impact Analysis: An Applied Anthropology Manual*. Oxford: Berg, 2000. This book provides a good overview of current practice drawing primarily from Australian materials.

Interorganizational Committee on Guidelines and Principles for Social Impact Assessment, U.S. Department of Commerce, National Oceanic and Atmospheric Administration, National Marine Fisheries Service. *Guidelines and Principles for Social Impact Assessment*. http://www.gsa.gov/pbs/pt/call-insiagide.htm, 1994.

Preister, Kevin. Issue-Centered Social Impact Assessment. In *Anthropological Praxis: Translating Knowledge into Action*. Robert M. Wulff and Shirley J. Fiske, eds. Pp. 39–55. Boulder, Colo: Westview Press, 1987. This documents anticipated impacts of the development of an area for skiing in Colorado.

Chapter 13

Evaluation

Evaluation is a kind of policy research. It shares some fundamental features with social impact assessment (SIA). First, both are concerned with impact or the effects of different actions on people. Second, both can make use of the same kinds of research methods and techniques. The two kinds of research are different in certain important ways. SIA is primarily concerned with discovering *before* the fact any costly unintended effects of an activity. That is, governments build dams to impound water so that floods are reduced, agricultural production is increased, or recreational opportunities can be developed. In this situation an SIA might be done to predict whether this would have adverse effects on nearby communities. The purpose of dams is not to displace communities, yet it is important to planners to identify all the effects. Evaluation is most often concerned with determining *after* the fact whether the intended benefits of an activity occurred, or alternatively, discovering whether a project with intended benefits is working. That is, an agency might establish a program to increase employment of high school dropouts and then do research to determine whether the dropouts became employed. In addition, evaluation can be used to examine program operations as well as program effects.

INTEGRATED RESEARCH METHODOLOGY

Our treatment of evaluation will focus primarily on research design. The discussion will start with consideration of classical experimental design. From this base we will consider a number of research design alternatives. Our perspective will be that of general social science as much as anthropology. The specific uses of ethnography in evaluation will be considered.

It is important to note that contemporary evaluation research makes use of many different research strategies and that these methods and techniques are used by evaluators regardless of the discipline in which they were trained. One is likely to pick up an ethnographically oriented evaluation research report, based on participant-observation, and find that no anthropologists were involved in the study. And, of course, the reverse is true; it is possible to find anthropologists involved in executing pre-test, post-test, control group experimental designs.

Ethnographic practice is one tool, a very useful tool, but only one tool. The implications of this are clear. Evaluation researchers need to know a number of different designs whether they are anthropologists, sociologists, psychologists, political scientists, economists, or other kinds of researchers. It is important to recognize that this statement on evaluation takes an integrated research methodology approach that may combine qualitative and quantitative research (Cook and Reichardt 1979).

The integrated research methodology approach requires that we control a variety of research designs and data collection techniques. This implies the possession of the necessary technical skill to process and analyze the data derived through a variety of techniques. The integrated research methodology approach means carefully identifying which research data collection technique is required to solve a research problem. What works? What carries us the furthest in understanding? What is efficient? What research technique is the most credible in a particular setting?

The criteria that we use to judge which design and technique we will use is quite broad. Of course, basic notions of validity and reliability are among the most important. Another important consideration is cost, both in money and time. The best design in the world is worthless if one cannot afford to implement it. Ethnographic practice sometimes involves a great deal of time in research. Yet, a good ethnographer can learn a lot about what is going on in a situation by interviewing one person. In any case, there is a large range of legitimate concerns in terms of research design and technique selection. A final, important question is: Does the researcher have the skill to do the task?

Anthropologists can be involved in evaluation in two different ways. First, and most important, is as a broadly trained social scientist who is prepared to do a variety of evaluation research tasks as are needed. The second is as a specialized evaluation ethnographer, who contributes to evaluation through nonexperimental, unobtrusive, qualitative, and participatory research techniques as these skills are needed. In this second role, the anthropologist may also be valued because he or she has knowledge of the group within which the evaluation is taking place, as much as knowledge of technique. While ethnographic skills are very useful in the evaluation process, as we will discuss later, the most promising approach is an integrated multidimensional approach.

One implication of the view expressed here is that there is not an anthropological way of evaluating. It is more useful to think of a multifaceted social science of evaluation in which individual problems in evaluation are addressed using a variety of techniques. Anthropologists can do their job better if they have control of a variety of techniques. The task is not to mimic sociology or psychology, but to participate in a larger contemporary tradition in social or behavioral science. The effect of this on anthropology will be positive.

This chapter will have two parts: (1) a discussion of the evaluation process, with description of alternatives for evaluation design and (2) case studies in evaluation done by anthropologists.

THE PROCESS OF EVALUATION

Warning! Because this single chapter treatment of evaluation is necessarily brief, our presentation of evaluation may make the field seem much more orderly than it really is. Evaluation encompasses all the disarray that you would expect in a relatively young field in which persons of many disciplines participate. This situation was exacerbated by the fact that important segments of the field, most notably educational evaluation, underwent rapid growth forced by huge federal subsidies. For example, the Elementary and Secondary Education Act of 1965 carried a provision that educators receiving grants in support of education programs had to submit evaluation reports which identified the effects of the program. Basically, a lot happened quickly, and there has been little synthesis. There are a number of competing viewpoints and substantial semantic difficulties. Now then, what is evaluation?

At its very core evaluation is what the dictionary says it is, that is, "The determination of the worth of something." While all of us are constantly evaluating things, activities, and ideas, evaluation in a technical sense requires much more than the casually subjective, and largely private assessments of worth that we produce every day. First, a general technical definition, "Evaluation is the determination of the worth of a thing. It includes obtaining information for use in judging the worth of a program, product, procedure, or objective, or the potential utility of alternative approaches designed to attain specified objectives" (Worthen and Sanders 1973:19).

When evaluation is done, it is almost always done in reference to activity which is intended to affect people in one way or another. Evaluation can be used to determine worth in both negative and positive aspects. While many research designs used in evaluation stress the determination of whether planned objectives were accomplished, evaluation can also be used to discover unintended consequences of programs and projects. The activities evaluated are always motivated by some desired end state. The evaluation process is a process by which values are rationalized. The idea of treatment borrowed from the literature on experimental design is useful as a label for the actions, projects, programs, and such which are carried out to achieve goals. Other dimensions to the evaluation process are the nature and characteristics of both the agency providing the service and the individuals and groups which are the focus of the agency.

At a general level there are three types of evaluations. These are described below.

Effects Studies

The basic task here is the determination of whether a program (or other entity) is achieving its goals. This is the classic evaluation task. It has also been referred to as product evaluation (Stufflebeam 1973) or outcome evaluation. Effects studies done during the life of a program that are intended to inform program managers or sponsors about program operations can be thought of also as process evaluations (Stufflebeam 1973). Effects studies can be directed at dissemination of practices to other settings as guiding decisions about continuance, enhancement, curtailment, and modification.

Process Studies

The basic task here is to determine how a program is operating. This is a managerial task. Both process and effects studies may be designed in the same way. Process evaluations may consist of long-term program monitoring.

Needs Assessment

The basic task here is to determine the needs of a potentially served population (McKillip 1987; Neuber 1980; Scriven and Roth 1978). One could include needs assessment in a discussion of planning. Needs assessment can also occur during the life of a program so as to allow program redefining. That is, it can be part of program planning and management. Needs assessment can be ongoing.

This general typology implies a number of dimensions. These include the purpose or role of the evaluation, the timing of the research, and, to some indirect extent, the design. There are a number of very useful discussions in the evaluation literature which address these dimensions. Let us first talk about design, and then, role and timing.

Research design is what is unique about evaluation research when compared to other types of research. Measurement and data analysis techniques are quite comparable in evaluation and basic research. Let us start our discussion of design by considering the classical design pattern and then expanding from that base.

Carol H. Weiss depicts the "traditional formulation" of evaluation research in the following way (1972:6):

1. Finding out the goals of the program;
2. Translating the goals into measurable indicators of goal achievement;
3. Collecting data on the indicators for those who have been exposed to the program;
4. Collecting similar data on an equivalent group that has not been exposed to the program (control group);
5. Comparing the data on program participants and controls in terms of goal criteria.

This is, of course, a generalized version of experimental design used in behavioral science. Your understanding of this basic pattern can be supplemented by reading the classics *Experimental and Quasi-experimental Designs for Research* by D. T. Campbell and J. C. Stanley (1965), or *Quasi-experimentation: Design and Analysis Issues for Field Settings* by Thomas D. Cook and Donald T. Campbell (1979). Still in print, these volumes very clearly lay out research design alternatives. Campbell and Stanley define five different research designs. These are very briefly discussed below.

The list starts with the least rigorous, the "one-shot case study." In the one-shot case study of a program, one would measure the effects of the program only once—after the research subjects had participated in the program. What is absent is a baseline measurement or what is called a pre-test to determine the "before condition." One has to assume a great deal about the program participants' prior state. Some researchers attempt to strengthen this design by using documentary evidence or reconstructions based on self-reports. At worst, one-shot case studies take the form of program-serving testimonials. Fortunately, there are many circumstances where the one-shot case study can be valuable, because the design is very common. Much ethnographic evaluation takes the form of a one-shot case study.

An enhancement of the one-shot case study is the "one-group, pre-test, post-test design." In this approach a pre-test is added. The addition of the pre-test allows one to measure change more objectively. It, however, does not allow one to conclusively attribute the change to the program. Change can occur because of other events, normal change through time, the pre-test's effects, ineffective measurement, or participant fatigue, as well as other factors.

Also used is the "static group comparison" which adds a control group to the one-shot case study design. In this case, a group which has experienced the program is compared with a group which has not experienced it. The weakness is that the design does not allow certainty about the differences between the groups before the treatment. It is possible to strengthen this design through matching of participants and the use of retrospective measures.

The fourth design is "pre-test, post-test, control group," which involves setting up two groups before the program. In terms of research design quality, the best way of doing this is by random assignment. There is a before and after measurement to determine effects of the program. This design, although very good, does not control for the effects of the research procedure.

This is controlled for through the use of the Solomon four-group design, in which there are six groups, some with treatment, some without, some with pre-test, some without. This set of design alternatives does not address issues relating to needs assessment but is applicable to many contexts in both effect and process studies. The problems with needs assessment mostly revolve around having the research sample be consistent with the group which actually receives the service after program implementation.

While these are standard designs, each of which represents an incremental increase in the capacity to specify cause, there are costs associated with increases in experimental control. This is a reason why, therefore, much evaluation is carried out using a one-shot-case study design. The more complex, error-reducing designs are used quite extensively in education to evaluate curriculum in anticipation of wider use. It is clear why; the treatments are usually more readily definable and control groups are easier to find and match. Treatments will consist of a set of test materials administered in an adequately standardized way, and, if you need a control group, other classes of student "subjects" are available. Similar patterns occur in the evaluation of drug treatment programs in which the participants have diminished control because they are in the program by order of the courts. Outside of the certain specialized areas, it may be very difficult to apply the more complex designs.

While there are many statements in the literature on evaluation which present the more complex designs as ideals, it is very important to view these designs as alternatives to be selected for application as appropriate. Selection should always be referenced to the most appropriate, and not the most elegant. There are a very large array of factors which need to be considered in evaluation planning, in addition to basic research design. Perhaps most important is the intended purpose of the evaluation. Some researchers may place too high a value on the elegance of their design, and too low a value on assisting the program to serve its clients better. Anthropologists in evaluation seem to be more committed to clients needs than others. Other factors to consider in design are cost, available time, and the nature of the service population.

REASONS WHY SOFT DESIGNS ARE THE MOST APPROPRIATE

As we know, in many circumstances soft and fuzzy is good. Much of the research methodology literature from outside anthropology idealizes formal measurement and statistical analysis. This has changed a great deal as the users of research have had more experience with qualitative research and become disenchanted with positivism. Yet one still finds defensiveness on the part of soft methodologists. Again, hard or soft are not the same as good or bad. Both approaches are subject to their own problems of quality. By soft, we mean, among other things, research that stresses qualitative methods, naturalistic observation, discovery, induction, and holism. By hard, we mean, among other things, quantitative methods, structured observation, verification, deduction, and particularism (Cook and Reichardt 1979:10). By way of example, ethnography with its emphasis on key informants and participant-observation tends toward softness. While survey research with emphasis on randomly selected subjects and instrumented observation (i.e., questionnaires) tends toward hardness. Again, we are not arguing for anything other than the selection of appropriate methods. Back to the question—Where are soft methods appropriate?

Soft methods are useful because they are often less of a burden for the program staff. The more structured the research design is, the greater the chance of the evaluation interfering with program functioning. It is very difficult to burden useful programs with certain kinds of highly structured research. The selection of softer designs is called for where obtrusiveness is an issue. Soft methods are useful where program goals are less well defined, or are especially complex and diverse. Soft approaches are really useful for discovery. Ethnographers seem to do research more to raise questions than to answer them. Soft methods are the only way to realistically handle complex situations. The more structured the research design, the fewer variables it can consider. Program goals are often not very well defined. Soft techniques can be fit into ongoing program development better than hard approaches. The before and after measures specified in the experimental designs can be replaced with the during-during-during measures which are more workable with softer techniques.

Softer methods often prepare the way for implementation of results better than hard methods because the researchers often end up with an excellent understanding of the persons managing programs and the constraints under which they must operate. In fact, it may be best to have the evaluation include continued feedback to the program with correction. This kind of arrangement is unworkable with hard designs because it interferes with the outcome of the research. Further, hard research designs assume too much about the stability of programs while they are being evaluated. Mid-study change in program administration disrupts the hard studies, but for the soft designs this kind of activity simply represents more data relevant to the program. We might say that soft techniques are useful in rapidly changing circumstances.

REASONS WHY HARD DESIGNS ARE THE MOST APPROPRIATE

Hard research designs are especially appropriate if the program has clear-cut, measurable objectives that are identified with the program. Hard designs are appropriate where program staff are familiar with, and value, research along with their commitment to service. This orientation is appropriate to situations where control groups are readily available. The idea of the control group is sometimes antithetical to the service orientation of program administrators. In some circumstances, establishing control groups requires one to deny access. Hard approaches work well where there is relative program stability and lower expectation or need for mid-course feedback. A useful application of hard approaches is in the production of the final evaluation of demonstration projects, with the goal being to inform potential adopters of the program.

It is worth pointing out that either hard or soft techniques must be executed in a way that allows their results to be applied to real world decision making. The inflexibility of the hard techniques can relate to less timeliness—that is, research has to run its course. Soft techniques can be so unfocused that the researcher meanders through a program without attending to the needed research issues. It is important to remember that the primary use of evaluation is to provide information for decision making. Late research is bad research.

PERSPECTIVES ON THE ROLE OF EVALUATION

Evaluation has a number of different roles, both legitimate and illegitimate. Useful understanding about the role of evaluation can be derived from the ideas of Michael Scriven and David L. Stufflebeam. Both have developed concepts of evaluation which can serve to direct it toward greater utility.

In a very important and frequently reprinted article entitled "The Methodology of Evaluation," Michael Scriven provides a number of concepts useful for thinking about the role of evaluation. Although his discussion is focused on evaluation in education, with emphasis on the evaluation of new teaching methods and curricula, his ideas are very widely applicable. As he notes, the roles of evaluation can be quite variable. All these roles relate to the primary goal of evaluation: to determine worth. The role of evaluation in some ways structures the evaluation itself. Relating to this,

Scriven conceives of two types of evaluation research, formative evaluation and summative evaluation.

Formative evaluation is carried out in the course of a project with the goal of improving project functions or products. The evaluation may be done by an outside consultant, but the information produced by the evaluation is for the use of the agency. As Scriven notes, "The evaluation feedback loop stays *within* the developmental agency (its consultants), and serves to improve the product" (1973:62). Formative evaluation, is conceptualized as a midterm outcome study of the product or effects of the program rather than a more general kind of process study which might answer the question: What is going on here?

Summative evaluation serves to determine worth at the end of the process and is intended to go outside the agency whose work is being evaluated. The evaluation serves to increase utilization of the product of the project and its recognition. According to Scriven, program monitoring is a hybrid type of summative evaluation in that it is intended to go outside the agency being evaluated, but at an intermediate time.

Both formative and summative evaluation can make use of the same research designs. However, because of their different roles they require different communication strategies. The essence of the formative-summative contrast rests in the direction and purpose of the communication of evaluation results.

Scriven also contrasts what he calls *intrinsic* and *pay-off* evaluation. Intrinsic evaluation evaluates the content of the project's product or treatment, whereas pay-off evaluation is focused on effects. These four concepts are useful because they focus the evaluation on a specific purpose.

Scriven's ideas make us sensitive to the various roles of evaluation; Stufflebeam's work served to model an entire process of evaluation. His work, developed in the context of educational evaluation, rested on the assumption that evaluation is done to aid decision making. The information that it provides should be useful to decision makers. Evaluation is a continuing process and is best organized in coordination with the implementation. Data collection needs to be consciously targeted on decision-making needs. The total evaluation process ultimately involves collaboration between evaluator and decision maker.

This view of evaluation is integrated by Stufflebeam into a comprehensive process referred to as the CIPP evaluation model. The model specifies various kinds of evaluation which serve various purposes and inform various types of decisions. These decision types are (1) "*planning decisions* to determine objectives," (2) "*structuring decisions* to design procedures," (3) "*recycling decisions* to judge and react to attainments," and (4) "*implementing decisions* to utilize, control and refine procedures" (Stufflebeam 1973:133).

The four types of decisions are served by four types of evaluation. These are *context evaluation, input evaluation, product evaluation* and *process evaluation.*

Context evaluation supports planning decisions. This category would include what is called needs assessment by others, but would also identify resources that are not being used, and constraints that affect needs. Products of context evaluation include identification of client population, general goals, and objectives.

Input evaluation supports structuring decisions. The important task here is the identification of resources that relate to project objectives. Part of the process involves the determination of current agency capability. Also included is the identification of alternate strategies for accomplishing objectives. Input evaluation will also involve costing out alternatives.

Process evaluation supports implementing decisions. This type of evaluation is used to find defects in procedures and implementation, to inform ongoing decisions, and to document activities of the program.

Product evaluation informs recycling decisions. The task here is to evaluate project accomplishments at various points in the life of the project. Product evaluation requires operational definition of objectives, development of a measurement strategy, and standards against which measurements are compared.

The three case studies illustrate contemporary involvement in evaluation and needs assessments.

SUMMER OF SAFETY PROGRAM EVALUATION FOR THE CORPORATION FOR NATIONAL SERVICE: A CASE STUDY

The Corporation for National Service (CNS) is a federal government agency that administers programs like AmeriCorps, VISTA, National Civilian Community Corps, Learn and Serve America, and National Senior Service Corps, among other programs. The first national program CNS implemented was the Summer of Safety (SOS). This seven- to ten-week summer program, which involved more than 7,000 participants in 34 states and the District of Columbia, was focused on public safety issues. The project was a concrete manifestation of the idea for a "season of service" expressed by President Clinton in his inaugural address. He exhorted the nation to invest their efforts to benefit people in need and the larger community. All CNS program components were involved in the project. SOS provided CNS with an opportunity to integrate all of its units around a central theme. Program participants carried out a number of public safety activities including organizing neighborhood block watches, helping community policing, and creating safety zones for children. Participants also conducted self-defense classes, counseled crime victims, removed graffiti, boarded-up abandoned buildings, escorted older people, taught mediation and conflict resolution, and worked to prevent drug problems.

The Summer of Safety evaluation director was anthropologist David Rymph, Director, Office of Policy Research for CNS. The research, focused on 91 local programs, made use of several methods. These included enrollment data analysis, cost/benefit analysis, customer satisfaction surveys, accomplishment surveys, and ethnographies of nine local projects. Ethnographic evaluation studies were done in Oakland, California, Denver, Colorado, Jemez, New Mexico, Baltimore, Maryland, Chicago, Illinois, St. Petersburg, Florida, Lansing, Michigan, New York, New York, and Fort Devens, Massachusetts.

Anthropologist Mitchell Ratner designed and managed the multisite ethnographic component. Ratner saw participant-observation as a "defining element" of the ethnographic research. This core was supplemented with qualitative interviewing with the goal of understanding the viewpoints of staff, participants, and other community members. The local studies were designed to be accomplished within a 60-day period for field work, analysis, and writing. Qualifications included a MA in applied anthropology, experience in conducting ethnographic research, good writing ability, and interest in the content area. The ethnographers had a two-day training session at the CNS headquarters to orient them to project procedures and the intent and purpose of both CNS and SOS. Ethnographers submitted field notes regularly and progress reports weekly.

The analysis process involved condensing and ordering the field notes produced through observation and interviewing resulting in the identification of pattern, association, and theme. The analysis also focused on community context, program processes, and program accomplishments. This process was aided by periodic field visits by Ratner and a meeting of all the ethnographers for discussion of their draft reports. CNS staff and program officers were able to participate in these sessions. According to Ratner, "The draft ethnographic reports and the analytic meeting provided vehicles through which intense discussions could take place on programmatic and policy questions" (Ratner 1995:4). The traditional anthropological task of comparison can be seen in program reports that drew together content from the nine studies which focused on community context and program accomplishment and their relationship.

EDUCATIONAL REFORM ASSESSED IN KENTUCKY: A CASE STUDY

Starting in 1990, a team conducted a qualitative study of the implementation of the Kentucky Education Reform Act of 1990 (KERA) with the goal of providing information to policymakers on the impacts of this legislation. The research continued for 10 years and was funded by a grant to AEL, Inc. from the U.S. Department of Education. AEL, formerly known as the Appalachia Educational Laboratory, serves Kentucky, Tennessee, Virginia, and West Virginia. It is a not-for-profit organization mostly supported by federal grants.

KERA is a large-scale, statewide, systemic educational reform effort mandated by the Supreme Court of Kentucky. This was done in response to a court case through which it was found that the Kentucky education system was unconstitutional because of inequality in the financial support of education in the various districts and because of inadequate education statewide. The verdict charged the state legislature with reestablishing an adequate and equitable education system. The outcome was one of the first truly systemic educational reform efforts in the United States. The KERA reforms are comprehensive and demanding. KERA included a unifying set of educational goals applicable to all students, a system of instructional guidance, and a governance system (Kannapel, Aagaard, Coe, and Reeves 2000:vii).

These educational goals provided a conceptual framework for the study. The study focused on issues relating to the implementation of KERA in four small rural school districts in three different regions of the state during a 10-year period. The research team included anthropologists Patricia J. Kannapel and Cynthia A. Reeves in prominent roles. Educational anthropologists Beth Goldstein and Fred Hess served on program review panels.

Early in the study the research focused on administrative and implementation issues. Later the research team began to focus on classroom effects of the reforms on curriculum, instruction, and student learning. The team made an effort to develop an understanding of local culture. Data collection processes included classroom observations (300 hours) and interviews (ca. 400) with educators, parents, students, and community members. In addition, the researchers examined documents including student work, test results, the minutes of school-based, decision-making councils and school planning documents. Some of the issues raised in the interviews were reexamined in focus groups with educators.

During the final phase of the research, the research team followed a single class of primary students throughout the study period mostly focusing on their experiences in third, fourth, and fifth grades.

The research focused on whether the schools helped students achieve the goals established by the reform act and how KERA-specified practices were implemented in the schools. The involvement of local people in what were called site-based, decision-making councils and other aspects of school decision making was also studied.

The researchers found that student achievement improved following KERA's implementation. There was evidence that the school with the highest proportion of low-income students improved more on assessment scores than the other schools. This particular school had adopted a strategy that raised expectations of each and every student. With the exception of this school, teachers and administrators had trouble increasing the expectations of students, especially those who were from minority or low-income families. There was evidence in five of the six schools that KERA's overall objective of improving learning for every student got lost in the process of implementing all the specific KERA initiatives.

The researchers found a number of changes in curriculum and instruction. There was much more emphasis on writing. In addition, teachers expanded their instructional repertoires to include a wider variety of instructional strategies. Even so, teachers had difficulty going beyond teaching the facts to an approach that emphasized problem solving, integration of subject matter knowledge, and real-life application of skills. KERA brought with it a new testing system known as "performance-based assessment" that required students to demonstrate their knowledge through real-life writing and performance tasks. Schools received financial rewards for improving student performance on these state tests, or received state intervention if they failed to improve enough. There was also the expectation that teachers would assess students continually in the classroom and adapt instruction to meet individual student needs. In reality, most teachers focused more on improving state test scores than on improving the learning of each student.

Another important aspect of the reform is the provision for school-based, decision-making (SBDM) councils consisting of administrators, teachers, and parents to make key policy decisions relating to learning at the schools themselves. The study found that few school councils took on meaningful decision-making roles in their schools, and that parent council members were not on an equal footing with educators. The team felt that the councils needed much more information, better guidelines, and training to achieve this aspect of the reform.

ASSESSING COMMUNITY NEEDS IN SASKATOON: A CASE STUDY

The Saskatoon Needs Assessment Project was carried out by a team from the Department of Anthropology and Archaeology of the University of Saskatchewan and led by A. M. "Sandy" Ervin (Ervin, Kaye, Marcotte, and Belon 1991). The idea for the project developed from the board of the United Way. The Executive Director of the agency approached Ervin about doing the research. The project was funded by a community foundation, the university, and the United Way. Saskatoon's population is about 200,000. The economy of this prairie city is diversified and includes agriculture, mining, and forestry, as well as a growing manufacturing segment. Recent unemployment figures are over 10 percent. There are increases in the use of food banks and soup kitchens.

The project was to provide baseline information for the agency to support their decision making in a number of areas. These are "identifying needs and public perceptions to assist agencies in meeting those needs; allocating funds by working with agencies to target programs in identified needs; evaluating new agencies which have applied to join United Way [and] fundraising by focusing marketing efforts on identified needs which the United Way serve" (Ervin 1991:1).

The research design was developed by the project leader in consultation with an advisory committee, United Way's staff and board, and the research staff. Designs of other Canadian United Way needs assessments were consulted. The assessment process called for six data collection activities. The team reviewed available reports relevant to Saskatoon needs. These reports, including those from the city government, nongovernment organizations, and academic programs, were abstracted for the final report. They attempted to review social and economic indicators with the assistance of Statistics Canada. These included census data, household structure, birth rates, labor force, employment, income, disability, and other data. The research team organized three public forums that were highly publicized. There were 135 interviews carried out with key informants from community agencies. Five focus groups were held with client groups and one was held with representatives of self-help groups (Merton, Fiske, and Kendall 1990). Data were also collected using a three-stage Delphi procedure with an expert panel consisting of 28 United Way agency executive directors. Overall the needs assessment had remarkable breadth of contact with community groups. Over 140 agencies or organizations participated in the interviews, forums, or submitted written briefs.

Delphi procedure was developed as a means of collating the opinions of a panel of experts in a way that allows them to be aware of each other's opinion during the process, without them being able to influence each other through their personalities. It is also discussed in Chapter 12, Social Impact Assessment. In this case the process started with posing the experts with a single task: "Please list what you consider to be the most important social or human needs that should be addressed in Saskatoon, regardless of what agencies or levels of government are responsible for them." They were to type in their answers in 10 boxes. The expert panel never spoke with each other directly, yet they communicated to each other through the research team. The research team analyzed the responses and put them into standardized phrasing and related clusters. This produced a list of 108 needs. In the second round they were asked to choose the top 12 in ranked order and to make comments. This produced another ranked list of 86 needs, ranked in terms of their raw scores. They were then asked for any adjustments. The need that was ranked highest was "to eliminate hunger and, therefore, the necessity of food banks." Other highly ranked needs were "need for more emphasis on preventive services," "need for accessible, affordable, quality accommodation; perhaps based on income (i.e. not low income ghettos)," and the "need to increase core funding for non-government agencies to enable long term planning and development."

The Delphi panel data were used, along with data from all other sources, to produce an abstract of community needs or "the widespread social problems that are confronting Saskatoon" (1991:20). Also reported were the needs of organizations, referred to here as metaneeds. The more than 200 needs identified were organized by 17 sectors including general health, mental health, seniors, native issues, racism and discrimination, immigrant and refugee resettlement, and rehabilitation, among others. The sectors were derived from a directory of community information published by the public library. The research team produced a series of recommendations for the United Way itself.

SUMMARY

Evaluation research is a rapidly growing area in applied anthropology. Preparation for careers in evaluation should include training in both experimental and case-study design as well as the appropriate data collection techniques. Research methods traditionally associated with anthropology are useful for a number of important evaluation tasks, but these need to be supplemented to meet the entire array of evaluation problems which emerge. The utility of ethnographic evaluation methods is highly related to the purpose of the evaluation. Ethnographic evaluation techniques are especially useful where one of the purposes of the evaluation is the documentation of program operations, or the discovery of what went wrong with a program which failed. Ethnographic techniques serve as a good foundation for providing recommendations for program improvement.

Anthropologists in evaluation do not make extensive use of experimental designs. Usually they rely on various kinds of case-study approaches. These approaches are quite variable and represent a significant array of research tools in their own right. The utility of the case-study approach can be seen in the interest in these approaches shown by nonanthropologists. The literature on evaluation methodology places an emphasis on the use of experimental designs other than the case study. It is important to recognize that in spite of this, much evaluation is done using the case-study approach. The reasons for this are largely practical. It is expensive and politically awkward to use the more complex experimental designs in many settings. In addition, there are many problems in evaluation where the best and perhaps only approach is the case-study method. In spite of the continued importance of the case-study method there is relatively little attention in the literature to refinements in the case-study methodology.

FURTHER READING

Cook, Thomas D. and Charles S. Reichardt, eds. *Qualitative and Quantitative Methods in Evaluation Research*. Sage Research Progress Series in Evaluation, Vol. 1. Beverly Hills, Calif.: Sage, 1979. This contains a number of good articles which deal with the qualitative-quantitative contrast.

Fetterman, David M. and M. Pitman, eds. *Educational Evaluation: Ethnography in Theory, Practice, and Politics*. Beverly Hills, Calif.: Sage, 1986. David Fetterman has provided leadership in the use of ethnography in evaluation.

Chapter 14

Cultural Resource Management

Cultural resource management (CRM) is "the management both of cultural resources and the effects on them that may result from land use and other activities of the contemporary world" (King 1998:265). CRM is primarily concerned with managing the resources associated with "historic places of archeological, architectural, and historical interest" and compliance with a wide range of cultural resource laws. While public or contract archaeology is an important part of the CRM endeavor, there is much more to CRM than just archaeology. The CRM process includes architectural historians, museum curators and collection managers, materials specialists, folklorists, and cultural anthropologists (Knudson 1986:395).

While CRM archaeology accounts for the largest portion of archaeological research performed in the United States (and the largest sector of employment in archaeology), the range of applications in archaeology extends well beyond CRM. Downum and Price (1999) present a typology of applied archaeology which clearly shows the broad range of applications in this subfield. Their typology includes "resource claims, archaeological contributions to cultural identity and representation, technological applications, public education, cultural tourism, environmental and ecosystems applications" as well as CRM (Downum and Price 1999:227–232). Applications in *resource claims* include the use of archaeology to document prehistoric land use in support of indigenous peoples' land claims and archaeological work in the context of repatriation of human remains and important artifacts to Native Americans under the provisions of the Native American Graves Protection and Repatriation Act (NAGPRA). *Archaeo-*

The authors of this chapter are John van Willigen and Donald W. Linebaugh.

logical contributions to cultural identity and representation include the recovery and display of archaeological materials in a way that increases the presence of underrepresented people in the historic record. Archaeology can also be used to investigate *technological applications* of the past for possible reuse in the present. For example, ancient farming practices revealed through archaeology have been recycled to solve problems in Israel and Peru (Downum and Price 1999:228–229). *Public education* and *cultural heritage tourism* are also important areas of application. *Environmental and ecosystems applications* are especially important in that archaeology is often the only source of information about environmental change in the past. For this reason, "archaeology offers some of the world's most important information for environmental analysis, planning, and ecosystem management" (Downum and Price 1999:231).

The term cultural resource management (CRM) was originally coined by archaeologists in the late 1970s to describe their contribution to the recently enacted environmental impact assessment process. The name is intended to emphasize the parallels between the more established field of natural resources management and the developing legislative framework for managing cultural resources, particularly within the discipline of archaeology; it also sought to escape the marginalization associated with the then widely used term "salvage archaeology" that carried a negative connotation.

In general, a cultural resource is "any resource (i.e., a thing that is useful for something) that is of a cultural character" (King 1998:265). The concept is used broadly and varies from context to context. For archaeologists, cultural resources primarily include sites, artifacts, and archaeological museum collections; however, the category is much larger and also includes historic buildings and landscapes, Native American graves and cultural items, shipwrecks, historical documents, religious sites, cultural use of natural resources, folk life, tradition and other social institutions, and community cultural amenities.

Managing these resources may require engaging in a complex, even contentious process, sometimes largely focused on professional concerns about research design and archaeological method, and at other times very engaged with public concerns about control of the past and its meaning and power in the present.

In a culturally pluralistic country there can be significant differences in what is regarded as possessing cultural value. The determination of cultural value ultimately is a matter of public discussion. An important task in CRM is negotiating the relationships between agencies advocating projects, the different publics that attach meaning to those resources, the cultural patrimony of the country, the archaeological data base, and, of course, the resource itself. Given the laws and regulations that establish and regulate the CRM process, improper cultural assessment can result in expensive project delays. This is illustrated by the following case.

THE CASE OF THE AFRICAN BURIAL GROUND

The case of the African Burial Ground illustrates the potential for public misunderstanding about cultural values and points out the significant costs (both monetary and social) associated with these misunderstandings (Harrington 1993). The African Burial Ground came into being in the late seventeenth and early eighteenth centuries as a burial place for slaves just outside the walls of New Amsterdam on the island of Manhattan. This cemetery eventually became covered and forgotten as New Amsterdam and later New York City expanded. During the late 1980s the U.S. General Services Administration began the process of constructing a new federal office building on Manhattan. As with most "federal actions" an environmental impact assessment was required and performed. The EIA process usually involves the consideration of the impact of a project on cultural resources. As part of the initial research, a map was discovered that depicted the African Burial Ground and suggested that it was located within the project area. Project planners responded to the identification of this historic resource in a typical way, treating it as an archaeological site to be excavated, analyzed, and reported on in what had come to be an established, routine procedure. However, there was no attempt to contact New York's African-American community to find out what this important resource meant to them. As it turned out, the large and very intact site held great meaning for the local African-American community. They responded negatively to the planned CRM process, including the excavation and removal of several hundred burials, and strongly protested the projected construction as blatant desecration. At this point, as Thomas King (1998:8) later observed, "all hell broke loose." A congressional investigation was launched, the construction was delayed at great cost, and the design of the project was considerably changed.

There are a number of key points to be learned from this case. First "cultural value" is, in the final analysis, a public concept, and determination of those values requires a carefully crafted project that draws its strength from both professional work and public discourse. Second, public discussion of cultural values associated with resources is essential in order to have effective projects, and this dialogue must start very early in the planning of the project.

THE LAWS AND REGULATIONS

Much of the work of cultural resource management archaeologists is indistinguishable from that of other, for example, academically-based archaeologists. They excavate all types of sites (and destroy them in the process); they analyze and interpret artifacts and features; and they report their findings. The key difference is that the professional work of CRM archaeologists is governed by law and regulation as well as scientific and intellectual curiosity. Thus, the research programs of CRM archaeologists are driven by development and commercial interests responding to cultural resource law and regulations that have little connection to specific research issues or site types. In this sense, study areas and sites are randomly selected for the CRM archaeologist who must then place them within a research context. As with practice in many disciplines, this regulatory and commercial atmosphere can make longer-term, larger-scale research goals much more difficult, although not impossible, to pursue. Of all the areas of professional practice we consider in this book, in fact, CRM has the most complex and influential legal basis. It is essential to understand these laws and regulations because they motivate so much of what is done.

The legal basis of CRM in the United States is formed by several principal federal laws (National Park Service 1993); similar laws and regulations do exist at the state and local level, but these are sporadic at best and vary greatly in terms of regulatory authority. Some of the state and local legislation mirrors the federal provisions; however, these non-federal laws and regulations are often without much regulatory punch and thus difficult to enforce. The laws governing CRM change periodically and can be subject to political, commercial, and public pressure. For example, the important National Historic Preservation Act was originally passed in 1966 and then was amended in 1980 and 1992. Anthropologists are often active in the process of revising these kinds of legislation by providing expert testimony in congressional hearings, consulting with legislators, and advocating support. Speaking subjectively, it seems that it is in this realm that anthropologists have had the most significant impact on legislation. It is very useful to read the laws to obtain a clear idea of what actions they mandate and what opportunities they create. The U.S. National Park Service publishes a summary collection of the federal laws that is available from the U.S. Government Printing Office (National Park Service 1993) and provides a website (www.cr.nps.gov/linklaws.htm) with up-to-date, downloadable versions of the CRM laws and regulations.

The legal basis for the ownership of archaeological resources varies from country to country. For a number of interesting reasons, ownership of these resources in the United States is ambiguous (Knudson 1986:396). First, in the case of prehistoric sites, there is no genetic relationship between the mainstream and politically dominant population of the United States and the persons who originally created the archaeological resources. Second, with some exceptions, archaeological resources were more or less unknown and therefore unaddressed constitutionally. Third, at the time that U.S. legal institutions were formed, reaction against the concepts of monarchy and the associated idea of royal property fostered the protection of private property rights. As a result, the idea of state ownership of cultural resources, such as archaeological sites, that is found in some other countries is absent in the United States. Thus, a comprehensive national policy on cultural resources in the United States has developed in the context of a cultural value on private property.

There is a large body of law relevant to CRM in the United States, and many of these laws specially address archaeological resources. Important early legislation, such as the Antiquities Act of 1906, set the tone for later federal policy. The Antiquities Act, for example, applied only to federal land thus escaping the private property issue (McGimsey and Davis 1984: 118). The most important pieces of legislation guiding CRM are the National Environmental Policy Act of 1969 (NEPA) and the National Historic Preservation Act of 1966 (NHPA) (amended in 1992).

The definition of the environment in NEPA includes sociocultural aspects, and therefore it specifically addresses cultural resources. NEPA is especially important because it "provided a land use and resource management legal mechanism that overrides the concept of private ownership" (Knudson 1986:397). NEPA provides a vehicle for open public consideration of the possible impacts of federal actions, including federally funded, permitted, or licensed projects. Ideally the process results in decisions which "balance environmental protection—including cultural resource protection—with other public values" (King 1998:269). This is very closely related to the process for the environmental impact assessment document discussed in Chapter 12, social impact assessment. The implementation of the process can range from being an important tool for democratic environmental decisions, sensitive to cultural diversity and environmental justice, to a kind of bureaucratic documentation of resources (King 1998:269). This means that the legal basis of CRM shares a great deal with the legal basis of social impact assessment which was discussed earlier.

Beyond the environmentally focused NEPA there are a range of important laws that specifically address historic preservation and structure and guide CRM practice. The NHPA, passed in 1966, established the federal government's policy concerning protection and preservation of historic properties. The category "historic properties" includes archaeological sites, artifacts, and records as well as things more narrowly historical. So just as NEPA's environment is broadly conceived to include archaeological resources, so too is NHPA's conception of history so inclusive that it includes prehistorical archaeology.

NHPA mandates that organizations involved in federal undertakings (funding, permitting, and licensing) must consider the effect of their project on cultural resources that are eligible for inclusion on the National Register of Historic Places (NRHP). The National Register listing, currently containing over 71,000 entries, is maintained by the Secretary of the Interior and is "composed of districts, sites, buildings, structures, and objects significant in American history, architecture, archaeology, engineering, and culture" (National Park Service 1993:7). The determination of NRHP eligibility for listing in the National Register is a central aspect of cultural resource management. If a resource is regarded as eligible for, or is actually listed in, the NRHP, then the impact of any planned federal or federally assisted project on the resource would be assessed. This entire process of identifying and evaluating resources is usually referred to as the "Section 106 process."

National Historic Preservation Act—Section 106

The head of any federal agency having direct or indirect jurisdiction over a proposed federal or federally assisted undertaking in any state and the head of any federal department or independent agency having authority to license any undertaking shall, prior to the approval of the expenditure of any federal funds on the undertaking or prior to the issuance of any license, as the case may be, take into account the effect of the undertaking on any district, site, building, structure, or object that is included in or eligible for inclusion in the National Register.

As stated above, Section 106 of NHPA requires that heads of federal agencies with direct or indirect jurisdiction over a proposed federal or federally assisted project evaluate the impacts of the project on any resource(s) listed in or eligible for listing in the National Register. This process, which must be completed before project construction is started, involves resource identification and evaluation and consultation with relevant organizations. The regulations make it possible for state and local governments, Native American groups, private citizens, and other "interested parties" to be involved in a meaningful way in the planning of federal or federally assisted projects. Much of the work of CRM archaeologists and other historic resource specialists revolves around the Section 106 process.

In addition to the Section 106 process, NHPA mandates a number of practices, including development of coordinated historic preservation plans, public education, support of local programs, and financial aid to local preservation efforts; many of these activities are delegated to state preservation offices. To accomplish this program, the law creates the position of State Historic Preservation Officer (SHPO) to be appointed by the governor of each state and territory. The SHPO has a number of important regulatory and coordinating roles under NEPA and NHPA, including compliance and review of all Section 106 projects. Because of their "domestic sovereign nation" status, tribal governments have their own historic preservation officers (HPO) that function similarly to SHPOs.

Another entity created by NHPA is the Advisory Council on Historic Preservation (ACHP). The ACHP is an independent federal agency that serves as a watchdog on activities associated with the Section 106 process. The council advocates for historic preservation, mediates controversial Section 106 cases, and provides training and public information about the Section 106 review process. The council cannot stop projects but it can publically criticize and even rebuke an agency if they are uncooperative or have ignored the intent of the Section 106 legislation. The council's 20 members include presidentially appointed private citizens, agency heads, and representatives of state, local, and tribal governments.

There are a number of other laws that are relevant to CRM. The Historic Sites Act of 1935 (HSA) defined an important role in historic preservation for the National Park Service (NPS). This role involves a special responsibility for interpreting and commemorating the nation's history through documenting, describing, and owning significant historic properties, including archaeological resources. This responsibility is implemented through the National Historic Landmarks (NHL), Historic American Buildings Survey (HABS), and Historic American Engineering Records (HAER) programs. As mentioned earlier the Antiquities Act of 1906 protects "objects of antiquity" on public lands and provides for the creation of national monuments. It is important to remember that much of the United States is publically owned or held land, and thus the Antiquities Act is important for the protection and management of historic resources across huge portions of the United States. The Archeological Resources Protection Act of 1979 (ARPA) provides clarification of the protection provisions of the Antiquities Act by defining "archeological resources." It also provides for the creation of a permitting system among many federal agencies to regulate and monitor archaeological activities on public land. The Archeological Data Preservation Act of 1974 also known as the "Moss-Bennett Act" provides a means for funding archaeological research made necessary due to federal actions, authorizing the use of up to 1 percent of a project's budget for archaeological research. The Abandoned Shipwrecks Act of 1987 establishes that the United States owns wrecks in territorial waters. This law was motivated by the need to protect wrecks from commercial salvage interests.

Of special interest to CRM are the laws that focus on Native American archaeological resources. Two laws are relevant to our concerns: the American Indian Religious Freedom Act of 1978 (AIRFA) and the Native American Graves Protection and Repatriation Act of 1990 (NAGPRA). AIRFA establishes the principle that the U.S. government works to protect free religious expression by Native Americans. The scope of this legislation is much broader than archaeological resources and includes religious practices themselves. NAGPRA provides for the repatriation of Native American ancestral human remains and related cultural items from agencies (like universities and museums) that have received federal funding to entities that have a genetic or cultural association with the ancestral population.

NAGPRA creates especially complex challenges for cultural resource managers. Native American and Native Hawaiian human and cultural remains have been collected for their research value for many years. As a result skeletal and artifactual materials taken from the consecrated context where they were originally placed have been invested in by the dominant society with an entirely different set of meanings (as scientific specimens) from those of Native American groups. Standard practice has been to store or display these materials in public and private museums and other research facilities. As a result of their growing outrage over the past treatment of these materials, Native American groups mobilized politically to bring change to the handling and ownership of these objects and this effort resulted in the passage of NAGPRA. The purpose and spirit of NAGPRA is to invest the contested materials with proper respect. Managers of collections that contain Native American or Native Hawaiian materials have become involved in the process of inventorying all collections and consulting with native groups about the materials; this process can result in the repatriation of these collections to their original or descendant owners. The repatriation process can sometimes involve reburial of skeletal remains in a sacred ritual context. NAGPRA also addresses materials that are still "in the ground" and thus requires coordination in the initial planning process of Section 106 projects that may identify Native American sites or properties (this has been reinforced and strengthened by recent changes to the NHPA regulations). If Native American materials covered by the law are discovered accidentally in the process of completing a federal project, those responsible must report it to the head of the lead agency. This starts a consultation process for dealing with the materials in a mutually acceptable way. Furthermore it results in a 30-day moratorium on further work in the area of the discovery. An alternative approach would be for persons involved in activities that may result in finding NAGPRA-eligible remains to prepare a "plan of action" which describes how Native American materials found will be managed as they are found. This document is to be developed in consultation with Native American representatives and provides for things such as custody and treatment of materials, from both a research and religious aspect, and disposition (King 1998:153–155).

THE CULTURAL RESOURCE IMPACT ASSESSMENT PROCESS[1]

Cultural resource assessment involves the integration of law and regulation with various archaeological practices such as site survey and excavation. The parallels with social impact assessment are very clear.

Scoping

Scoping is done as part of the planning of an impact-producing project such as the construction of a highway or excavation of a sewer line. This

1. This section is based upon King (1998:219–231). We follow his outline.

is something that occurs in social impact assessment also. In the case of CRM, the development of a scope is often done as part of an environmental impact assessment (EIA) or environmental impact study (EIS) as mandated by NEPA, a process that includes attention to cultural resources. If NEPA does not apply, it is possible that the resources would be assessed from the perspective of other cultural resource laws such as the National Historic Preservation Act.

It is necessary to determine whether a particular project is subject to federal regulations, and this involves the determination of federal agency involvement, either directly or as federal assistance, and an assessment of whether the project will impact historic properties. Federal agency involvement includes projects financed and/or regulated by federal government agencies as well as projects performed for the government or directly by the government.

Following a determination of whether the project is covered by NEPA, NHPA, or other similar legislation, an evaluation of the project's *area of potential effects* (APE) must be completed. This is not as straightforward as one might think because it goes beyond the direct physical effects of the project to include indirect and cumulative effects, for example both auditory and visual impacts.

The scoping exercise is largely a process of gathering information and assessing this information in terms of the location of known or suspected resources. Thus, scoping involves background research and evaluation of previous studies in an effort to document previously identified resources and aid in assessing the potential for various types of resources in the project area. Scoping also requires consultation with relevant officials such as the State Historic Preservation Officer (SHPO) and other stakeholders. Scoping often involves public input, and this is achieved through venues such as public meetings. Therefore, it is important for CRM professionals to develop skills for effectively consulting and coordinating with colleagues and managing public meetings.

Various regulations specify that during the scoping process attention should be directed to areas of special concern that may be impacted by the project. These areas include Native American sacred sites, Native American religious practices, cultural concerns of low-income and minority populations, historic documents, and historical, scientific or archaeological data (King 1998:220). Consultation is a key word in this phase of the assessment process. The diversity of cultural resources means that a wide range of expertise may be needed to properly perform the impact assessment study. Thus, consultation is often necessary with a variety of agencies and stakeholders. Regulations requires consultation with SHPO and HPO, Native American and Native Hawaiian groups, and low-income and minority groups.

Identification of Cultural Resources

While the range of possible resources is very large, the actual resources considered in each case will depend on the situation. It is important to remember that the category of cultural resources, as used here, is a complex and somewhat arbitrary product of regulation, law, and executive order. In general, the NHPA and implementing regulations use the term historic properties to describe a segment of cultural resources.

Historic properties are places which are listed in, or eligible to be listed in, the National Register of Historic Places. There is a wide range of criteria that can be applied to determine if a property is eligible, and these will be discussed in more detail below. The category of historic places includes buildings, structures, sites, and districts which are "significant" in terms of history, archaeology, architecture, engineering, or culture. Although the category is labeled "historical," it includes prehistoric resources as well. *Native American cultural materials*, human remains, funerary items, sacred objects, and objects of cultural patrimony associated with Native Americans are included. These materials may come under the provisions of NAGPRA. This is only relevant on federal or Native American lands. *Archaeological, historical and scientific data*, in various contexts are included. *Native American religious practices* are under the provisions of AIRFA. Native American *sacred sites* are included as significant cultural resources under the provisions of Executive Order 13007. *Community cultural practices* of various kinds are defined as cultural resources and included in NEPA. *Historical documents* may also be included.

The identification process results in the first substantial need for field research in the Section 106 process. The identification stage is frequently divided into two portions: Phase I survey and Phase II evaluation or assessment. Usually, a survey is performed to determine whether an area to be impacted by a project includes "significant" resources, such as prehistoric and historic archaeological sites and architectural or engineering resources. Surveys typically involve a literature review to determine whether any previously identified sites or structures are located in the project area and field testing to locate previously unknown resources. These projects are typically called Phase I Archaeological Surveys. The resulting survey reports document areas of high, low, and no archaeological potential, gather evidence from the sites that may be disturbed, and make preliminary assessments of NRHP eligibility. Some sites will be recommended as not eligible for the NRHP for various reasons and will drop out of the process at this point; others will be considered potentially eligible for the NRHP and will move onto the Phase II evaluation-of-significance and assessment-of-impact stage. Artifacts and other materials discovered during this process must be inventoried and stored in an approved curation facility, as are all field excavation records. The reports and photos produced are made available to the state through the SHPO.

In addition to these very typical CRM projects there may be a wide range of different topical surveys. Some foci include architecture, engineering resources, culturally significant places, and historic records. All of these studies are done with stakeholder and cross-disciplinary consultation.

Determination of Significance

The criteria for significance of "historic properties" is specified in regulation, although these criteria are, of necessity, general and subject to varying interpretations. The task in this stage of work is determining whether a specific resource meets the National Register criteria for listing. Evaluation of the significance of the sites identified during Phase I survey as potentially eligible for the NRHP is often referred to as a Phase II evaluation or testing study. Typically, if a resource is considered not eligible for NRHP listing at either the Phase I or Phase II stage, impacts will not be assessed any further. As a practical matter, significance has to be determined for a wide range of cultural resource types making the process difficult and open to criticism. The determination of significance is guided by a set of standard NRHP guidelines.

The Elusive Concept—Significance

The NRHP was established to list properties that were considered significant to the archaeological, historic, architectural, engineering, or cultural heritage of the United States. Thus, the evaluation of significance is at the core of determining the NRHP eligibility of a property. The difficulty in this arises in defining what is significant, and to whom. The process is subjective and requires the investigator to make certain value judgments about a site or structure and its importance to our nation's heritage. Fortunately, the NHPA has established some guidelines, *The National Register Criteria for Evaluation of Cultural Resources* (U.S. Department of the Interior 1983), for making the decisions that guide us through the process and help us move from making an unsubstantiated guess to an informed assessment of significance. The *Criteria for Evaluation* states that significance is present in "districts, sites, buildings, structures, and objects" that possess integrity and meet at least one of four broad criteria, discussed in this chapter, labeled A–D. Keatinge has provided a simple shorthand for remembering the criteria for evaluation. Criterion A is for "association," B is for "big people," C is for "cute buildings," and D is for "data" (most often used for archaeological sites) (Keatinge quoted in King 1998:75).

The process of determining significance and thus NRHP eligibility has been summarized by Hardesty, Little, and Fowler (2000:11–52) in their book *Assessing Site Significance: A Guide for Archaeologists and Historians*. The authors lay out five principal steps in evaluating a property's eligibility for the NRHP. Step 1 involves categorizing the property (i.e., is it an object, building, structure, site, or district?). Step 2 involves determining which historic context the property represents and the property type's relationship to the context. A historic context is "a broad pattern of historical development" (Hardesty, Little, and Fowler 2000:13). The NPS provides some guidance in terms of their *Revised Thematic Framework* (NPS 1996) for developing contexts, and most states have plans that detail historic contexts for the state and region. Step 3 calls for the evaluation of significance using the NRHP criteria A–D (i.e., considering the resource's significance within the appropriate historic context in terms of the four NRHP criteria). Step 4 involves applying several special criteria considerations that exclude certain property types from eligibility; for example, properties less than 50 years old, cemeteries and graves, birthplaces, and religious properties. Step 5 requires an assessment of the property's integrity and involves asking the question, "Does it retain sufficient integrity to convey its significance?" For example, in the case of Criterion D and archaeological sites we ask the question, "Does the site retain enough integrity to provide important research data?" Each of these five steps require careful analysis and judgment on the part of the researcher. Guidance can be sought from the SHPO staff, NPS, and NRHP staff, and by using previous NRHP nominations and eligibility determinations for resources similar to the one under evaluation.

The Guidelines

The quality of significance in American history, architecture, archaeology, engineering, and culture is present in districts, sites, buildings, structures, and objects that possess integrity of location, design, setting, materials, workmanship, feeling, and association, and:

A. That are associated with events that have made a significant contribution to the broad patterns of our history; or

B. That are associated with the lives of persons significant in our past; or

C. That embody the distinctive characteristics of a type, period, or method of construction, or that represent the work of a master, or that possess high artistic values, or that represent a significant and distinguishable entity whose components may lack individual distinction; or

D. That have yielded or may be likely to yield, information important in prehistory or history.

Thus, a resource must pass the significance test by possessing both integrity and falling within one or all of the criteria (A–D). In addition to the guidelines, one can also use the previous register nominations to guide the significance evaluation process, drawing on significance arguments presented for similar sites or structures. In the case of Native American sacred sites,

Native American consultants may be reluctant to disclose the reasons why a site is significant making it difficult to determine eligibility.

Assessing Effects

Having determined NRHP eligibility, it is necessary to identify possible negative effects to the resource or to document that there will be no adverse effects. While "criteria of adverse effect" are published in government regulations, the determination of effect is often a matter of judgment by CRM professionals and stakeholders. Some of the possible adverse effects as categorized by King (1998:226) include physical damage or destruction, alteration of the visual and auditory environment, introducing incompatible uses in the area; neglect of a resource in charge of an agency, and transfer of property out of federal care.

Seeking Mitigation Measures

Once adverse effects are identified and agreed upon, a plan for mitigating them is necessary. Mitigation can involve "avoiding the impact altogether, minimizing impacts, rectifying impacts, reducing or eliminating impacts over time [and/or] compensating for impacts" (King 1998:227). Like other aspects of the cultural resource impact assessment process, open consultation with stakeholders is needed and is essential for establishing a workable and acceptable mitigation plan.

Establishing and Documenting Mitigation Measures

Once mitigation measures are agreed upon, they need to be documented. In the case of historic properties, documentation takes the form of what is called "Memoranda of Agreement" prepared by the lead agency, the SHPO, and other stakeholders (King 1998:228). The ACHP provides oversight in this process. For projects that involve NAGPRA issues or claims, there is a similar document called a Plan of Action (POA) and Comprehensive Agreement (CA). Negotiating mitigation measures may be very difficult and conflict ridden. For example, this process may engender bureaucratic power struggles, interest group pressures, political maneuvering, and public divisiveness. Yet, in most cases, this can be avoided by full involvement of stakeholders and clear, well-researched presentations of the problem and the proposed resolution strategy. Excavation and data recovery are often used as appropriate means of mitigation of adverse effects that cannot be avoided for projects with significant archaeological resources.

ACHP Comments

The ACHP can become involved in the process if agreement on mitigation cannot be reached. In the absence of a suitable agreement, the ACHP is solicited for comments. This provision, invoking the full advisory council, has the effect of increasing the likelihood that an agreement will be reached between the parties. King (1998:229) writes that, "this sort of high-level attention can have career implications for those farther down the agency food chain, so the great bulk of Section 106 consultations *do* result in agreements."

Implementing Mitigation

It is important to incorporate a means of monitoring progress in the mitigation plan. This can involve the use of third-party monitors, inclusion of monitoring provisions in contracts, issuance of periodic reports by specific deadlines, and public disclosure with opportunities for public comment. Project mitigation may include extensive excavation and analysis.

DOCUMENTATION

A large portion of the public investment in archaeological research in the United States occurs through the Section 106 process and CRM projects in general. One effect of this is that most "print material" on cultural resources in the United States, particularly archaeological and architectural sites, is in the form of what is known as "gray literature." The term "gray literature" refers to unpublished, uncatalogued, and limited circulation technical reports. Unfortunately, this material has very limited bibliographic control making it difficult to obtain by researchers not familiar with the project or sponsoring organization. One institution which documents these materials is the National Archeological Database—Reports. NADB—Reports is a bibliographic inventory of over 240,000 limited circulation reports. The data base can be searched on-line using a variety of descriptors. A recent development in distributing these materials is the use of on-line, downloadable formats and thematic collections of reports available at low cost on CD-ROM. For example, the Jamestown Rediscovery project in Virginia (www.jamestownrediscovery.org) now offers their technical excavation reports as downloadable files that can be printed by the user. The Virginia Department of Transportation has also just released a new CD-ROM-based series that presents thematically grouped CRM reports for wide, cost-effective distribution. It is likely that much of the problem with using "gray literature" will be solved with electronic and digital applications.

We have included three cases to illustrate aspects of professional work of the anthropologists involved in CRM. The first illustrates a CRM project done in response to the construction of a bus parking lot. This is coupled with a description of the Federal Aid Interstate-270 Archaeological Mitigation Project. The latter was selected because it is very large, of long duration, and often cited as a model project. These two cases are supplemented with CRM work done by a cultural anthropologist in the American Southwest.

THE PENTRAN BUS PARKING LOT PROJECT, A TYPICAL SECTION 106 CRM PROJECT: A CASE STUDY

The Pentran Bus Parking Lot project began as do most Section 106 projects with a request from the Virginia Department of Transportation (VDOT) (on behalf of the City of Hampton) to the Virginia Department of Historic Resources (VDHR) (Virginia SHPO) to review the undertaking. Due to the project's location in an area of the city of Hampton known to have been utilized prehistorically and historically from early settlement to the present, the VDHR requested a Phase I survey of the approximately one-acre property. This initial survey was performed by a staff archaeologist at the VDOT's Suffolk District Office.

The Phase I survey consisted of a series of 17 shovel test pits (measuring 25–30 centimeters in diameter and dug to sterile subsoil) spaced across the property. These tests produced 1,999 artifacts, of which 50 (2.5%) dated to the seventeenth and nineteenth centuries; the remainder of the artifacts were related to a former auto junkyard on the site. The presence of a very small number of seventeenth-century artifacts, coarse earthenware, dark green bottle glass, wrought nails, and white and red clay tobacco pipestems, combined with the large number of previously identified early settlement period sites in Hampton, suggested to the VDOT archaeologist the potential for an important early site on the property. Thus, the site was considered potentially eligible for nomination to the National Register and avoidance of a Phase II evaluation was recommended (Stuck and Downing 1995).

The Phase II evaluation project was contracted by the VDOT to the William & Mary Center for Archaeological Research. Fieldwork consisted of additional shovel test pits, test unit excavation, and machine stripping of the plowzone or upper layer of disturbed, mixed soils. This work identified over 1,000 artifacts and 40 cultural features, including a cellar pit, structural postholes, slot fence trenches, and sheet refuse dating to the second half of the seventeenth century. Historical research on the property suggested that the site might be a trading plantation belonging to early Hampton residents William Claiborne and Thomas Jarvis. The Phase II fieldwork concluded with a recommendation that the site be considered eligible for the National Register because of its potential to provide valuable information about early life on a Hampton plantation and how this site fit into the surrounding cultural and economic landscape (Stuck and Downing 1995).

With the site taking up most of the project parcel, there was little hope of redesigning the project to avoid damage to the archaeological resources. Thus, a Phase III data recovery mitigation plan was prepared that detailed the research design and goals, including the methodology for additional excavation, historical research, analysis, and research questions. The subsequent excavation resulted in a collection of over 17,000 artifacts and excavation of hundreds of cultural features dating to the seventeenth century, including a large post-in-ground dwelling house, a post-in-ground barn, several smaller outbuildings, a well, and numerous fenced enclosures (Higgins, Downing, and Linebaugh 1999). The analysis included the work of historians, artifact specialists and faunal analysts to study the over 6,000 animal bones to ascertain diet, and so forth; and archaeobotanists to study the plant remains (seeds and leaves) to reconstruct the environment around the plantation.

This multidisciplinary research provided a detailed understanding of the plantation of Thomas Jarvis, from approximately 1661 to about 1700, and its place within the emerging settlement of Kecoughtan (later the city of Hampton). Another particularly important aspect of the project was the opportunity for a public archaeology component. A very successful open house was held near the end of the fieldwork, allowing the public (over 500 visitors) to tour the site, view the artifacts, and talk with the archaeologists. This type of public interpretation and participation is now integrated in most large mitigation projects, as regulators and archaeologists come to appreciate the importance of including stakeholders in the project, particularly through educational opportunities.

THE FAI-270 PROJECT, A LARGE-SCALE MITIGATION PROJECT: A CASE STUDY

The Federal Aid Interstate-270 Archaeological Mitigation Project was a collaboration between the Illinois Department of Transportation (IDOT) and University of Illinois archaeologists. The project, directed by Charles J. Bareis and James W. Porter of the University of Illinois at Urbana–Champaign and monitored by archaeologist Bennie C. Keel of the U.S. Department of the Interior, is significant because of both its magnitude and duration. It is a large and very successful CRM project. This mitigation project benefitted from a long history of cooperation between the Illinois Department of Transportation and its engineers and the archaeological community of Illinois. It was focused on mitigating the impact on archaeological resources caused by the construction of a six-lane highway that would cross about 1,000 acres of land in southern Illinois.

The project is located on the American Bottom, part of the Mississippi

River flood plain located in three Illinois counties across the Mississippi from metropolitan St. Louis. This alluvial plain is very productive land, and this productivity relates directly to the large number of archaeological sites that it contains. An effect of this number of sites is that it is difficult to change the location of the highway right-of-way to avoid significant sites; virtually any location would compromise cultural resources. The best known site on the American Bottom is Cahokia Mounds, a Mississippian site dating from 800 to 1400 A.D. It consists of a large mound and a surrounding settled area thought to have a population of about 20,000 to 25,000. Today it is encompassed by the Cahokia Mounds State Park, located a few miles across the Mississippi from downtown St. Louis. Important archaeological research has been underway at Cahokia since the 1920s. The FAI-270 project started in 1975 with a careful reconnaissance survey of the highway right-of-way by IDOT crews.

An important component of the research was the development of a research design or plan which specifies sampling and analysis methodology and summarizes basic research questions. The research design allowed the project to address scientific questions "to answer local and regional archaeological questions as perceived by those who knew well the archaeology of the American Bottom" (Bareis and Porter 1984:3).

Ultimately nearly 100 archaeological sites were excavated and documented. About two-thirds were on or near the highway right of way, and the rest were located on nearby bluffs. Here excavations were done to mitigate the effects of removing or placing the fill used for constructing the road bed. The result was a massive data base located at the University of Illinois.

SOUTHERN PAIUTE COLORADO RIVER CORRIDOR PROJECT, ETHNOGRAPHY IN CRM: A CASE STUDY

Although with much less frequency than in archaeology or architecture, ethnography is also used in the context of cultural resource assessment. A series of interrelated ethnographic projects was initiated in 1992 in order to begin a detailed consultation process with the Southern Paiute people, regarding cultural resource management within their traditional territory. The first stage of the project, concluded in 1994, investigated cultural resources within the Colorado River corridor. The first report of the project described the ethnographic concerns of the Southern Paiute people, and the second, presented in 1995, described the impact of the Glen Canyon Dam and the changes it caused on the Colorado River. The 1997 project areas were Zion National Park, Utah, and Pipe Spring National Monument, Arizona. Each project utilized on-site interviews of Paiute elders, previously documented interviews of Paiute elders, and other legal and general documents on this and related subjects. The projects included investigations of ethnoarchaeology, ethnobotany, ethnozoology, rock art, traditional cultural properties (often known by Indian peoples as power places), ethnogeography, and cultural landscapes. An interdisciplinary team, led by anthropologist Richard W. Stoffle, was assembled to address the interrelations of these various aspects. The process informs extensive integration, Stoffle wrote, "Ideally, the process of cultural resource assessment studies entails separate studies of specific, bounded *cultural domains*, or categories of knowledge regarding certain domains such as plants, animals, water, culture history, and the like" (Stoffle, Austin, Halmo, and Phillips 1997: 93). Part of the project included work with an environmental education program for Southern Paiute youth that focused on the "*integration of concepts* through experiential activities, presentations, and discussions" (Stoffle, Austin, Fulfrost, Phillips, and Drye 1995:142). The 1997 project also investigated the legal history of both locations and found that "park service personnel and tribal representatives have demonstrated a readiness to move beyond minimal legal compliance to establish a meaningful partnership for the interpretation and preservation of cultural resources" (Stoffle et al. 1997:67). Site by site information is included in each report along with recommendations. The project calls for a long-term commitment to combining the knowledge and skills of both the National Park Service and the Southern Paiute tribes.

SUMMARY

Cultural resource management is a robust area of professional practice shaped by law and national values. Since the emergence of this area of practice there has been a consistent growth of job opportunities at all degree levels (i.e., BA, MA, and Ph.D.). This is one of the few areas where a degree in anthropology represents a technical qualification within the field. Archaeology done for cultural resource management purposes dominates the subdiscipline in terms of numbers of persons involved and the amount of research done. Most archaeology done in the United States is for cultural resource management purposes, and a large portion of this is performed by private-sector consulting firms. The needs of all of these persons has stimulated the development of special training and certification programs. Persons working in this area experience the daily intersection of policy decisions and their professional training. While this is mostly the domain of archaeology, cultural anthropologists are also involved in CRM. Furthermore, there are clear conceptual and practical parallels and interaction with the domain of social impact assessment.

FURTHER READING

Downum, Christian E. and Laurie J. Price. Applied Archaeology. *Human Organization* 58(3):226–239, 1999. This is a useful review of the diversity of applied work in archaeology.

King, Thomas F. *Cultural Resource Laws and Practice: An Introductory Guide.* Walnut Creek, Calif.: AltaMira Press, 1998. This is a readable, comprehensive review of the legal context of CRM. Some of this carries over to social impact assessment.

RELATED WEBSITES

Advisory Council on Historic Preservation: http://www.achp.gov/aboutcouncil. html.

American Bottom archaeology publications: http://www.anthro.uiuc.edu/itarp/ publications.html.

National Register of Historic Places: http://www.cr.nps.gov/nr/about.htm.

Part IV

Being a Professional

Chapter 15

Making a Living

Here we discuss various aspects of professional life after training. Most important is the process of finding a job. The job market for anthropologists is based on demand for persons with skills in social science research methodology for the most part. While this is changing, the job market is not very much aware of anthropologists as such, there being a limited market for anthropology graduates as such except in North American archaeology. And, while there are many opportunities for professional work, very few are for "anthropologists only." In spite of this, it is possible to be meaningfully employed doing things that are consistent with your training in anthropology. This circumstance is not limited to anthropology, it is typical of many of the social sciences and humanities. It is because of these conditions that the anthropologist seeking work must be ready to deal with employers who are unfamiliar with the true capabilities of well-trained, contemporary anthropologists, or who hold grossly inaccurate stereotypes of the anthropologist's capabilities. The most adaptive response to these conditions includes a commitment on the part of the anthropologist to educating the employer, and a strategy of self-presentation that is based on experience and capabilities rather than diploma and transcript. This does not represent a problem because these days, except for a very few occupations, it works this way for almost everyone.

LOOKING FOR WORK

Success in the job hunt requires special preparation and tactics. The key to success is continual self-assessment in terms of your employment goals, and the continual investment of a substantial amount of creative energy.

One might start the process by reading one of the useful guides to the creative job search. Two which make sense to me are *What Color Is Your Parachute? A Practical Manual for Job Hunters and Career Changers* by Richard Bolles (2001) and *Who's Hiring Who* by Richard Lathrop (1989).

The Bolles and Lathrop volumes taken together provide an excellent general approach to the job search. While neither make specific reference to the problems of anthropologists, their advice on finding employment is excellent. The Bolles volume stresses an overall approach based on detailed self-assessment, including the specification of individual career goals and research into the characteristics of the potential employing organizations. This is complemented by the idea that the job-hunter assume control of his or her occupational destiny. The Lathrop volume provides good advice on individual career goal assessment, resume writing, letter writing, and employment interviews.

The first step toward meaningful work is based upon a complex of difficult decisions concerning what you are to do and where you want to do it. These decisions should not be made haphazardly or by default. *Who's Hiring Who* provides useful career analysis guidelines which would serve one well at this phase. Lathrop's scheme will lead you through a number of steps which will result in an assessment of your abilities as these relate to job functions. The process results in specification of an ideal job from a number of different standpoints, including location, work relationships, job flexibility, work environment, pay goals, and fields of work which have a high potential for you.

No matter what technique for assessment you use, you should document what you learn about yourself, the job hunt, and employers. Therefore, early in the process of job hunting, start a "job-hunt field notebook" in which you record your observations about the process in much the same way as you would in a field work situation. You might find it useful to list in your notes some possible jobs which represent meaningful careers to you. This is really just an extension of your self-study of the domain of application.

Career ideas may be obtained by regular reading of classified ads in local or out-of-town newspapers and professional newsletters. You might simply clip ads and paste them in your notebook so as to record as much information as possible about work opportunities. Other sources of information about jobs include the American Anthropological Association *Newsletter* which lists an increasing number of nonacademic jobs. One might also consult newsletters and other publications in your "domain of application," such as urban affairs, education, planning, health care delivery, and evaluation. College placement bureaus can also be useful sources, although these organizations vary in quality. Look also at the bulletin boards of academic departments who would be training the competition. Do not overlook state and local government employment offices. The federal government has a rather complex system of disseminating employment information. What are some other sources? Share them with your network.

Very early in the process you should begin to thoroughly document existing jobs within real organizations for which you would like to work. This should happen months or even years before the actual search. You can begin to eliminate organizations which are less attractive to you and concentrate your efforts on the best prospects. This screening will allow you to begin to research each organization with sufficient comprehensiveness to allow you to identify specific jobs and their requirements and needs. Relatively few employers have a clear conception of what anthropologists can do. This relates to three basic conditions which cultural anthropologists face on the job market.

1. You will be competing with persons who are not trained in anthropology, for example, social workers, sociologists, and urban planners.
2. You will be hired on the basis of what you can do, not who you are. This requires that you be able to communicate to people what you can do.
3. You will have to work to overcome stereotypes potential employers will have toward anthropologists. This will require that you focus on your skills in your presentations of self.

In your training you will need to continually focus on the acquisition of skills. You must be able to *do* things. The more the better. A skill such as doing statistical analysis using a computer program such as SPSS can make all the difference.

It is because of this that you must acquire a range of skills which are appropriate to the goals of the potential employing organizations. This is why training and the job-hunt are coincidental. Decisions about the training you will seek are decisions about seeking employment.

You must identify all your skills. In this case, "all" means skills which you acquired both within and outside anthropology. Skills should be stated in terms of *functions* rather than experiences, although you should also be able to provide evidence of where you used these skills. These skills should be listed in your job-hunting field notebook. The Richard Bolles volume referred to above provides a number of exercises that can lead to better self-assessment in this area. Bolles provides a set of activities that will produce a good self-assessment. The 2001 edition of the Bolles volume uses the metaphor of a flower to focus attention on self-assessment questions about geography, interests and special knowledge, people environments, values, purposes and goals, working conditions and salary, and responsibility.

ANTHROPOLOGISTS AND THE JOB MARKET

The job market for anthropologists is difficult to characterize. First of all, we anthropologists must be aware of a large number of different job markets, and that these markets exist at a number of different organizational levels. That is, we must be aware of jobs at the local, state, national, and international levels. We can also think in terms of various sectors of the economy, such as the educational sector, the health care sector, the business sector, the planning sector, the governmental sector, and so on. In addition, we might also think in terms of the public job market and the hidden job market. More about these distinctions later.

Many persons writing about job-hunting strategies stress the importance of a focused approach to the job market. It is argued that without focus you will ineffectively expend your energies. Focus is necessary if one is going to be in the position to carry out the research required for the successful job hunt. The requirement to know the market, which is generally important, is absolutely crucial in anthropology where so few employers are aware of the potentials and nature of anthropology. It will be necessary to "sell" anthropology by showing the usefulness of the skills which you have learned. It is your responsibility to do this. Attempts to tout the potentials of anthropology by the relevant associations and departments simply will not be of sufficient scale to have any meaningful effect upon you and your efforts. *You* must do it. Do not be resigned and fatalistic. Remember you are in a better position because of your acquired anthropological perspective in problem solving. They need you—they just don't know it yet.

The creative job-hunting anthropologist should be able to select potential employing organizations and do sufficient research into their nature so as to identify the organization's problems so that you can show them how you can help them and have them hire you. You must know enough about the organization to be able to identify their problems and to associate your skills with solutions to their problems. As Bolles asserts, you must identify "the person who has the power to hire you for the job that you are interested in" (2001:188). The matching of skills with problems occurs at the individual level. It is necessary to make direct contact with the person who needs you. If you are isolated from the person by a personnel department, you will not have the opportunity to tell your story where it counts. This means that even when you are applying for a civil service position, you must contact the person directly prior to the decision to hire. Remember, you will not be hired on the basis of your being the best anthropologist. They must see you as a skills-possessing problem solver that relates to their organization's need to be more efficient, more sensitive, more effective, more responsive, or more profitable.

To review, the effective job search is based on:

1. Early synthesis of job-hunting strategies and anthropology training.
2. Continual research into potential work roles, potential employers, and needed skills.
3. Continual self-assessment of your values and skills.
4. Research into the specific potential employer and his or her needs and problems.
5. Individual presentation as a skilled problem solver.

THE RESEARCH MARKET

Another aspect of the job search is the research market. Obtaining research support through grants and contracts is both a highly marketable skill and the most important means of job development. It should be clear that if you can earn your keep from outside monies, many organizations will hire you. Further, it is possible, as some anthropologists have, to create your own research firm based on grants and contracts which would then "hire" you. Another employment situation to consider is that of the consultant. Before launching into this role, it would be useful to read a volume like Herman Holtz's *How to Succeed as an Independent Consultant* (1993).

BEING A CONSULTANT

There are many reasons why consultants are hired. One might suggest that the client's need for information which the consultant can provide is a less frequent motivation than one would imagine. In any case, let us consider the reasons for the client-consultant relationship being established. The reasons relate to the special skills of the consultant, the special needs of the client organization, and the limitations of the client organization. Although consultant-like roles can develop internal to an organization, we are going to regard consultancy as essentially an outsider's role. The consultant may have a substantially reduced stake in the organization. In some cases the fact that the consultant is an outsider is essential to his or her contribution. In other words, he or she may be hired as an outsider, and less as an expert. In addition to these factors, consultants may be hired on the basis of requirements of law.

REASONS FOR USING CONSULTANTS

1. The consultant's knowledge of a specific region or aspect of culture may not be available within the organization.
2. The consultant's special research skills may not be available within the organization. These skills may be derived from the generalized pool of social science techniques (e.g., questionnaires and survey techniques) as well as techniques

specific to anthropology (e.g., excavation, ethnosemantic techniques, and participant-observation).

3. The consultant's special problem-solving skills are not available within the organization. This may relate to the goal of improving the organization functioning of the client's group.

4. The consultant may possess skills which, although available in the client organization, are required to meet temporary short-falls in manpower.

5. The consultant may be "certified" to have the skills necessary to meet certain legal requirements which the client must satisfy.

6. The consultant's status as a credible outsider may allow him or her to provide a noninvolved, and therefore objective, evaluation of the client group's functioning.

7. The consultant's status as a credible outsider may be used by the client to reduce the social cost of certain organizational or policy changes. That is, the interventions for change may be designed by the client for application by the consultant.

8. The consultant's teaching skills coupled with her knowledge may allow her to contribute to the development of the client organization's knowledge and skill levels.

9. The consultant may provide the client with a mechanism for increasing organizational prestige, or a "headliner" attraction for a conference or other meeting.

THE CONSULTING PROCESS

Useful sources on the consulting process include Edgar Schein's *Process Consultation: Its Role in Organizational Development* (1988) and *Process Consultation Revisited: Building the Helping Relationship* (1999). This is a classic written by a social psychologist. The consulting process is very effectively addressed, from the anthropologist's perspective, by Maureen J. Giovannini and Lynne M. H. Rosansky in *Anthropology and Management Consulting: Forging a New Alliance* (1990:10–16).

The consultant and the client must develop mutual understandings and expectations concerning the desired outcome of the consultant process. There should be a shared understanding between the consultant and client concerning expectations. The problem definition stage may result in a formal written statement, perhaps in the form of a contract, or the understanding may be more informal. The most important area of negotiation and specification would be client needs. Further, it is important to note that there may be major discrepancies between the client's perceptions of need and the anthropologist's ultimate assessment of the situation. Needs assessment is a complex process which should ultimately focus on the total situation. This process can be particularly difficult when the client is a service-providing agency whose links to the target population may be poorly developed. The anthropologist may soon discover in such cases that the needs perceived by the client are different from and perhaps contradictory to the needs discovered in the community at large. As is consistent with the holism of anthropology, the anthropologist may identify a significantly larger range of needs within the total community served by the agency. A key question is whether or not the needs are attributed to the community or the agency. The negotiation concerning needs has to consider the needs of the anthropologist as a professional. A number of issues must be considered. It is important for the client to have a clear understanding of the resources needed for the work to be completed. The anthropologist's need for information access has to be clearly explained and understood by the client. During planning the anthropologist may discover that effective consulting is not possible in a setting and "walk away" from it (Giovannini and Rosansky 1990:11–12). Giovannini and Rosansky cite "lack of organizational readiness," "lack of fit between consultant capability and client needs," "inability to accept client's goals or policies," and "lack of client commitment" as reasons for not proceeding (1990:12).

The client must understand the professional ethics of the anthropologist. Presenting a copy of the Society for Applied Anthropology or the National Association for the Practice of Anthropology's ethics statement may be called for. One of the products of the negotiation process will usually be an improved understanding of the nature of anthropology as an applied discipline. Although the potential "consumers" of applied anthropology services represent a rather substantial group, it would seem reasonable to say that applied anthropology does not have a large informed constituency among policy makers, community leaders, and other potential consumers. It is important that the anthropologist clearly discusses the nature of anthropology as a research discipline so the client is made into an informed consumer. It is surprising how immutable is the image of the anthropologist as a researcher of the exotic, remote, and preindustrial.

An M.A. graduate of the University of Kentucky's applied anthropology program was hired by the Kentucky State Police as a program coordinator in the planning department. As soon as his coworkers found out that he was an anthropologist, they started to bring in cigar boxes full of "arrow heads" for him to "identify." These conceptions are not difficult to deal with once the encounter was developed, but these views tend to limit the number of encounters which might lead to consulting relationships. Many potential consumers may never see the need for hiring the bush-jacketed, sun-helmeted comic stereotype of the anthropologist.

While one of the results of the negotiation process should be an improvement of the client's understanding of anthropology, the criterion for engaging a problem or complex of problems should not be "whether or not it's an anthropological problem." We might strongly assert here that there are no such things as anthropological problems—there are only client problems or community problems. This is not to say that anything is fair game or that there are no criteria for engaging a problem. We cannot practically limit ourselves to what is the "common understanding of what anthropology is." As applied anthropologists we cannot afford compulsively maintained boundaries. Attempts to rigidly define what is or is not anthropology are unproductive. Further, in certain contexts it can be irresponsible. The focus of concern of an applied anthropologist is not our discipline, but reality, a reality that we see through what we have learned as anthropologists.

It is assumed that the anthropologist like any other consultant will not necessarily engage in a formal research project in every consultancy situation. In many situations it is simply not necessary to engage in research at all. It is possible to "just know it." In fact, the importance of old-fashioned scholarly expertise is consistently underemphasized in much of the material written about applied anthropology. Much of this material stresses the nature of the applied role, ethical problems and concerns, and special research contexts and strategies. But when one reviews the history of the field, it is clearly apparent that applied anthropologists who have sustained involvement as consultants are often recruited as area experts rather than social scientists. This reality is rarely recognized in applied training programs. It is important to note that much of contemporary applied anthropology is *not* based on area knowledge but on knowledge of research techniques either as part of social science or specific to anthropology (such as participatory fieldwork). It should be obvious that consultancy serves a large number of purposes. As purposes vary so do the consumers of the consultants' products. Consultants may produce materials which are directly "consumed" by the client. Although this would seem to be the most typical, consultants very frequently produce material for third parties. Such is the case when the consultant is hired to provide legally required documentation or evaluation of aspects of a specific program. Such consultation may be specified in the conditions of funding support.

Client organizations may use consultants to produce an impact on third parties. The consultant may be hired to "tell the client's story" or to improve or enhance the client's image in the community. Presumably the client needs the special expertise of the anthropologist in these cases, but frequently it would seem that clients hire consultants for "cosmetic" reasons, thereby increasing the credibility of the message. This statement is not intended to represent a cynical criticism of certain types of consultancy situations, it is just that clients have many legitimate needs which can be best met by consultants.

When one engages in consultancy, one very quickly discovers the "political" implications of information. Information can be used as the "substance" from which power is formed. Clients may use the anthropologist as a means of solidifying, protecting, or enhancing the political position of the client. Because of the centrality of the anthropologist in the information acquisition process, he or she can be buffeted by various political forces. As a corollary, the anthropologist can use his or her position of centrality to increase control and access to information. This may be done through selective control of the release of information. Information management has very important ethical implications.

Consultants rarely have a well-developed political constituency. Yet such a constituency may be very important for an anthropologist working in a community setting. An applied anthropologist working on an evaluation of a social service agency may find that, if he or she wants to maximize his impact on the agency, it may be necessary to build an auxiliary clientele in the "service population" of the agency. This will have two potential effects. First, it will help provide the anthropologist with useful information about the community being served, and, second, it also will serve to buffer the anthropologist's position politically.

COMMUNICATION TO CLIENTS

The process of communication is of course very important and often associated with difficulty. The source of difficulty is the contrast in the language and concepts of the anthropologist and his or her client. This source of difficulty is inevitably present to varying degrees. When the anthropologist engages a client's problem, he or she must to some extent conceptualize the problem in anthropological terms. This allows the anthropologist to deal with the problem, but it also causes the need for translation of the results back to the meanings which are significant to the client. A translation process must always occur for effective communication because anthropologists, like any other scientists, communicate using their own special code.

It should be apparent that client-anthropologist communication can be difficult. Not only must knowledge be transferred, but there must be a certain number of conceptual shifts. That is, the knowledge conveyed most probably must be reconceptualized by the client. To the extent that it is possible, the anthropologist should attempt to avoid much of the reconceptualization by communicating in the client's cognitive framework. The standard wisdom is "Don't use jargon." Clearly, the purging of technical reports of complex terminology is an important first step, but it is not sufficient to insure effective communication. It is also important to control the complexity of the message in order to maintain a higher level of comprehensibility. The consulting anthropologist must use facts parsimoniously and decisively, limiting communication to essentials so as to not confound the message.

The style of communication can vary with the length of time spent in the consultancy and the urgency and concern communicated by the client concerning the issues. When one thinks of the communication process, one

often thinks of a technical report submitted at the conclusion of the consultancy period. It is very clear that the one-shot, written, end-of-term report can be limited in its effectiveness. Assuming that the anthropologist
and client have sufficient time to develop rapport, communication of useful
knowledge should start early and continually proceed. This may allow the
client to participate in the discovery process, perhaps to better understand
and assimilate the results. This process can result in increasingly effective
use of the anthropologist's skills, and therefore, a potential for improving
the efficiency of meeting client needs. Such interaction can obviate the need
for the "big report" because all the data may have been communicated less
formally. In such cases the report may merely serve as historic documentation or a means of meeting a contractual obligation.

THE RESEARCH MARKET

The major source of funding of both grants and contracts is the federal
government. The U.S. government's commitment to research support
started long ago. As early as 1803 the government provided funds for the
Lewis and Clark expedition. The first research project funded by congressional action occurred in 1842, when Samuel F. B. Morse was awarded
$20,000 to test the commercial feasibility of the electromagnetic telegraph.
Since these beginnings, expansion has been dramatic with most growth in
federal research spending occurring after World War II. Prior to the war
most research was done "in-house." Funding is made available for various
types of research activities. These include basic research, applied research,
and development programs which have a research component. These distinctions are important to our discussions in that each is a discrete category
with an appropriate funding mechanism unto itself (Scurlock 1975:ix).

Opportunities for the academic and nonacademic applied anthropologist
occur in all these categories. Each funding program is subject to compliance
with certain statutes, regulations, and administrative policies. It is beyond
the scope of this chapter to account for the complexities of the procedures.
We will, however, consider in general terms some of the important issues
in federal research funding. The need to know procedures and policies is
highest for the small-scale consulting firm. Academic applied anthropologists at larger universities usually have access to an "office of sponsored
research" and a support staff. Anthropologists hired by larger-scale consulting firms also have the benefit of such specialists. It is often necessary
to have the support of specialists who continually search for research opportunities, provide preliminary support, assist in proposal preparation,
and negotiate contracts properly in order to be consistently successful. It
must be made clear that all these processes are highly competitive and that
success is based upon competence in both the research and the funding
process.

DOING RESEARCH FOR THE FEDERAL GOVERNMENT

An anthropologist may do federally sponsored research in a number of ways. First, an anthropologist may be engaged on a direct-hire or consultant basis to do in-house research for a federal agency. One might also be hired as a staff member of an organization which has agreed to carry out a project on the basis of a grant or contract. In this section we will deal with the opportunities afforded by applying for contracts rather than the direct-hire means. A number of different kinds of organizations compete for the federal research funding. These include universities, profit-making firms, not-for-profit research organizations, individual consultants, and the government agencies themselves. Each of these organizations has specific characteristics which influence their competitiveness. In some ways the academic department is in the worst position to compete because of inherent lack of flexibility in scheduling and staffing. Further, departments are usually staffed by persons of a single discipline which can cause conceptual and methodological narrowness. The problems associated with this bias have led to the establishment of alternative kinds of organizations on university campuses to better compete for grants and contracts.

Profit-making consulting firms have certain advantages. Their staffing is much more flexible and diverse than academic departments. The not-for-profit organizations are perhaps somewhat less flexible; further, they probably are poorly capitalized for the most part and therefore can afford less "internal seed-money."

CONTRACTS AND GRANTS

Here we are concerned with the source of the basic ideas which when expanded and elaborated can serve as the basis for an applied research proposal. We are less concerned with the so-called unsolicited proposal which is more typical in the basic research areas, although it is clear that this too can result in significant opportunities for the applied anthropologist. Here our concern is with research done in response to specifications provided by entities other than an individual researcher. Design criteria may vary extensively in terms of level of specificity. It should also be recognized that the researcher may arrange to have a research contract procurement procedure set up so as to allow bidding on a research idea generated by the researcher. In these cases it usually involves the researcher submitting an unsolicited proposal and the agency responding by putting out a request for proposals in response to the idea. In subsequent deliberations the original submitter of the idea is in a competitively good position.

Research support can be obtained through either grants or contracts. Both are subject to their own special kind of procedures and regulation. Although at times it is difficult to distinguish between grants and contracts, it is possible to point out certain differences. Contracts provide a means of paying for an activity which meets a specific need identified by an agency. In most cases the agency has clearly determined the actual format of the desired service, including expected outcomes, schedule, and cost. The agency selects the contractor on the basis of proximity to the research site, budget bids, professional qualifications, and previous performance. Contracts are more strictly managed than grants. Grants tend to be more frequently used where researcher-initiated experiment and development is involved. Grantees are not subject to such rigorous reporting requirements. Although the term *grant* connotes some type of gift, it is subject to many of the same controls as a contract. For the purposes of fostering untrammeled scientific inquiry, the conception of the grant as a gift is a useful fiction; however, one must remember that it, for legal administrative reasons, is best to think of it as what it is, a kind of contract. The consistent principle in case law is that the acceptance of a grant establishes a contractual relationship between grantor and grantee.

There are a number of important concepts concerning grant budgeting which will be noted in passing here. Fundamental to the budgeting process is the notion of "allowable costs" which includes those expenses "which are related to the conduct of the research" (Scurlock 1975:4). Allowable costs are of two types, direct and indirect. Direct costs are expended solely on the activities of the research project, whereas indirect costs are for support and maintenance of the research personnel and equipment.

Indirect costs are rarely budgeted directly. Usually a research group calculates the portion of their total enterprise which bears on research support. Facts relating to these costs are presented in negotiations with the relevant federal agencies. These negotiations result in an indirect cost rate which would apply in all cases of grants to the research group. The rate is often expressed as a percentage of salaries and wages. The indirect cost rate, often labeled "overhead," varies from agency to agency. Further, the various types of research groups, that is, universities, consulting firms, and so forth, charge different rates. I have heard of ranges from about 25 percent of salaries and rates to over 100 percent. Large-scale consulting firms tend to be the highest.

Government procurement is dominated by certain themes. The most important is the goal of receiving "acceptable goods or services at the lowest practical price in order to avoid waste in the use of public monies" (Scurlock 1975:11). In addition, procedures are established so as to avoid favoritism and corruption. Originally, the preferred method of procurement was based on formal advertising and the submission of a firm bid by the potential contractor. As time passed and the scale of government expenditures increased, this single procedure proved inadequate and was supplemented by the so-called negotiated contract. This system allows the federal government to use a wider range of criteria than just price, and more closely resembles the procedures used in the private sector.

Agencies may formulate a problem in a number of ways. The idea for the research may be developed within the agency and then put out for competition. Sometimes the unsolicited proposal can serve as the basis for a government-sponsored competitive solicitation or negotiated contract. The decisions concerning form are usually up to the agency. Normally the agency will use the competitive bidding process where it is possible to specify the required research procedure, to involve sufficient qualified bidders for adequate competition, and to have enough time for adequate bidding. Two-step formal advertising is used in cases where the problem to be researched may have a range of possible solutions, thus making it somewhat more difficult for the agency to specify procedures and outcomes. At times, an agency may use this procedure to support research which will result in a research plan which would be put out on bids for final implementation. In a manner similar to standard advertising, a researcher submits a so-called technical proposal. This proposal does not have a cost component. The agency may consult with the researchers in order to improve the proposal. All persons who submit a qualified technical proposal will then be issued an "invitation for bid." If only one bid is submitted, it may be contracted, in which case it would be a so-called sole source contract.

In certain cases the research goals and procedures may be very difficult to specify, as is typical in basic research projects. In addition, the range of proposal evaluation criteria necessary may be more complex than price and design. As Scurlock notes, "The skills, interest and availability of research personnel and the resources at their disposal are all factors to be considered in selecting the research contractor" (1975:14). There may still be competition, but it goes beyond the formal narrow range of criteria characteristic of the more formal procedures. The negotiated contracts process starts in very much the same way as the more formal types.

The most important source of information on contract and other federal research opportunities is the *Commerce Business Daily* (*CBD*). *CBD* is a daily publication of the United States Department of Commerce which lists government procurement invitations, contract awards, subcontracting leads, sales of surplus property, and foreign business opportunities. In *CBD*, one will find notices concerning ongoing negotiations as well as notifications for more open opportunities. In addition to *CBD*, some agencies have their own publications for announcing contract opportunities. An example is the *NIH Guide for Grants and Contracts*. These publications are available on the Web. Qualified individuals may ask for and receive the so-called Request for Proposals (RFP). The important component of the RFP is the Scope of Work, which is rather like a proposal in reverse. The work scope specifies what needs to be done. Evaluation criteria may also be stated. Proposals submitted in this way are subject to substantial modification in the review and funding process. The proposal review is usually carried out by a specialized review board consisting of scientists from the specific area of inquiry. Contact between the researcher and the agency is maintained through a contracting officer, who solicits answers to questions raised in the analysis process. The negotiation process produces a final research design which is hoped to be the most efficient and appropriate and least costly. After a defined period of time, the negotiations are closed, review is complete, and the contract is awarded.

One way of facilitating the obtaining of research funds is to create one's own not-for-profit research organization. Information on establishing such an organization may be obtained by writing to the Internal Revenue Service for publication 557 entitled *Tax-Exempt Status for Your Organization* (1988). This booklet outlines the procedure for being exempt from the income tax. Incorporation may also be recommended so as to limit liability. The Federal Tax Code allows such organizations to be established if the research is in the public interest. The definition of "public interest" seems quite broad. Research is considered to be in the public interest if the results are made available to the public "on a nondiscriminating basis" (U.S. Internal Revenue Service 1988). Research carried out for federal, state, and local government can also justify exemption. Various other activities are included. There are anthropologists who have established such organizations.

TIES TO THE ACADEMIC WORLD

Except in rare cases (excluding archaeologists), the nonacademically employed anthropologist will infrequently have other anthropologists as work associates. This raises some questions about how the anthropologist can maintain theoretical and methodological currency as well as obtain the emotional sustenance so necessary for work satisfaction. Nonacademically employed anthropologists may have some of their needs met by joining national general-purpose organizations, such as the American Anthropological Association, or the national and international specialized groups, such as the Society for Applied Anthropology, National Association for the Practice of Anthropology, Society for Medical Anthropology, and the Council on Anthropology and Education. Another alternative is joining the many regional general-purpose organizations, such as the Southern Anthropological Society, Central States Anthropological Society, Northeastern Anthropological Association, Alaska Anthropological Association, and the Anthropological Society of Washington. Other relevant organizations include the American Ethnological Society, American Folklore Society, American Society for Ethnohistory, Association for Political and Legal Anthropology, Association for Social Anthropology in Oceania, and the Society for Cross-Cultural Research.

Most of the organizations listed above have memberships which are virtually all academic. Being of and for academics, their programs and organizational structures are clearly addressed to the needs of this constituency. The most important need of academics is addressed by providing a medium for publishing research output. The competition for publication slots is substantial, and it would appear that the academic anthropologists will continue to dominate the pages of journals such as the *American Anthropologist, American Ethnologist,* and *Human Organization*. Annual programs of these associations will probably continue to be dominated by academics in spite of many positive accommodations to the needs of non-academic applied anthropologists.

The Society for Applied Anthropology has been committed to the advancement of applied anthropology for a longer time than the older American Anthropological Association. Both of these associations have an important complementary role to play at the national level. The Society for Applied Anthropology was founded in 1941. According to Spicer, "The SAA was not enthusiastically welcomed into the world of anthropology. The newborn was regarded as something of a monstrosity and as a consequence it began its first growth in the limbo of illegitimacy" (1976:335). Today it is a mature and successful association with a robust annual meeting and publication program. The leadership of the Society for Applied Anthropology is strongly committed to maintaining lower student membership fees. The leadership works very hard to maintain low student costs through special fund-raising activities. Student membership costs $25 per year and includes a quarterly journal, *Human Organization*, the career-oriented publication, *Practicing Anthropology*, and a newsletter. Fees can be sent to the Society for Applied Anthropology, P.O. Box 24083, Oklahoma City, OK 73124 (http://www.sfaa.net).

In 1984, the National Association for the Practice of Anthropology was formed as a unit within the American Anthropological Association. This association is made up of members of the American Anthropological Association who opt for participation in this unit. NAPA has provided the ideas and energy that have made the American Anthropological Association annual meetings more useful for practicing anthropologists. *NAPA Bulletins*, the organization's monograph series, provides an alternative publishing format for practitioners. Recent numbers have dealt with a variety of useful topics including ethnicity (Keefe 1989), government employment (Hanson, Conway, Alexander, and Drake 1988), and various aspects of consulting (Davis, McConochie, and Stevenson, 1987; Giovannini and Rosansky 1990), as well as other useful content. NAPA publishes a directory, has a student award, and has a mentoring program for young professionals. To belong to NAPA, you must first join the American Anthropological Association. One can contact the American Anthropological Association at

4350 North Fairfax Drive, Suite 640, Arlington, VA 22203 or http://www.aaanet.org/ about details.

Spicer divides the history of the Society for Applied Anthropology into four phases. These coincide, more or less, with each of the decades from the 1940s through the 1970s. During the first phase there was a great deal of debate concerning the nature of applied anthropology. This seems to relate to the general quest for legitimacy for applied anthropologists. Often expressed in the pages of the journal of the society was the notion that there was an inadequate body of anthropological theory and knowledge. Publication policy stressed the case study based on direct observation. A large segment of both the members and authors of the society and its journal were not anthropologists.

During the 1950s the society made its "most important contribution to anthropology as a whole" (Spicer 1976:336). The society was the first anthropology organization to actively deal with the issue of professional ethics. The society developed a succession of schemes before other organizations dealt with this serious issue. During this period Spicer notes that there was a somewhat greater identification with academic careers. This was the trend for the next two decades. In the next two phases, the society comes to be an organization appropriate to the needs of the academic who on occasion serves as an academic consultant. Although the society has been dominated by academics, it is making a number of accommodations to its nonacademic members. Currently its executive committee, as well as its nominations and elections committee, is elected from both academic and nonacademic slates. In addition, its annual meeting includes "skills sessions" on topics such as social impact assessment.

Probably the best organizations for "keeping in touch" are the local practitioner organizations often refered to as LPOs. These vary considerably in their size and the complexity of their programs. The LPOs offering the most comprehensive programs are the Washington Association of Professional Anthropologists (WAPA) and the High Plains Society for Applied Anthropology (HPSAA). WAPA has a largely local membership and is concerned with the practical needs of the nonacademically employed anthropologists. WAPA fosters such activities as job-hunting skills workshops, "theoretical up-date sessions," a job network to assist members, and a newsletter publication. The High Plains Society for Applied Anthropology includes members from Arizona to Montana. Their program is geared to the low density of the distribution of anthropologists in the Rocky Mountain West. They offer a journal and a lively annual meeting. The active list of local practitioner organizations changes from time to time. Linda A. Bennett wrote a descriptive account of these worthwhile organizations that was published by NAPA (1988). It is very important to both support and make use of these organizations. A NAPA page at the American Anthropological Association website currently lists the Chicago Association for Practicing Anthropologists, Great Lakes Associations of Practicing Anthropologists, Mid-South Association of Practicing Anthropologists, North Florida Network of Practicing Anthropologists, Philadelphia Association of Practicing Anthropologists, Southern California Applied Anthropology Network, and Sun Coast Organization of Practicing Anthropologists, as well as WAPA and HPSAA.

SUMMARY

As you complete your course of study in anticipation of a career in applied anthropology, it is very important to assess who you are and what you want to accomplish in the future. This requires continual self-assessment. Self-assessment makes sense only if it is the foundation for the strategic acquisition of new skills and experience in their use. An excellent way to learn about yourself is the process of putting together a resume geared to a specific job. This forces you to think about who you are and what you are capable of doing to help meet societal needs.

The number of work opportunities for anthropologists *as* anthropologists is quite small. The opportunities for people who know and do what anthropologists know and do, are large. The basis for employment is what you can do, not what the market believes about anthropology. Except for a few cases, we will compete with people with many different kinds of training. Therefore, we have to be aware of other disciplines and their relationship with the job market.

The job search starts as soon as training begins. As students, we have to work for the skills needed in the job market. Success is not based on indifferently following a course of study with individual curiosity the only guide. Success requires clear specification of goals as these relate to the needs of potential employers. The end point is not a cynical market orientation, but a careful assessment of what society needs and then action in terms of those needs.

Applied anthropologists often have to master special knowledge about doing business as an anthropologist. Which is to say, they need to be able to assume the responsibilities of being a consultant if that is the employment framework within which they are working. This includes special attention being paid to working with clients to solve their problems, and solving the problems of communication.

FURTHER READING

Bennett, Linda A. *Bridges for Changing Times: Local Practitioner Organizations in American Anthropology*. Washington, D.C.: National Association for the Practice of Anthropology, 1988. This provides historical background on LPOs.

Bolles, Richard N. *What Color Is Your Parachute? A Practical Manual for Job*

Hunters and Career Changers. Berkeley, Calif.: Ten Speed Press, 2001. This book, revised every year, must be read cover to cover if you are serious about the job search. Read it as soon as possible because it will help you think more clearly about your training needs. Get a copy and do the exercises in it.

References

Aberle, David F. Introducing Preventative Psychiatry into a Community. *Human Organization* 9(3):5–9, 1950.

Academy for Educational Development. *Public Health Communication Model.* Washington, D.C.: Academy for Educational Development, 1987.

Achatz, Mary and Crystal A. MacAllum. *Young Unwed Fathers: Report from the Field.* Philadelphia: Public/Private Ventures, 1994.

Aiyappan, A. *Report on the Socio-Economic Condition of Aboriginal Tribes of Madras.* Madras: Government of Madras, 1948.

Alexander, Jack and William Chapman. *Initial Security Classification Guidelines for Young Males Classification Improvement Project.* Working Paper XI. State of New York, Department of Correction Services, 1982.

Alkin, Marvin. *A Guide for Evaluation Decision Makers.* Beverly Hills, Calif.: Sage, 1985.

Allen, W., Max Gluckman, D. U. Peters, and C. G. Trapnell. *Land Holding and Land Use among the Plateau Tonga of Mazabuka District.* Rhodes-Livingstone Papers No. 14. Livingstone: Rhodes-Livingstone Institute, 1948.

Altman, D. G., J. A. Flora, S. P. Fortman, and J. W. Farquhar. The Cost-Effectiveness of Three Smoking Cessation Programs. *American Journal of Public Health* 77:162–165, 1987.

American Anthropological Association. Resolution. *American Anthropologist* 44: 289, 1942.

American Anthropological Association. 1990 PhD Survey Results. *Anthropology Newletter* 32(5):1, 44, 1991.

American Medical Association. *Cultural Competence Compendium.* Washington, D.C.: American Medical Association, 2001.

American Medical Student Association. *Cultural Competency in Medicine.* http://www.amsa.org/programs/gpit/cultural.htm, 2000.

Andreasen, A. *Marketing Social Change: Changing Behavior to Promote Health,*

Social Development, and the Environment. San Francisco: Jossey-Bass, 1995.

Angrosino, Michael V., ed. *Do Applied Anthropologists Apply Anthropology?* Southern Anthropological Society Proceedings No. 10. Athens: University of Georgia Press, 1976.

Arensberg, Conrad M. Report on a Developing Community, Poston, Arizona. *Applied Anthropology* 2(1):2–21, 1942.

Arensberg, Conrad M. and Solon T. Kimball. *Culture and Community.* New York: Harcourt, Brace and World, 1965.

Argyris, Chris and Donald A. Schon. Participatory Action Research and Action Science Compared: A Commentary. In *Participatory Action Research.* William Foote Whyte, ed. Pp. 85–96. Newbury Park, Calif.: Sage, 1991.

Asad, Talal, ed. *Anthropology and the Colonial Encounter.* London: Ithaca Press, 1973.

Bainton, Barry R. Society of Professional Anthropologists Formed in Tucson. *Anthropology Newsletter* 16(8):4–6, 1975.

Balderston, F. E. and Roy Radner. *Academic Demand for New Ph.D.'s 1970–90: Its Sensitivity to Alternate Policies.* Paper P-26. Berkeley: Ford Foundation Program in University Administration, University of California, Berkeley, 1971.

Ballard, Steven C. and Thomas E. James. Participatory Research and Utilization in the Technology Assessment Process. *Knowledge* 4(3):409–427, 1983.

Barber, Bernard. *Effective Social Science.* New York: Russell Sage Foundation, 1987.

Bardolf, Paul. Scaling-up PRA: Lessons from Vietnam. In *Who Changes? Institutionalizing Participation in Development.* James Blackburn with Jeremy Holland, eds. Pp. 18–22. London: Intermediate Technology Publications, 1998.

Bareis, Charles J. and James W. Porter. *American Bottom Archaeology: A Summary of the FAI-270 Project Contribution to the Culture History of the Mississippi River Valley.* Urbana: University of Illinois Press for the Illinois Department of Transportation, 1984.

Barnett, H. G. Applied Anthropology in 1860. *Applied Anthropology* 1:19–32, 1942.

Barnett, H. G. *Anthropology in Administration.* New York: Harper and Row, 1956.

Bascom, William R. *Economic and Human Resources—Ponape.* Ponape, Eastern Carolines: U.S. Commercial Company, 1947.

Bateson, Gregory and Margaret Mead. Principles of Morale Building. *Journal of Educational Sociology* 15:206–220, 1941.

Beaglehole, E. and P. Beaglehole. *Some Modern Maoris.* Wellington: New Zealand Council for Education Research, 1946.

Beals, Ralph L. *Politics of Social Research: An Inquiry into the Ethics and Responsibilities of Social Scientists.* Chicago: Aldine, 1969.

BEBASHI. *Focus Groups: Process for Developing HIV Education Materials.* HIV Education Case Studies No. 2. Washington, D.C.: U.S. Conference of Mayors, 1990.

Bell, M., Stephen L. Schensul, and M. Just. *Coping in a Troubled Society: An*

Environmental Approach to Mental Health. Washington, D.C.: Lexington Books, 1974.

Belshaw, Cyril S. *The Sorcerer's Apprentice: An Anthropology of Public Policy*. New York: Pergamon Press, 1976.

Benedict, Ruth. *The Chrysanthemum and the Sword*. Boston: Houghton Mifflin, 1946.

Bennett, John W. Community Research in the Japan Occupation. *Clearing House Bulletin of Research, Human Organization* 1(3):1–2, 1951.

Bennett, John W. Anthropological Contributions to the Cultural Ecology and Management of Water Resources. In *Man and Water: The Social Sciences in the Management of Water Resources*. Lexington: University Press of Kentucky, 1974.

Bennett, Linda A. *Bridges for Changing Times: Local Practitioner Organizations in American Anthropology*. NAPA Bulletin 6. Washington, D.C.: American Anthropological Association, 1988.

Bennett, Linda A. Developing a Consortium of Applied and Practicing Anthropology (CAPA) Programs: A Status Report. Presented at a meeting of the Society for Anthropology in Community Colleges, 2000.

Berger, Peter L. *Pyramids of Sacrifice*. New York: Basic Books, 1974.

Bernard, H. Russell and Willis E. Sibley. *Anthropology and Jobs: A Guide for Undergraduates*. A Special Publication of the American Anthropological Association. Washington, D.C.: American Anthropological Association, 1975.

Berreman, Gerald. Academic Colonialism: Not So Innocent Abroad. *The Nation*, November 10, pp. 505–508, 1969.

Best Start, Inc. *WIC at the Crossroads: The Texas WIC Marketing Study*. Tampa, Fla.: Best Start, 1994.

Beyer, Janice M. and Harrison M. Trice. The Utilization Process: A Conceptual Framework and Synthesis of Empirical Findings. *Administrative Science Quarterly* 27:591–622, 1982.

Blustain, Harvey. *Resource Management and Agricultural Development in Jamaica: Lessons for a Participatory Approach*. Ithaca, N.Y.: Cornell University Rural Development Committee, 1982.

Boas, Franz. Correspondence: Scientists as Spies. *The Nation*, December 20, p. 797, 1919.

Bolles, Richard N. *What Color Is Your Parachute? A Practical Manual for Job Hunters and Career Changers*. Berkeley, Calif.: Ten Speed Press, 2001.

Briody, Elizabeth K. Profiles of Practice: Anthropological Careers in Business, Government, and Private Sector Associations. In *Anthropology for Tomorrow: Creating Practitioner-Oriented Applied Anthropology Programs*. Robert T. Trotter II, ed. Washington, D.C.: American Anthropological Association, 1988.

Britan, Gerald M. *An Assessment of AID's Project Evaluation System*. Office of Evaluation Working Paper No. 34. Evanston, Ill.: Office of Evaluation, Northwestern University, 1980.

Brokensha, David and Peter Hodge. *Community Development: An Interpretation*. San Francisco: Chandler Publishing, 1969.

Brokensha, David F., Michael M. Horowitz, and Thayer Scudder. *The Anthropol-*

ogy of Rural Development in the Sahel. Binghamton, N.Y.: Institute for Development Anthropology, 1977.

Brown, Judith et al. *Identifying the Reasons for Low Immunization Coverage: A Case Study of Yaounde.* United Republic of Cameroon: World Health Organization, EPI/GEN/80/4, 1980.

Brownrigg, Leslie Ann. *Al Futuro Desde la Experiencia: Los Pueblos Indigenias y el Manejo del Medio Ambiente.* Quito: Ediciones Abya-Yula, 1986.

Brundtland Report. World Commission on Environment and Development. *Our Common Future.* Oxford: Oxford University Press, 1987.

Bryant, Carol A. Counseling Guide. In *Breastfeeding for Healthy Mothers, Healthy Babies: Training Manual for Motivation and Training Tapes.* Tampa, Fla.: Best Start, 1990.

Bryant, Carol A. and Doraine F. C. Bailey. The Use of Focus Group Research in Program Development. In *Soundings: Rapid and Reliable Research Methods for Practicing Anthropologists.* NAPA Bulletin 10. John van Willigen and Timothy J. Finan, eds. Washington, D.C.: American Anthropological Association, 1991.

Bryant, Carol A., Minda Lazarov, Richard Light, Doraine Bailey, Jeanine Coreil, and Sandra L. D'Angelo. Best Start: Breastfeeding for Healthy Mothers, Healthy Babies—A New Model for Breastfeeding Promotion. *Journal of the Tennessee Medical Association* (December):642–643, 1989.

Bryant, Carol A. and James H. Lindenberger. Social Marketing: Realizing Its Potential as a Social Change Strategy. Unpublished paper, 1992.

Bryant, Carol A., James H. Lindenberger, Chris Brown, Ellen Kent, Janet Mogg Schreibert, Marta Bustillo, and Marsha Walker Canright. A Social Marketing Approach to Increasing Enrollment in a Public Health Program: A Case Study of the Texas WIC Program. *Human Organization* 60(3):234–245, 2000.

Buehler, Karen L. *Perceptions of Hispanic Employment.* China Lake, Calif.: Management Division, Office of Finance and Management, Naval Weapons Center, 1981.

Bunker, Robert and John Adair. *The First Look at Strangers.* New Brunswick, N.J.: Rutgers University Press, 1959.

Burchell, Robert W. and David Listokin. *The Environmental Impact Handbook.* New Brunswick, N.J.: Center for Urban Policy Research, Rutgers University, 1975.

Burdge, Rabel J. *A Conceptual Approach to Social Impact Assessment.* Middleton, Wis.: Social Ecology Press, 1994.

Burns, Allan. An Anthropologist at Work: Field Perspectives on Applied Ethnography. *Council on Anthropology and Education Quarterly* 6(4):28–33, 1975.

Callaway, Donald G., Jerrold E. Levy, and Eric Henderson. *The Effects of Power Production and Strip Mining on Local Navajo Populations.* Lake Powell Research Bulletin No. 22. Los Angeles: Institute of Geophysics and Planetary Physics, University of California, Los Angeles, 1976.

Campbell, Donald T. and J. C. Stanley. *Experimental and Quasi-experimental Designs for Research.* Chicago: Rand-McNally, 1965.

Caplan, Nathan. A Minimal Set of Conditions Necessary for the Utilization of

Social Science Knowledge in Policy Formulation at the National Level. In *Using Social Research in Public Policy Making*. Carol H. Weiss, ed. Pp. 183–198. Lexington, Mass.: D.C. Heath, 1977.

Caplan, Nathan, Andrea Morrison, and Russell J. Stambaugh. *The Use of Social Science Knowledge in Policy Decisions at the National Level*. Ann Arbor: Institute for Social Research, University of Michigan, 1975.

Carley, Michael J. and Eduardo S. Bustelo. *Social Impact Assessment and Monitoring: A Guide to the Literature*. Boulder, Colo.: Westview Press, 1984.

Cartter, Alan M. The Academic Labor Market. In *Higher Education and the Labor Market*. M. S. Gordon, ed. New York: McGraw-Hill, 1974.

Cellarius, Barbara A., Deborah Crooks, Patricia Kannapel, Juliana McDonald, Cynthia Reeves, and John van Willigen. Cultural Action: Theory, Process and Practice. *High Plains Applied Anthropologist* 16(1):9–18, 1996.

Cernea, Michael M. *Putting People First: Sociological Variables in Rural Development*. 2nd ed. New York: Oxford University Press for the World Bank, 1991a.

Cernea, Michael M. What Policy-Makers Require of Anthropologists. Unpublished paper presented at the annual meetings of the Society for Applied Anthropology, 1991b.

Chambers, Erve. Anthropologists in Nonacademic Employment. *Anthropology Newsletter* 18(6):14–17, 1977.

Chambers, Erve. *Applied Anthropology: A Practical Guide*. Prospect Heights, Ill.: Waveland Press, 1989.

Chambers, Robert. *Rural Development: Putting the Last First*. London: Longman, 1983.

Chambers, Robert. The Origins and Practices of Participatory Rural Appraisal. *World Development* 22(7):953–969, 1994.

Chambers, Robert. *Whose Reality Counts? Putting the First Last*. London: Intermediate Technology Publications, 1997.

Chambers, Robert, Arnold Pacey, and Lori Ann Thrupp. *Farmer First: Farmer Innovation and Agricultural Research*. London: Intermediate Technology Publications, 1989.

Chapple, Eliot D. Applied Anthropology in Industry. In *Anthropology Today: An Encyclopedic Inventory*. Sol Tax, ed. Chicago: University of Chicago Press, 1953.

Chatelain, Agnes B. and Louis F. Cimino. *Directory of Practicing Anthropologists*. A Special Publication of the American Anthropological Association, No. 13. Washington, D.C.: American Anthropological Association, 1981.

Childhood Development Center, Georgetown University. *Towards a Culturally Competent System of Care*. Vol. 1. Washington, D.C.: CASSP Technical Assistance Center, Georgetown University Child Development Center, 1989.

Clark, Barton M. and John van Willigen. Documentation and Data Management in Applied Anthropology. *Journal of Cultural and Educational Futures* 2(2–3):23–27, 1981.

Clemmer, Richard O. Resistance and the Revitalization of Anthropologists: A New Perspective on Culture Change and Resistance. In *Reinventing Anthropology*. Dell Hymes, ed. Chicago: University of Chicago Press, 1969.

Clift, Elayne. Social Marketing and Communication: Changing Health Behavior in the Third World. *American Journal of Health Promotion* 3(4):17–23, 1989.

Clifton, James A. *Applied Anthropology: Readings in the Uses of the Sciences of Man.* New York: Houghton Mifflin, 1970.

Clinton, Charles A. 1975. The Anthropologist as Hired Hand. *Human Organization* 34(2):197–204, 1975.

Clinton, Charles A., ed. *Social Impact Assessment in Context: The Tensas Documents.* Occasional Papers in Anthropology, Mississippi State University. Mississippi State: Mississippi State University, 1978.

Cochrane, Glyn. *Development Anthropology.* New York: Oxford University Press, 1971.

Cochrane, Glyn. *What We Can Do for Each Other: An Interdisciplinary Approach to Development Anthropology.* Amsterdam: B. R. Gruener, 1976.

Cochrane, Glyn. *The Cultural Appraisal of Development Projects.* New York: Praeger, 1979.

Collier, John. *Instruction to Field Workers, Applied Anthropology Unit.* Washington, D.C.: Office of Indian Affairs, Applied Anthropology Unit, 1936.

Collins, Jane L. and Michael Painter. *Settlement and Deforestation in Central America: A Discussion of Development Issues.* Binghamton, N.Y.: Institute for Development Anthropology, 1986.

Committee on Ethics, Society for Applied Anthropology. *Statement on Professional and Ethical Responsibilities.* Washington, D.C.: Society for Applied Anthropology, 1983.

Conklin, Harold C. *Hanunoo Agriculture: A Report on an Integral System of Shifting Cultivation in the Philippines.* Northford, Conn.: Elliot's Books, 1975.

Cook, Thomas D. and Donald T. Campbell. *Quasi-experimentation: Design and Analysis Issues for Field Settings.* Chicago: Rand-McNally, 1979.

Cook, Thomas D. and Charles S. Reichardt, eds. *Qualitative and Quantitative Methods in Evaluation Research.* Beverly Hills, Calif.: Sage, 1979.

Coreil, J., C. Bryant, and N. Henderson. *Social and Behavioral Foundations of Public Health.* Thousand Oaks, Calif.: Sage, 2001.

Coreil, Jeannine. Lessons from a Community Study of Oral Rehydration Therapy in Haiti. In *Making Our Research Useful.* John van Willigen et al., eds. Pp. 143–157. Boulder, Colo.: Westview Press, 1989.

Coreil, Jeannine and J. Dennis Mull. Preface. In *Anthropology and Primary Health Care.* Jeannine Coreil and J. Dennis Mull, eds. Pp. xiii–xiv. Boulder, Colo.: Westview Press, 1990.

Council on Environmental Quality. *Preparation of Environmental Impact Statements, Guidelines 38(147) Pt. II.* Washington, D.C.: Council on Environmental Quality, 1973.

Cushman, Frances and Gordon MacGregor. *Harnessing the Big Muddy.* Lawrence, Kans.: Indian Service, 1949.

D'Andrade, R. G., E. A. Hammel, D. L. Adkins, and C. K. McDaniel. Academic Opportunity in Anthropology 1974–90. *American Anthropologist* 77(4): 753–773, 1975.

Davidson, Judith R. The Delivery of Rural Reproductive Medicine. In *Anthropological Praxis.* Robert M. Wulff and Shirley J. Fiske, eds. Pp. 262–272. Boulder, Colo.: Westview Press, 1987.

Davis, Nancy Yaw. Cultural Dynamics: A Case History of a Research and Consulting Business. In *Research and Consulting as a Business*. NAPA Bulletin 4. By Davis, Nancy Yaw, Roger P. McConochie, and David R. Stevenson. Washington, D.C.: American Anthropological Association, 1987.

Davis, Nancy Yaw, Roger P. McConochie, and David R. Stevenson. *Research and Consulting as a Business*. NAPA Bulletin 4. Washington, D.C.: American Anthropological Association, 1987.

Dawson, Judith A. and Joseph J. D'Amico. Involving Program Staff in Evaluation Studies: A Strategy for Increasing Information Use and Enriching the Data Base. *Evaluation Review* 9(2):173–188, 1985.

Derman, William and Scott Whiteford, eds. *Social Impact Analysis and Development Planning in the Third World*. Boulder, Colo.: Westview Press, 1985.

DeWalt, Billie R. Anthropology, Sociology, and Farming Systems Research. *Human Organization* 44(2):106–114, 1985.

DeWalt, Billie R. Halfway There: Social Science in Agricultural Development and the Social Science of Agricultural Development. In *The Social Sciences in International Agricultural Research: Lessons from the CRSPs*. Boulder, Colo.: Lynne Rienner, 1989.

DeWalt, Billie R. and Kathleen M. DeWalt. *Farming Systems Research in Southern Honduras, Report No. 1*. Lexington: Department of Sociology, Department of Anthropology, Agricultural Experiment Station, University of Kentucky, 1982.

Dixon, Mim. *What Happened to Fairbanks? The Effects of the Trans-Alaska Oil Pipeline on the Community of Fairbanks, Alaska*. The Social Impact Assessment Series, No. 1. Boulder, Colo.: Westview Press, 1978.

Dobyns, Henry F. Taking the Witness Stand. In *Applied Anthropology in America*. E. M. Eddy and W. L. Partridge, eds. New York: Columbia University Press, 1978.

Dobyns, Henry F., Paul Doughty, and Harold Lasswell, eds. *Peasants, Power and Applied Social Change: Vicos as a Model*. Beverly Hills, Calif.: Sage, 1971.

Doughty, Paul L. Vicos: Success, Rejection and Rediscovery of a Classic Program. In *Applied Anthropology in America*. 2nd ed. E. M. Eddy and W. L. Partridge, eds. New York: Columbia University Press, 1986.

Doughty, Paul L. Against the Odds: Collaboration and Development at Vicos. In *Collaborative Research and Social Change: Applied Anthropology in Action*. Donald D. Stull and Jean J. Schensul, eds. Boulder, Colo.: Westview Press, 1987.

Downum, Christian E. and Laurie J. Price. Applied Archaeology. *Human Organization* 58(3):226–239, 1999.

Du Bois, Cora. *People of Alor: A Social-Psychological Study of an East Indian Island*. Cambridge, Mass.: Harvard University Press, 1944.

Dupree, Louis. The Jungle Survival Field Test. Maxwell Air Force Base, Ala.: ADTIC, 1956a.

Dupree, Louis. The Desert Survival Field Test. Maxwell Air Force Base, Ala.: ADTIC, 1956b.

Dupree, Louis. The Water Survival Field Test. Maxwell Air Force Base, Ala.: ADTIC, 1958.

Eddy, Elizabeth M. and William L. Partridge. Training for Applied Anthropology.

In *Applied Anthropology in America*. Elizabeth M. Eddy and William L. Partridge, eds. New York: Columbia University Press, 1978a.

Eddy, Elizabeth M. and William L. Partridge, eds. *Applied Anthropology in America*. New York: Columbia University Press, 1978b.

Eddy, Elizabeth M. and William L. Partridge, eds. *Applied Anthropology in America*. 2nd ed. New York: Columbia University Press, 1987.

Eiselein, E. B. and Wes Marshall. Mexican-American Television: Applied Anthropology and Public Television. *Human Organization* 35(2):147–156, 1976.

Elmendorf, Mary L. and Patricia K. Buckles. *Socio-cultural Aspects of Water Supply and Excreta Disposal*. The World Bank, Energy, Water and Telecommunications Department, Public Utilities Notes (P.U. Report No. RES 15). Washington, D.C.: The World Bank, 1978.

Elmendorf, Mary L. and Raymond B. Isely. The Role of Women as Participants and Beneficiaries in Water Supply and Sanitation Programs. Water and Sanitation for Health Project (WASH) Technical Report No. 11 prepared for the Office of Health, Bureau for Science and Technology. Washington, D.C.: U.S. Agency for International Development, 1981.

Elwin, Verrier. Growth of a Philosophy. In *Anthropology in the Development Process*. Hari Mohan Mathur, ed. New Delhi: Vikas Publishing House, 1977.

Embree, John F. Resistance to Freedom—An Administrative Problem. *Applied Anthropology* 2(4):10–14, 1943a.

Embree, John F. Dealing with Japanese-Americans. *Applied Anthropology* 2(2):37–43, 1943b.

Embree, John F. Community Analysis—An Example of Anthropology in Government. *American Anthropologist* 46(3):277–291, 1944.

Embree, John F. Military Government in Saipan and Tinian: A Report on the Organization of Susupe and Chuco, Together with Notes on the Attitudes of the People Involved. *Applied Anthropology* 5(1):1–39, 1946.

Embree, John F. American Military Government. In *Social Structure: Studies Presented to A. R. Radcliffe-Brown*. M. Fortes, ed. London: Oxford University Press, 1949.

Erasmus, Charles J. *Man Takes Control: Cultural Development and American Aid*. Minneapolis: University of Minnesota Press, 1961.

Ervin, Alexander M. *Applied Anthropology: Tools and Perspectives for Contemporary Practice*. Boston: Allyn and Bacon, 2000.

Ervin, Alexander M., Antonet T. Kaye, Giselle M. Marcotte, and Randy D. Belon. *Community Needs, Saskatoon—The 1990's: The Saskatoon Needs Assessment Project*. Saskatoon: University of Saskatchewan, Department of Anthropology, 1991.

Esber, George S., Jr. Designing Apache Homes with Apaches. In *Anthropological Praxis: Translating Knowledge into Action*. R. Wulff and S. Fiske, eds. Boulder, Colo.: Westview Press, 1987.

Escobar, Arturo. *Encountering Development: The Making and Unmaking of the Third World*. Princeton, N.J.: Princeton University Press, 1994.

Espaldon, Victoria O. and Annielyn O. Magsino. *Participatory Landscape Lifescape Appraisal (PLLA) for Community Resource Management*. SANREM CRSP Southeast Asia, 2001.

Everhart, Robert B. Problems in Doing Fieldwork in Educational Evaluation. *Human Organization* 34(2):205–215, 1975.

Fabrega, Horatio, Jr. Medical Anthropology. In *Biennial Review of Anthropology*. B. J. Siegel, ed. Stanford, Calif.: Stanford University Press, 1972.

Fals-Borda, Orlando and Muhammad A. Rahman, eds. *Action and Knowledge: Breaking the Monopoly with Participatory Action Research*. New York: Apex Press, 1991.

Fenton, William N. and Elizabeth L. Moore. *Introduction to Customs of the American Indians Compared with the Customs of Primitive Times*. Toronto: Champlain Society, 1974.

Fetterman, David M. A National Ethnographic Evaluation of the Career Intern Program. In *Anthropological Praxis: Translating Knowledge into Action*. R. Wulff and S. Fiske, eds. Boulder, Colo.: Westview Press, 1987.

Fetterman, David M. *Ethnography: Step by Step*. Newbury Park, Calif.: Sage, 1989.

Fetterman, David M. and M. Pitman, eds. *Educational Evaluation: Ethnography in Theory, Practice, and Politics*. Beverly Hills, Calif.: Sage, 1986.

Fine, S. H. *The Marketing of Ideas and Social Issues*. New York: Praeger, 1981.

Fishbein, M., C. Guenther-Grey, W. Johnson, R. J. Wolitski, and A. McAlister. Using a Theory-Based Community Intervention to Reduce AIDS Risk Behaviors: The CDC's AIDS Community Demonstration Projects. In *Social Marketing: Theoretical and Practical Perspectives*. M. E. Goldberg and S. Middlestadt, eds. Mahwah, N.J.: Lawrence Erlbaum Associates, 1997.

Fiske, Shirley. Report to the Governing Council of the National Association for the Practice of Anthropology, Washington, D.C., 1991.

Fitzsimmons, Stephen J. The Anthropologist in a Strange Land. *Human Organization* 34(3):183–196, 1975.

Folch-Lyon, Evelyn, Luis de la Macora, and S. Bruce Schearer. Focus Groups and Survey Research on Family Planning in Mexico. *Studies in Family Planning* 12(12):409–412, 1981.

Forde, E. Daryll. Applied Anthropology in Government: British Africa. In *Anthropology Today*. A. L. Kroeber, ed. Chicago: University of Chicago Press, 1953.

Fortes, Meyer. *Social Anthropology at Cambridge since 1900*. Cambridge: Cambridge University Press, 1953.

Foster, George M. Use of Anthropological Methods and Data in Planning and Operation. *Public Health Reports* 68(9):841–857, 1953.

Foster, George M. *Traditional Cultures and the Impact of Technological Change*. New York: Harper and Row, 1962.

Foster, George M. *Applied Anthropology*. Boston: Little, Brown, 1969.

Freire, Paulo. *Pedagogy of the Oppressed*. New York: Continuum, 1970.

Freire, Paulo. *Pedagogy of the Oppressed*. New York: Continuum, 1997.

Fuchs, Estelle and Robert J. Havighurst. *To Live on this Earth: American Indian Education*. New York: Doubleday, 1970.

Gadotti, M. *Reading Paulo Freire: His Life and Work*. Albany: State University of New York Press, 1994.

Gandhi, Sunita. Morocco: Enhancing the Participation of Women in Development. In *The World Bank Participation Sourcebook*. Washington, D.C.: The World Bank, 1996.

Gardner, Katy and David Lewis. *Anthropology, Development, and the Post-modern Challenge*. Chicago: Pluto Press, 1996.

Garfinkel, Harold. *Studies in Ethnomethodology*. Englewood Cliffs, N.J.: Prentice-Hall, 1967.

Gaviria, M., G. Stern, and S. Schensul. Sociocultural Factors and Perinatal Health in a Mexican American Community. *Journal of the National Medical Association* 74(10):983–989, 1982.

Gearing, Frederick O. *The Face of the Fox*. Sheffield, Wis.: Sheffield Publishing of Waveland Press, 1988.

Gearing, Frederick O., Robert McC. Netting, and Lisa R. Peattie, eds. *Documentary History of the Fox Project*. Chicago: University of Chicago, Department of Anthropology, 1960.

Gilbert, E. H., David W. Norman, and F. E. Finch. *Farming Systems Research: A Critical Appraisal*. Michigan State University Development Paper No. 8. East Lansing: Michigan State University, 1980.

Gilbert, M. Jean. Training for Cultural Competence in the Clinical Encounter: Successful Techniques. National Conference for Quality Health Care for Culturally Diverse Populations: Provider and Community Collaboration in a Competitive Market Place, New York, October 1–4, 1998.

Giovannini, Maureen J. and Lynne M. H. Rosansky. *Anthropology and Management Consulting: Forging a New Alliance*. NAPA Bulletin 9. Washington, D.C.: American Anthropological Association, 1990.

Gladwin, Thomas. Civil Administration on Truk: A Rejoinder. *Human Organization* 9(4):15–23, 1950.

Glaser, Barney G. and Anselm L. Strauss. *The Discovery of Grounded Theory: Strategies for Qualitative Research*. Hawthorne, N.Y.: Aldine de Gruyter, 1967.

Glaser, Edward M., Harold H. Abelson, and Kathalee N. Garrison. *Putting Knowledge to Use: Facilitating the Diffusion of Knowledge and the Implementation of Planned Change*. San Francisco: Jossey-Bass, 1983.

Glasser, Irene. Homelessness in Hartford: A Preliminary Study. Eastern Connecticut State University, 1996.

Gluckman, Max. *Administrative Organization of the Barotse Native Authorities*. Communication 1. Northern Rhodesia: Rhodes-Livingstone Institute, 1943.

Gluckman, Max. *The Judicial Process among the Barotse of Northern Rhodesia*. Manchester: University of Manchester Press, 1955.

Goldman, Laurence R., ed. *Social Impact Analysis: An Applied Anthropology Manual*. Oxford: Berg, 2000.

Goldschmidt, Walter C. *As You Sow: Three Studies in the Social Consequences of Agribusiness*. Glencoe, Ill.: Free Press, 1947.

Goldschmidt, Walter C. *The Uses of Anthropology*. A Special Publication of the American Anthropological Association. Washington D.C.: American Anthropological Association, 1979.

Goldschmidt, Walter C. and Theodore H. Haas. A Report to the Commissioner of Indian Affairs: Possessory Rights of the Natives of Southeastern Alaska. Mimeograph, 1946.

Goodenough, Ward H. *Cooperation in Change: An Anthropological Approach to Community Development*. New York: Russell Sage Foundation, 1963.

Gough, Kathleen. *Anthropology, Child of Imperialism*. London: London University, School of Oriental and African Studies, Third World Study Group, 1968.

Gouldner, Alvin W. Theoretical Requirements of the Applied Social Sciences. *American Sociological Review* 22:92–102, 1957.

Greaves, Tom. *Intellectual Property Rights for Indigenous Peoples: A Source Book*. Oklahoma City, Okla.: Society for Applied Anthropology, 1994.

Green, Edward C. *Knowledge, Attitudes, and Practices Survey of Water and Sanitation in Swaziland*. Swaziland: Health Education Unit, Ministry of Health and Water Borne Disease Control Project, 1982.

Green, Edward C. and Michael G. Wessels. Mid-term Evaluation of the Province-Based War Trauma Team Project: Meeting the Psychosocial Needs of Children in Angola. A Project of the Christian Children's Fund, Richmond, Virginia. Ashland, Va.: TvT Associates/Health Technical Services and Randolph-Macon College, 1997.

Greenwood, Davydd J. and Morten Levin. *Introduction to Action Research: Social Research for Social Change*. Thousand Oaks, Calif.: Sage, 1998.

Greenwood, Davydd J. et al. *Industrial Democracy as Process: Participatory Action Research in the Fagor Cooperative Group of Mondragon*. Assen-Maastricht: Van Gorcum, 1992.

Grinstead, M. J. Poverty, Race and Culture in a Rural Arkansas Community. *Human Organization* 35(1):33–34, 1976.

Hall, Edward T. Military Government on Truk. *Human Organization* 9(2):25–30, 1949.

Halpern, Joel. *Some Reflections on the War in Laos, Anthropological or Otherwise*. Brussels: Centre d'Etude du Sud-Est Asiatique et de l'Extreme Orient, 1972.

Hammel, E. A. Training Anthropologists for Effective Roles in Public Policy. In *Anthropology and the Public Interest*. Peggy Reeves Sanday, ed. New York: Academic Press, 1976.

Hansen, Asael T. Community Analysis at Heart Mountain Relocation Center. *Applied Anthropology* 5(3):15–25, 1946.

Hanson, Karen J. ed., John J. Conway, Jack Alexander, and H. Max Drake. *Mainstreaming Anthropology: Experiences in Government Employment*. NAPA Bulletin 5. Washington, D.C.: American Anthropological Association, 1988.

Hardesty, Donald L., Barbara J. Little, and Don Fowler. *Assessing Site Significance: A Guide for Archaeologists and Historians*. Walnut Creek, Calif.: AltaMira Press, 2000.

Harrington, Spencer P. M. Bones and Bureaucrats: New York's Great Cemetery Imbroglio. *Archaeology* 46:28–38, 1993.

Harza Engineering Company. *Environmental Design Considerations for Rural Development Projects*. Washington, D.C.: U.S. Agency for International Development, 1980.

Hastings, G. B., L. MacFadyen, A. M. Mackintosh, and R. Lowry. New Debate: Assessing the Impact of Branding and Tobacco Marketing Communications on Young People in Britain. *Social Marketing Quarterly* 4(4):54–60, 1998.

Heider, Karl G. *Ethnographic Film*. Austin: University of Texas Press, 1976.

Held, Jan G. Applied Anthropology in Government: The Netherlands. In *Anthro-*

pology Today. A. L. Kroeber, ed. Chicago: University of Chicago Press, 1953.

Hess, G. Alfred, Jr. Using Time-Effective Ethnographic Evaluation to Reshape a Private-Public Partnership. In *Soundings: Rapid and Reliable Research Methods for Practicing Anthropologists.* NAPA Bulletin 10. John van Willigen and Timothy J. Finan, eds. Washington, D.C.: American Anthropological Association, 1991.

Higgins, Thomas F. III, Charles M. Downing, and Donald W. Linebaugh. Traces of Historic Kecoughtan: Archaeology at a Seventeenth-Century Plantation. Data Recovery at Site 44HT44, Associated with the Proposed Pentran Bus Parking Lot, City of Hampton, Virginia, Project: U000–114–V19, PE101. Williamsburg, Va.: William & Mary Center for Archaeological Research for the Virginia Department of Transportation, 1999.

Hildebrand, Peter. *Generating Technology for Traditional Farmers: A Multidisciplinary Approach.* Guatemala: Instituto de Ciencia y Tecnologia Agricolas, 1976.

Hildebrand, Peter. Combining Disciplines in Rapid Appraisal: The Sondeo Approach. *Agricultural Administration* 8:423–432, 1981.

Hill, Carole E. *Training Manual in Medical Anthropology.* Carole E. Hill, ed. Washington, D.C.: American Anthropological Association, 1984.

Hinsley, Curtis M., Jr. Amateurs and Professionals in Washington Anthropology, 1879 to 1903. In *American Anthropology, the Early Years.* John V. Murra, ed. 1974 Proceedings of the American Ethnological Society. New York: West Publishing, 1976.

Hinsley, Curtis M., Jr. Anthropology as Science and Politics: The Dilemmas of the Bureau of American Ethnology, 1879 to 1904. In *The Uses of Anthropology.* Walter Goldschmidt, ed. Washington, D.C.: American Anthropological Association, 1979.

Hoben, S. J. *The Sociolinguistic Context of Literacy Programs: A Review of Nonformal Adult Literacy.* AID Contract 147–PE–70. Washington, D.C.: U.S. Agency for International Development, 1980.

Holmberg, Allan R. The Research and Development Approach to the Study of Change. *Human Organization* 17:12–16, 1958.

Holtz, Herman. *How to Succeed as an Independent Consultant.* New York: John Wiley and Sons, 1993.

Honadle, George. Rapid Reconnaissance for Development Administration: Mapping and Moulding Organizational Landscapes. *World Development* 10(8): 633–649, 1982.

Honigmann, John J. *Information for Pakistan: Report of Research on Intercultural Communication through Films.* Chapel Hill: Institute for Research in Social Science, University of North Carolina, 1953.

Honigmann, John J. *The Development of Anthropological Ideas.* Homewood, Ill.: Dorsey Press, 1976.

Horowitz, Irving, ed. *The Rise and Fall of Project Camelot: Studies in the Relationship between Social Sciences and Practical Politics.* Cambridge, Mass.: M.I.T. Press, 1967.

Hostetler, John A. Amish Schooling: A Study in Alternatives. *Council on Anthropology and Education* 3(2):1–4, 1972.

Huizer, Gerrit. A-social Role of Social Scientists in Underdeveloped Countries: Some Ethical Considerations. In *Current Anthropology in the Netherlands.* Peter Kloos and Henri J. M. Claessen, eds. Rotterdam: Anthropological Branch of the Netherlands Sociology and Anthropology Society, 1975.

Hyland, Stanley, Linda A. Bennett, Thomas W. Collins, and Ruthbeth Finerman. Developing Purposeful Internship Programs. In *Anthropology for Tomorrow: Creating Practitioner-Oriented Applied Anthropology Programs.* Robert T. Trotter II, ed. Washington, D.C.: American Anthropological Association, 1988.

Hyland, Stanley and Sean Kirkpatrick. *Guide to Training Programs in the Applications of Anthropology.* 3rd ed. Memphis, Tenn.: Society for Applied Anthropology, 1989.

Hymes, Dell, ed. *Reinventing Anthropology.* New York: Random House, 1974.

Ingersoll, Jasper. Mekong River Basin Development: Anthropology in a New Setting. *Anthropological Quarterly* 41:147–167, 1968.

Ingersoll, Jasper. *The Social Feasibility of PaMong Irrigation: A Report to the U.S. Bureau of Reclamation and the U.S. Agency for International Development.* Washington, D.C.: U.S. Agency for International Development, 1969.

Ingersoll, Jasper, Mark Sullivan, and Barbara Lenkerd. *Social Analysis of A.I.D. Projects: A Review of the Experience.* Washington, D.C.: U.S. Agency for International Development. 1981.

International Cooperation Administration. *Community Development Review.* No. 3. Washington, D.C.: International Cooperation Administration, 1955.

International Maize and Wheat Improvement Center. *Planning Technologies Appropriate to Farmers: Concepts and Procedures.* Mexico City: CIMMYT, 1980.

Interorganizational Committee on Guidelines and Principles for Social Impact Assessment, U.S. Department of Commerce, National Oceanic and Atmospheric Administration, National Marine Fisheries Service. *Guidelines and Principles for Social Impact Assessment.* Washington, D.C., 1994.

Jacobs, Sue-Ellen. *Social Impact Assessment: Experiences in Evaluation Research, Applied Anthropology and Human Ethics.* Mississippi State University Occasional Papers in Anthropology. John H. Peterson, ed. Mississippi State: Department of Anthropology, Mississippi State University, 1977.

Jacobsen, Claire. *The Organization of Work in a Pre-school Setting: Work Relations Between Professionals and Para-professionals in Four Head Start Centers.* New York: Bank Street College of Education, 1973.

Jenks, Albert E. The Relation of Anthropology to Americanization. *The Scientific Monthly* 12:240–245, 1921.

Johnson, Jeffery and David Griffith. Perceptions and Preferences for Marine Fish: A Study of Recreational Fishermen in the Southeast. Raleigh: University of North Carolina Sea Grant Program, 1985.

Jones, Delmos J. Social Responsibility and Belief in Basic Research: An Example from Thailand. *Current Anthropology* 12(3):347, 1971.

Jones, Delmos J. Applied Anthropology and the Application of Anthropological Knowledge. *Human Organization* 35:221–229, 1976.

Jones, Jeffrey. *Diagnostico Socio-economico Sobre el Consumo y Produccion de Lena in Fincas Pequenas de la Peninsula de Azuero, Panama.* Turrialba,

Costa Rica: Centro Agronomico Tropical de Investigacion y Ensenanza, 1982.

Jorgensen, Joseph G. On Ethics and Anthropology. *Current Anthropology* 12(3): 321–334, 1971.

Joseph, Alice, Rosamond B. Spicer, and Jane Chesky. *The Desert People: A Study of the Papago Indians.* Chicago: University of Chicago Press, 1949.

Kaiser Permanente. *Provider's Handbook on Culturally Competent Care.* Kaiser Permanente National Diversity Council, 1996.

Kannapel, Patricia J., Lola Aagaard, Pamelia Coe, and Cynthia A. Reeves. *Elementary Change: Moving toward Systemic School Reform in Rural Kentucky.* Charleston, W.Va.: AEL, 2000.

Kasmir, Sharryn. *The Myth of Mondragon: Cooperatives, Politics, and Working-Class Life in a Basque Town.* Albany: State University of New York Press, 1996.

Keefe, Susan Emley, ed. *Negotiating Ethnicity: The Impact of Anthropological Theory and Practice.* NAPA Bulletin 8. Washington, D.C.: American Anthropological Association, 1989.

Keith, Arthur. How Can the Institute Best Serve the Needs of Anthropology? *Journal of the Royal Anthropological Society* 47:12–30, 1917.

Kemmis, Stephen. Action Research in Retrospect and Prospect. Presented at the annual meetings of the Australian Association for Research in Education, 1980.

Kendall, Carl. The Use and Non-Use of Anthropology: The Diarrheal Disease Control Program in Honduras. In *Making Our Research Useful: Case Studies in the Utilization of Anthropological Knowledge.* John van Willigen, Barbara Rylko-Bauer, and Ann McElroy, eds. Boulder, Colo.: Westview Press, 1989.

Kennard, Edward A. and Gordon MacGregor. Applied Anthropology in Government: United States. In *Anthropology Today.* A. L. Kroeber, ed. Chicago: University of Chicago Press, 1953.

Kennedy, Raymond. Applied Anthropology in the Dutch East Indies. *Transactions of the New York Academy of Sciences* (Ser. 2) 6:157–162, 1944.

Kerri, James N. A Social Analysis of the Human Element in Housing: A Canadian Case. *Human Organization* 36(2):173–185, 1977.

Kessing, Felix M. Experiments in Training Overseas Administrators. *Human Organization* 8(4):20–22, 1949.

Khoury, Amal J., Amal Mitra, Agnes Hinton, and Syed W. Moazzem. Evaluation of the Loving Support Campaign in Mississippi. Paper presented at the meeting of the American Public Health Association, 2001.

Kimball, Solon T. *Community Government in the War Relocation Centers.* Washington, D.C.: Government Printing Office, 1946.

Kimball, Solon T. Some Methodological Problems of the Community Self-Survey. *Social Forces* 31:160–164, 1952.

Kimball, Solon T. and Marion Pearsall. *The Talladega Story: A Study in Community Process.* University: University of Alabama Press, 1954.

Kimball, Solon T. and John H. Provinse. Navaho Social Organization in Land Use Planning. *Applied Anthropology* 1(4):18–25, 1942.

King, Thomas F. *Cultural Resource Laws and Practice: An Introductory Guide.* Walnut Creek, Calif.: AltaMira Press, 1998.

Kiste, Robert C. *The Bikinians: A Study in Forced Migration*. Menlo Park, Calif.: Cummings Publishing Company, 1974.

Kleinman, Arthur. *Patients and Healers in the Context of Culture*. Berkeley: University of California Press, 1980.

Kluckhohn, Clyde and Dorothea C. Leighton. *The Navaho*. Cambridge, Mass.: Harvard University Press, 1946.

Kluger, Richard. *Simple Justice: The History of Brown v. Board of Education and Black America's Struggle for Equality*. New York: Knopf, 1976.

Knudson, Ruthann. Contemporary Cultural Resource Management. In *American Archaeology Past and Future*. David J. Meltzer, Don D. Fowler, and Jeremy A. Sabloff, eds. Washington, D.C.: Smithsonian Institution Press, 1986.

Koons, Adam, Beatrice Hackett, and John Mason. *Stalking Employment in the Nation's Capital: A Guide for Anthropologists*. Washington, D.C.: Washington Association of Professional Anthropologists, 1989.

Korten, David. Community Organisation and Rural Development: A Learning Process Approach. *Public Administration Review* (September/October), 1980.

Korten, David. Rural Development Programming: The Learning Process Approach. In *People-Centered Development*. David C. Korten and Rudi Klauss, eds. West Hartford, Conn.: Kumarian Press, 1984.

Kotler, Philip. *Marketing for Nonprofit Organizations*. Englewood Cliffs, N.J.: Prentice-Hall, 1975.

Kotler, Philip and G. Armstrong. *Principles of Marketing*. 7th ed. Englewood Cliffs, N.J.: Prentice-Hall, 1996.

Kotler, Philip and E. L. Roberto. *Social Marketing: Strategies for Changing Public Behavior*. New York: Free Press, 1989.

Kotler, Philip and Gerald Zaltman. Social Marketing: An Approach to Planned Social Change. *Journal of Marketing* 35(July):3–12, 1971.

Krueger, Richard A. *Focus Groups: A Practical Guide for Applied Research*. Newbury Park, Calif.: Sage, 1988.

Kumar, Krishna. *Conducting Group Interviews in Developing Countries*. A.I.D. Program Design and Evaluation Methodology Report No. 8. Washington, D.C.: Agency for International Development, 1987.

Kushner, Gilbert. Applied Anthropology Training Programs. *Practicing Anthropology* 1(2):23, 1978.

Lackner, Helen. Social Anthropology and Indirect Rule. The Colonial Administration and Anthropology in Eastern Nigeria: 1920–1940. In *Anthropology and the Colonial Encounter*. T. Asad, ed. New York: Humanities Press, 1973.

Lafitau, Joseph F. *Customs of the American Indians Compared with the Customs of Primitive Times*. Toronto: The Champlain Society, 1724 (reissued 1974).

Lample, Linda L. and Thomas A. Herbert. *The Integration of Fish, Seafood, and Aquaculture Products into the Florida Farmers' Market System*. Tallahassee, Fla.: T. A. Herbert and Associates, 1988.

Landman, Ruth H. and Katherine Spencer Halpern, eds. *Applied Anthropologist and Public Servant: The Life and Work of Philleo Nash*. NAPA Bulletin 7. Washington, D.C.: American Anthropological Association, 1989.

Landy, David. A Halfway House for Women: Preliminary Report of a Study. In *Mental Patients in Transaction*. Springfield, Ill.: Charles C. Thomas, 1961.

Langer, Elinor. Human Experimentation: New York Verdict Affirms Patient's Rights. *Science* 151:663–666, 1966.

Lantis, Margaret L. Anthropology as Public Service. *Applied Anthropology* 4:20–32, 1945.

Lantis, Margaret L. and Evelyn B. Hadaway. How Three Seattle Tuberculosis Hospitals Have Met the Needs of Their Eskimo Patients. Paper presented to the National Tuberculosis Association, Kansas City, Mo., 1957.

Lasswell, Harold D. and Allen R. Holmberg. Toward a General Theory of Directed Value Accumulation and Institutional Development. In *Comparative Theories of Social Change*. H. W. Peter, ed. Ann Arbor, Mich.: Foundation for Research on Human Behavior, 1966.

Lathrop, Richard. *Who's Hiring Who: How to Find that Job Fast.* 12th ed. Berkeley, Calif.: Ten Speed Press, 1989.

Leacock, Eleanor, Nancie L. Gonzales, and Gilbert Kushner, eds. *Training Programs for New Opportunities in Applied Anthropology.* A Symposium Sponsored by the Society for Applied Anthropology. Washington, D.C.: American Anthropological Association, 1974.

LeCompte, Margaret D., Jean J. Schensul, Margaret R. Weeks, and Merrill Singer. *Researcher Roles & Research Partnerships.* Walnut Creek, Calif.: AltaMira Press, 1999.

Lefebvre, R. Craig and June A. Flora. Social Marketing and Public Health Intervention. *Health Education Quarterly* 15(3):299–315, 1988.

Lefley, Harriet P. Approaches to Community Mental Health: The Miami Model. *Psychiatric Annals* 5(8):315–319, 1975.

Lefley, Harriet P. and Evalina W. Bestman. Community Mental Health and Minorities, a Multi-Ethnic Approach. In *The Pluralistic Society: A Community Mental Health Perspective.* Stanley Sue and Thom Moore, eds. New York: Human Sciences Press, 1984.

Leighton, Alexander. *Human Relations in a Changing World: Observations on the Use of the Social Sciences.* New York: Dutton, 1949.

Leighton, Alexander and Dorothea C. Leighton. *The Navaho Door.* Cambridge, Mass.: Harvard University Press, 1944.

Leighton, Alexander et al. Assessing Public Opinion in a Dislocated Community. *Public Opinion Quarterly* 7(4):652–658, 1943.

Leighton, Dorothea C. and John Adair. *People of the Middle Place: A Study of the Zuni Indians.* New Haven, Conn.: Human Relations Area Files, 1946.

Leviton, Laura C. and E.F.X. Hughes. Research on the Utilization of Evaluations: A Review and Synthesis. *Evaluation Review* 5:525–548, 1981.

Lindenberger, James H. and L. A. Bryant. Promoting Breastfeeding in the WIC Program: A Social Marketing Case Study. *American Journal of Health Behavior* 24(1):53–60, 2000.

Ling, J. C., B. A. Franklin, J. F. Lindsteadt, and S.A.N. Searon. Social Marketing: Its Place in Public Health. *Annual Review of Public Health* 13:341–362, 1992.

Little, Peter D. *The Illusive Granary: Herder, Farmer and State in Northern Kenya.* Cambridge: Cambridge University Press, 1992.

Low, Setha M. and Elaine L. Simon. *Working Landscapes: A Report on the Social*

Uses of Outside Space in Corporate Centers and Program Recommendations for Carnegie Center. Philadelphia, 1984.

Lurie, Nancy Oestreich. Anthropology and Indian Claims Litigation: Problems, Opportunities, and Recommendations. *Ethnohistory* 2:357–375, 1955.

MacArthur, John R., Sandra Dudley, and Holly Ann Williams. Approaches to Facilitating Health Care Acceptance: A Case Example from Karenni Refugees. In *Caring for Those in Crisis: Integrating Anthropology and Public Health in Complex Humanitarian Emergencies*. Holly Ann Williams, ed. NAPA Bulletin 21. Washington, D.C.: American Anthropological Association, 2001.

McCay, Bonnie J. and Carolyn F. Creed. Social Structure and Debates on Fisheries Management in the Atlantic Surf Clam Fishery. *Ocean and Shoreline Management* 13:199–229, 1990.

Maccoby, N. et al. Reducing the Risk of Cardiovascular Disease. *Journal of Community Health* 3:100–114, 1977.

McCorkle, Constance M. *The Social Sciences in International Agricultural Research: Lessons from the CRSPs*. Boulder, Colo.: Lynne Rienner, 1989.

McGimsey, Charles R. and Hester A. Davis. United States of America. In *Approaches to Archaeological Heritage: A Comparative Study of World Cultural Resource Management Systems*. Henry Cleere, ed. Pp. 116–124. New York: Cambridge University Press, 1984.

MacGregor, Gordon. *Warriors Without Weapons*. Chicago: University of Chicago Press, 1946.

MacGregor, Gordon. Anthropology in Government: United States. In *Yearbook of Anthropology—1955*. New York: Wenner-Gren, 1955.

McGuire, Thomas R. and Marshall A. Worden. *Socio-cultural Impact Assessment of the San Xavier Planned Community, Papago Indian Reservation, Pima County, Arizona*. Tucson: Bureau of Applied Research in Anthropology, University of Arizona, 1984.

McKillip, Jack. *Need Analysis: Tools for the Human Services and Education*. Newbury Park, Calif.: Sage, 1987.

McPherson, Laura, ed. *The Role of Anthropology in the Agency for International Development*. Binghamton, N.Y.: Institute for Development of Anthropology, 1978.

Maloney, Clarence, K.M.A. Aziz, and Profulla C. Sarker. *Beliefs and Fertility in Bangladesh*. Rajshahi, Bangladesh: Institute of Bangladesh Studies, Rajshahi University, 1980.

Manoff, R. K. *Social Marketing: New Imperative for Public Health*. New York: Praeger, 1985.

Manoff, R. K. *Rationale for Application of Social Marketing and Use of Mass Media in Prevention*. Washington, D.C.: Manoff Group, 1988.

Marcus, George E. and Michael M. J. Fischer. *Anthropology as Cultural Critique: An Experimental Moment in the Human Sciences*. Chicago: University of Chicago Press, 1986.

Mark, Melvin M. and R. Lance Shotland. Stakeholder Based Evaluation and Value Judgements. *Evaluation Review* 9(5):605–625, 1985.

Marshall, Patricia. *Executive Summary Interim Report: Rural Alcohol Initiative*. Ashland, Ky.: Lansdowne Mental Health Center, 1979.

Maruyama, Magorah. Cultural, Social and Psychological Considerations in the

Planning of Public Works. *Technological Forecasting and Social Change* 5: 135–143, 1973.

Mascarenhas, James. Participatory Rural Appraisal and Participatory Learning Methods: Recent Experiences from MYRADA and South India. *Forests, Trees, and People Newsletter* No. 15/16. Uppsala: Swedish University of Agricultural Sciences, 1992.

Mason, Leonard E. *Economic and Human Resources—Marshall Islands*. Ponape: U.S. Commercial Company, 1947.

Mason, Leonard E. The Bikinians: A Transplanted Population. *Human Organization* 9(1):5–15, 1950.

Mason, Leonard E. Kili Community in Transition. *South Pacific Commission Quarterly Bulletin* 18:32–35, 1958.

Mathur, Hari Mohan. Anthropology, Government, and Development Planning in India. In *Anthropology in the Development Process*. Hari Mohan Mathur, ed. New Delhi: Vikas Publishing House, 1977.

Matlon, P., R. Cantrell, D. King, and M. Benoit-Cattin. *Coming Full Circle: Farmer's Participation in the Development of Technology*. Ottawa: IDRC, 1984.

Mead, Margaret. Applied Anthropology: The State of the Art. In *Perspectives on Anthropology, 1976*. A.F.C. Wallace, ed. Washington, D.C.: American Anthropological Association, 1977.

Mead, Margaret, ed. *Cultural Patterns and Technical Change*. New York: American Library, 1955.

Mead, Margaret, Eliot D. Chapple, and G. Gordon Brown. Report of the Committee on Ethics. *Human Organization* 8(2):20–21, 1949.

Mekeel, H. Scudder. An Appraisal of the Indian Reorganization Act. *American Anthropologist* 46(2):209–217, 1944.

Merton, Robert K., Marjorie Fiske, and Patricia L. Kendall. *The Focused Interview: A Manual of Problems and Procedures*. 2nd ed. New York: Free Press, 1990.

Merton, Robert K. and Patricia L. Kendall. The Focused Interview. *American Journal of Sociology* 51:541–557, 1946.

Messing, Simon D. Application of Health Questionnaires to Pre-Urban Communities in a Developing Country. *Human Organization* 24(3):365–372, 1965.

Messing, Simon D. et al. Health Culture Research in a Developing Country. *American Behavioral Scientist* 7(8):29–30, 1964.

Miles, Matthew B. and A. Michael Huberman. *Qualitative Data Analysis: A Sourcebook of New Methods*. Beverly Hills, Calif.: Sage, 1984.

Miller, Barbara D. *Local Social Organizations and Local Project Capacity*. Syracuse, N.Y.: Local Revenue Administration Project, Maxwell School, Syracuse University, 1980.

Millsap, William. New Tools for an Old Trade: Social Impact Assessment in Community and Regional Development. In *Social Science Education for Development*. William T. Vickers and Glenn R. Howze, eds. Tuskegee, Ala.: Tuskegee Institute, Center for Rural Development, 1978.

Mooney, James. *The Ghost Dance Religion and the Sioux Outbreak of 1890*. Fourteenth Annual Report. Washington, D.C.: Bureau of American Ethnology, 1896.

Moore, John. Perspective for a Partisan Anthropology. *Liberation* (November):34–43, 1971.

Morgan, David L. *Focus Groups as Qualitative Research*. Newbury Park, Calif.: Sage, 1988.

Moser, C. and J. Holland. *A Participatory Study of Urban Poverty and Violence in Jamaica: Analysis of Research Results*. Washington, D.C.: The World Bank, Urban Development Division, 1995.

Mukerjee, Nilanjana. The Rush to Scale: Lessons Being Learnt in Indonesia. In *Who Changes? Institutionalizing Participation in Development*. James Blackburn with Jeremy Holland, eds. London: Intermediate Technology Publications, 1998.

Murdock, George P. et al. *Outline of Cultural Materials*. 5th rev. ed. New Haven, Conn.: Human Relations Area Files, 1982.

Murphy, Cullen. Pay Dirt. *Atlantic* 278(3):26–30, 39, 42, 1991.

Murray, Gerald F. The Domestication of Wood in Haiti: A Case Study in Applied Evolution. In *Anthropological Praxis: Translating Knowledge into Action*. R. Wulff and S. Fiske, eds. Boulder, Colo.: Westview Press, 1987.

Myres, J. L. The Science of Man in the Service of the State. *Journal of the Royal Anthropological Institute of Great Britain and Ireland* 59:19–52, 1928.

Nadel, S. F. *The Nuba: An Anthropological Study of the Hill Tribes of Kordofan*. London: Oxford University Press, 1947.

Narayan, D. and D. Nyamwaya. *Learning from the Poor: A Participatory Poverty Assessment in Kenya*. World Bank, Environmental Department Paper No. 34. Washington, D.C.: The World Bank, 1996.

National Association for the Practice of Anthropology. *NAPA Directory of Practicing Anthropologists*. Washington, D.C.: American Anthropological Association, 1991.

National Park Service (NPS). *Federal Historic Preservation Laws*. Washington, D.C.: Government Printing Office, 1993.

National Park Service (NPS). *Revised Thematic Framework*. Washington, D.C.: NPS, 1996.

Naylor, Larry L. *Native Hire on Trans-Alaska Pipeline. Report prepared for Arctic Gas Pipeline Company*. Fairbanks: Department of Anthropology, University of Alaska, 1976.

Nellemann, George. Hinrich Rink and Applied Anthropology in Greenland in the 1860s. *Human Organization* 28:166–174, 1969.

Neuber, Keith A. *Needs Assessment: A Model for Community Planning*. Beverly Hills, Calif.: Sage, 1980.

Nicaise, Joseph. Applied Anthropology in the Congo and Ruanda-Urandi. *Human Organization* 19:112–117, 1960.

Norman, David W. and Emmy B. Summons. *Farming Systems in the Nigerian Savanna: Research Strategies for Development*. Boulder, Colo.: Westview Press, 1982.

Nugent, Jeffery B., William L. Partridge, Antoinette B. Brown, and John D. Rees. *An Interdisciplinary Evaluation of the Human Ecology and Health Impact of the Aleman Dam*. Mexico: Center for Human Ecology and Health, Pan American Health Organization, 1978.

Oberg, Kalervo, Allan G. Harper, and Andrew R. Cordova. *Man and Resources in *the Middle Rio Grande Valley*. Albuquerque: University of New Mexico Press, 1943.

Office of Minority Health, U.S. Public Health Service. *Assuring Cultural Competence in Health Care: Recommendations for National Standards and Outcomes-Focused Research Agenda*. http://www.omhrc.gov/clas/, n.d.

Oliver, Douglas L., ed. *Planning Micronesia's Future: A Summary of the United States Commercial Company's Economic Survey of Micronesia, 1946*. Cambridge, Mass.: Harvard University Press, 1951.

Opler, Marvin K. A Sumo Tournament at Tule Lake Center. *American Anthropologist* 47:134–139, 1945.

Orbach, Michael. Qualifications for the Performance of Social Impact Assessment. Report submitted to the Executive Committee of the Society for Applied Anthropology for the Social Impact Assessment Committee. Typescript, 1979.

O'Reilly, Kevin R. and Michael E. Dalmat. Marketing Program Evaluation: Birth Attendant Training in Kenya. *Practicing Anthropology* 9(1):12–13, 1987.

Osteria, Trinidad S. and Pilar Ramos-Jimenez. Women in Health Development: Mobilization of Women for Health Care Delivery in a Philippine Community. *Soujourn* 3(2):217–235, 1988.

Padfield, Harland and Courtland L. Smith. Water and Culture. *Rocky Mountain Social Science Journal* 5(2):23–32, 1968.

Parker, Patricia L. and Thomas F. King. Intercultural Mediation at Truk International Airport. In *Anthropological Praxis: Translating Knowledge into Action*. R. Wulff and S. Fiske, eds. Boulder, Colo.: Westview Press, 1987.

Partridge, William L. *Training Manual in Development Anthropology*. Washington, D.C.: American Anthropological Association, 1984.

Partridge, William L. and Elizabeth M. Eddy. The Development of Applied Anthropology in America. In *Applied Anthropology in America*. Elizabeth M. Eddy and William L. Partridge, eds. New York: Columbia University Press, 1978.

Patton, Michael Quinn. *Utilization-Focused Evaluation*. 2nd ed. Beverly Hills, Calif.: Sage, 1986.

Paul, Benjamin D., ed. *Health, Culture, and Community*. New York: Russell Sage Foundation, 1955.

Pearsall, Marion and M. Sue Kern. Behavioral Science, Nursing Services, and the Collaborative Process: A Case Study. *Journal of Applied Behavioral Science* 3(2):253–270, 1967.

Peattie, Lisa R. Reflections on Advocacy Planning. *American Institute of Planners* 34:80–87, 1968.

Peattie, Lisa R. Conflicting Views of the Project: Caracas versus the Site. In *Regional Planning for Development: The Experience of the Guayani Program of Venezuela*. Lloyd Rodwin, ed. Cambridge, Mass.: M.I.T. Press, 1969a.

Peattie, Lisa R. Social Mobility and Economic Development. In *Regional Planning for Development: The Experience of the Guayani Program of Venezuela*. Lloyd Rodwin, ed. Cambridge, Mass.: M.I.T. Press, 1969b.

Peattie, Lisa R. Public Housing: Urban Slums under Public Management. In *Race, Change and Urban Society, Urban Affairs Annual Review*. P. Orleans and W. Ellis, eds. Beverly Hills, Calif.: Sage, 1971a.

Peattie, Lisa R. Conventional Public Housing. Working Paper No. 3. Cambridge, Mass.: Joint Center for Urban Studies, 1971b.

Pelto, Pertii J. and Gretel H. Pelto. Intra-cultural Diversity: Some Theoretical Issues. *American Ethnologist* 2(1):1–18, 1975.

Pelto, Pertii J. and Gretel H. Pelto. *Anthropological Research: The Structure of Inquiry.* New York: Cambridge University Press, 1978.

Pelto, Pertii J. and Jean J. Schensul. Theory and Practice in Policy Research. In *Applied Anthropology in America.* 2nd ed. E. Eddy and W. Partridge, eds. New York: Columbia University Press, 1986.

Pelzer, Karl and Edward T. Hall. *Economic and Human Resources—Truk Islands, Central Carolines.* Ponape: U.S. Commercial Company, 1947.

Peterson, John H., Jr. *Socio-economic Characteristics of the Mississippi Choctaw Indians.* Social Science Research Center Report No. 34. Mississippi State: Mississippi State University, 1970.

Peterson, John H., Jr. Assimilation, Separation and Out-Migration in an American Indian Community. *American Anthropologist* 74:1286–1295, 1972.

Peterson, John H., Jr. The Changing Role of an Applied Anthropologist. In *Applied Anthropology in America.* Elizabeth M. Eddy and William L. Partridge, eds. New York: Columbia University Press, 1978.

Peterson, John H., Jr. and Sue-Ellen Jacobs. Anthropologists in Social Impact Assessment. Presented at the Society for Applied Anthropology meetings, Philadelphia, 1977.

Pillsbury, Barbara. *Executive Summaries of Evaluations and Special Studies Conducted for A.I.D. in Asia in Fiscal Year 1985.* Washington, D.C.: Agency for International Development, 1989.

Pollard, Richard. *Social Marketing of Vitamin A. Final Creative and Promotional Strategy. West Sumatra Vitamin A Project Report.* Washington, D.C.: The Manoff Group, 1987.

Posner, Bruce G. The Future of Marketing Is Looking at You. *Fast Company* (October/November):105–109, 1996.

Powdermaker, Hortense. Summary of Methods of a Field Work Class Cooperating with the Committee on Food Habits. In *The Problem of Changing Food Habits.* Washington, D.C.: National Research Council, 1943.

Powell, John Wesley. *First Annual Report of the Bureau of American Ethnology.* Washington, D.C.: Government Printing Office, 1881.

Practical Concepts, Incorporated. *Planning Rural Energy Projects: A Rural Energy Survey and Planning Methodology for Bolivia.* Washington, D.C.: Practical Concepts, Inc., 1980.

Preister, Kevin. Issue-Centered Social Impact Assessment. In *Anthropological Praxis: Translating Knowledge into Action.* R. Wulff and S. Fiske, eds. Pp. 39–55. Boulder, Colo.: Westview Press, 1987.

Price, Derek and J. de Solla. Ethics of Scientific Publication. *Science* 144:655–657, 1964.

Price, John A. *Applied Anthropology: Canadian Perspectives.* Downsview, Ontario: SAAC/York University, 1987.

Prior, Julian. *Pastoral Development Planning.* Oxfam Development Guideline No. 9. Oxford: Oxfam, 1994.

Provinse, John H. Cultural Factors in Land Use Planning. In *The Changing Indian.* Oliver La Farge, ed. Norman: University of Oklahoma Press, 1942.

Provinse, John H. and Solon T. Kimball. Building New Communities during Wartime. *American Sociological Review* 11:396–410, 1946.

Quandt, Sara A. and Cheryl Ritenbaugh, eds. *Training Manual in Nutritional Anthropology.* Washington, D.C.: American Anthropological Association, 1986.

Ralston, Lenore, James Anderson, and Elizabeth Colson. *Voluntary Efforts in Decentralized Management, Final Report, Project on Managing Decentralization.* Berkeley: Institute of International Studies, University of California, 1981.

Ramesh, R., N. Narayanasamy, and M. P. Boraian. Getting Fisherfolk off the Hook: An Exploratory PRA in Southern India. *PLA Notes: Participatory Learning and Action* 30:54–58, 1997.

Rangun, V. K. and S. Karim. Teaching Note: Focusing the Concept of Social Marketing. Cambridge, Mass.: Harvard Business School, 1991.

Rappaport, J. Studies in Empowerment: Introduction to the Issue. In *Studies in Empowerment: Steps toward Understanding and Action.* J. Rappaport, C. Swift, and R. Hess, eds. New York: The Haworth Press, 1984.

Read, C. H. Anthropology at the Universities. *Man* 38:56–59, 1906.

Reining, Conrad C. A Lost Period of Applied Anthropology. *American Anthropologist* 64:593–600, 1962.

Rhoades, Robert E. *The Art of the Informal Agricultural Survey.* Training Document 1982–2. Lima, Peru: Social Science Department, International Potato Center, 1982.

Rhoades, Robert E. *Breaking New Ground: Agricultural Anthropology.* Lima, Peru: International Potato Center, 1984.

Rhoades, Robert E. and Robert H. Booth. Farmer-Back-to-Farmer: A Model for Generating Acceptable Agricultural Technology. *Agricultural Administration* 11:127–137, 1982a.

Rhoades, Robert E. and R. Booth. *Farmer-Back-to-Farmer: A Model for Generating Acceptable Technology.* Working Paper 1982–1. Lima, Peru: Social Science Department, International Potato Center, 1982b.

Rhoades, Robert E., R. Booth, R. Shaw, and R. Werge. The Involvement and Interaction of Anthropological and Biological in the Development and Transfer of Post-Harvest Technology at CIP. In *The Role of Anthropologists and Other Social Scientists in Interdisciplinary Teams Developing Improved Food Production Technology.* Los Banos, Philippines: International Rice Research Institute, 1982.

Rich, R. F. Selective Utilization of Social Science Related Information by Federal Policy Makers. *Inquiry* 12:239–245, 1975.

Riecken, Henry W. Memorandum on Program Evaluation, Ford Foundation. In *Evaluating Action Programs: Readings in Social Action and Education.* Carol A. Weiss, ed. Boston: Allyn and Bacon, 1972.

Rietbergen-McCracken, Jennifer and Deepa Narayan. *Participation and Social Assessment: Tools and Techniques.* Washington, D.C.: The International Bank for Reconstruction and Development/The World Bank, 1998.

Roberts, A. *The Social Impact of the Tangaye (Upper Volta) Solar Energy Dem-*

onstration: A Summary Report. Ann Arbor: University of Michigan, Center for Afro-American and African Studies, 1981.

Rodnick, David. *Report on the Indians of Kansas.* Applied Anthropology Unit Report Series. Washington, D.C.: Office of Indian Affairs, Department of the Interior, 1936.

Rodnick, David. *Postwar Germans: An Anthropologist's Account.* New Haven, Conn.: Yale University Press, 1948.

Rosaldo, Renato. *Culture and Truth: The Remaking of Social Analysis.* Boston: Beacon Press, 1993.

Rostow, W. W. *The Stages of Economic Growth: A Non-Communist Manifesto.* Cambridge: Cambridge University Press, 1960.

Rothman, Jack. *Using Research in Organizations.* Beverly Hills, Calif.: Sage, 1980.

Ruttan, V. W. The Green Revolution: Seven Generalisations. *International Development Review* 4:15–23, 1977.

Ryan, A. The Resurgence of Breastfeeding in the United States. *Pediatrics* 99(4):1–5, 1997.

Rylko-Bauer, Barbara and John van Willigen. A Framework for Developing Utilization-Focused Policy Research in Anthropology. In *Speaking the Language of Power: Communication, Collaboration, and Advocacy (Translating Ethnography into Action).* David Fetterman, ed. Washington, D.C.: Falmer Press, 1993.

Rynkiewich, Michael A. and James P. Spradley. *Ethics and Anthropology: Dilemmas in Fieldwork.* New York: John Wiley and Sons, 1976.

Sachchidananda. Planning, Development and Applied Anthropology. *Journal of the Indian Anthropological Society* 7:11–28, 1972.

Sackman, Harold. *Delphi Critique, Expert Opinion, Forecasting and Group Process.* Lexington, Mass.: Lexington Books, 1975.

Sanday, Peggy Reeves, ed. *Anthropology and the Public Interest.* New York: Academic Press, 1976.

Sandford, S. *Management of Pastoral Development in the Third World.* London: Wiley, 1983.

Sandoval, Mercedes C. and Leon Tozo. An Emergent Cuban Community. *Psychiatric Annals* 5(8):324–332, 1975.

Sands, Deborah Merrill. A Review of Farming Systems Research. Prepared for Technical Advisory Committee/CGIAR. Rome: CGIAR, 1985.

SANREM CRSP. Looking Back on the Landscape: Impacts and Lessons from the SANREM CRSP. Watkinsville, Ga.: SANREM CRSP, 2001.

Sasaki, Tom T. *Fruitland, New Mexico: A Navaho Community in Transition.* Ithaca, N.Y.: Cornell University Press, 1960.

Sasaki, Tom T. and John Adair. New Land to Farm: Agricultural Practices among the Navaho Indians of New Mexico. In *Human Problems in Technological Change.* Edward H. Spicer, ed. New York: Russell Sage Foundation, 1952.

Scaglion, Richard. *Samukundi Abelam* Conflict Management: Implications for Legal Planning in Papua New Guinea. *Oceania* 52:28–38, 1981.

Schapera, Isaac. *Migrant Labour and Tribal Life.* London: Oxford University Press, 1947.

Schearer, S. Bruce. The Value of Focus Group Research for Social Action Programs. *Studies in Family Planning* 12(12):407–408, 1981.

Schein, Edgar H. *Process Consultation: Its Role in Organizational Development.* Reading, Mass.: Addison Wesley, 1988.

Schein, Edgar H. *Process Consultation Revisited: Building the Helping Relationship.* Reading, Mass.: Addison Wesley, 1999.

Schellstede, W. P. and R. L. Ciszewski. Social Marketing of Contraceptives in Bangladesh. *Studies in Family Planning* 15(1), 1984.

Schensul, Jean J. Knowledge Utilization: An Anthropological Perspective. *Practicing Anthropology* 9(1):6–8, 1987.

Schensul, Jean J. and E. Caro. The Puerto Rican Research and Training Project. Final Report to the National Institute of Education, 1982.

Schensul, Jean J. and Margaret D. LeCompte. *Ethnographer's Toolkit.* Walnut Creek, Calif.: AltaMira Press, 1999.

Schensul, Jean J. and Stephen L. Schensul. Collaborative Research: Methods of Inquiry for Social Change. In *The Handbook of Qualitative Research in Education.* Margaret D. LeCompte, Wendy L. Millroy, and Judith Preissle, eds. San Diego, Calif.: Academic Press, 1992.

Schensul, Stephen L. Action Research: The Applied Anthropologist in a Community Mental Health Program. In *Anthropology Beyond the University.* A. Redfield, ed. Southern Anthropological Society Proceedings No. 7. Athens: University of Georgia Press, 1973.

Schensul, Stephen L. Skills Needed in Action Anthropology: Lessons from El Centro de La Causa. *Human Organization* 33(2):203–208, 1974.

Schensul, Stephen L. Commando Research: Innovative Approaches to Anthropological Research. *Practicing Anthropology* 1(1):1–3, 1978.

Schensul, Stephen L. The Area Health Education Center Program. *Practicing Anthropology* 3(3):15–16, 1981.

Schensul, Stephen L. and M. Bymel. The Role of Applied Research in the Development of Health Services in a Chicano Community in Chicago. In *Topias and Utopias in Health.* S. Ingram and J. Altschuler, eds. The Hague: Mouton, 1975.

Schensul, Stephen L. and Jean J. Schensul. Advocacy and Applied Anthropology. In *Social Scientists as Advocates: Views from the Applied Disciplines.* Pp. 121–166. G. H. Weber and L. Cohen, eds. Beverly Hills, Calif.: Sage, 1978.

Schensul, Stephen L. and Jean J. Schensul. Self-Help Groups and Advocacy: A Contrast in Beliefs and Strategies. In *Beliefs and Self-Help: Cross-Cultural Perspectives and Approaches.* G. Weber and L. Cohen, eds. New York: Human Sciences Press, 1982.

Schlesier, Karl H. Action Anthropology and the Southern Cheyenne. *Current Anthropology* 15(3):277–283, 1974.

Schoolcraft, Henry R. *Information Respecting the History, Condition and Prospects of the Indian Tribes of the United States.* Philadelphia: Lippincott, 1852–1857.

Schultz, T. W. *Transforming Traditional Agriculture.* New Haven, Conn.: Yale University Press, 1964.

Schumacher, E. F. *Small Is Beautiful.* London: Blond and Briggs, 1973.

Scoones, Ian and John Thompson. *Beyond Farmer First: Rural People's Knowledge,*

Agricultural Research and Extension Practice. London: Intermediate Technology Publications, 1994.

Scott, Eugenie C., Billie R. DeWalt, Elizabeth Adelski, Sara Alexander, and Mary Beebe. *Landowners, Recreationists, and Government: Cooperation and Conflict in Red River Gorge*. Lexington: University of Kentucky, Water Resources Research Institute, 1982.

Scrimshaw, Susan C. M. and Elena Hurtado. *Rapid Assessment Procedures for Nutrition and Primary Health Care: Anthropological Approaches to Improving Program Effectiveness (RAP)*. Los Angeles: UCLA Latin American Center Publications, 1987.

Scriven, Michael. The Methodology of Evaluation. In *Educational Evaluation: Theory and Practice*. Blaine R. Worthen and James R. Sanders, eds. Belmont, Calif.: Wadsworth Publishing, 1973.

Scriven, Michael and J. Roth. Needs Assessment: Concept and Practice. *New Directions for Program Evaluation* 1:1–11, 1978.

Scudder, Thayer. *The Ecology of the Gwembe Tonga*. Rhodes-Livingstone Institute, Kariba Studies, Vol. 2. Manchester: Manchester University Press, 1962.

Scudder, Thayer. Man-Made Lakes and Social Change. *Engineering and Science* 24:19–22, 1966.

Scudder, Thayer. Social Anthropology, Man-Made Lakes and Population Relocation in Africa. *Anthropological Quarterly* 41:168–176, 1968.

Scurlock, Reagan. *Government Contracts and Grants for Research: A Guide for Colleges and Universities*. Washington, D.C.: Committee on Governmental Relations, National Association of College and University Business Officers, 1975.

Seidel, J. et al. *The Ethnograph*. Version 3.0. Littleton, Colo.: Qualis Associates, 1988.

Seligman, C. G. *Pagan Tribes of the Nilotic Sudan*. London: G. Routledge, 1932.

Service, Elman R. *Primitive Social Organization*. New York: Random House, 1960.

Shaner, W. W., P. F. Philipps, and W. R. Schmehl. *Farming Systems Research and Development: A Guideline for Developing Countries*. Boulder, Colo.: Westview Press, 1982.

Siegel, Karolynn and Peter Tuckel. The Utilization of Evaluation Research: A Case Analysis. *Evaluation Review* 9(3):307–328, 1985.

Siegel, M. and L. Donner. *Marketing Public Health*. Gaithersburg, Md.: Aspen Publishers, 1998.

Simmonds, N. W. The State of the Art of Farming Systems Research. Paper prepared for the Agriculture and Rural Development Department of the World Bank, Washington, D.C., 1984.

Sinha, Surajit. *Nirmal Kumar Bose, Scholar-Wanderer*. New Delhi: National Book Trust, 1986.

Sjoberg, Gideon, ed. *Ethics, Politics and Social Research*. Cambridge, Mass.: Schenkman Publishing, 1967.

Smith, W. A. and S. E. Middlestadt. The Applied Behavioral Change Framework. In *The World Against AIDS: Communication for Behavioral Change*. W. A. Smith, ed. Washington, D.C.: Academy for Education Development, 1993.

Smucker, Glenn R. *Trees and Charcoal in Haitian Peasant Economy: A Feasibility*

Study of Reforestation. Port-au-Prince: U.S. Agency for International Development Mission, 1981.

Society for Applied Anthropology. *Practicing Anthropology: A Career-Oriented Publication of the Society for Applied Anthropology*. College Park, Md.: Society for Applied Anthropology, 1978.

Softestad, Lars T. On Evacuation of People in the Kotmale Hydro Power Project: Experience from a Socio Economic Impact Study. *Bistandsantropogen* [Development Anthropologist] 15:22–32, 1990.

Sorenson, John L. and Larry L. Berg. *Evaluation of Indian Community Action Programs at Arizona State University, University of South Dakota and University of Utah (CR-82–1)*. Santa Barbara, Calif.: General Research Corporation, 1967.

Southern Regional Council. *The Negro and Employment Opportunities in the South*. Atlanta, Ga.: Southern Regional Council, 1961.

Spicer, Edward H. The Use of Social Scientists by the War Relocation Authority. *Applied Anthropology* 5(2):16–36, 1946a.

Spicer, Edward H. *Impounded People: Japanese-Americans in the Relocation Centers*. Washington, D.C.: Department of the Interior, War Relocation Authority, 1946b.

Spicer, Edward H. *Human Problems in Technological Change*. New York: Russell Sage Foundation, 1952.

Spicer, Edward H. Beyond Analysis and Explanation? The Life and Times of the Society for Applied Anthropology. *Human Organization* 35(4):335–343, 1976.

Spicer, Edward H. Early Applications of Anthropology, 1976. In *Perspectives on Anthropology 1976*. A.F.C. Wallace et al., eds. Washington, D.C.: American Anthropological Association, 1977.

Spicer, Edward H. Anthropologists and the War Relocation Authority. In *The Uses of Anthropology*. Walter Goldschmidt, ed. Washington, D.C.: American Anthropological Association, 1979.

Spicer, Edward H. and Theodore E. Downing. Training for Non-Academic Employment: Major Issues. In *Training Programs for New Opportunities in Applied Anthropology*. E. Leacock, N. Gonzalez, and G. Kushner, eds. Washington, D.C.: American Anthropological Association, 1974.

Spillius, James. Natural Disaster and Political Crisis in a Polynesian Society: An Exploration of Operational Research II. *Human Relations* 10(2):113–125, 1957.

Stern, Gwen. Research, Action, and Social Betterment in Collaborative Research and Social Policy. *Applied Behavioral Scientist* 29(2):229–248, 1985.

Stevens, Patricia E. and Joanne M. Hall. Participatory Action Research for Sustaining Individual and Community Change: A Model of HIV Prevention Education. *AIDS Education and Prevention* 10(5):387–402, 1998.

Stewart, Frances. *Technology and Underdevelopment*. Boulder, Colo.: Westview Press, 1977.

Stewart, Omer C. Kroeber and the Indian Claims Commission Cases. Kroeber Anthropology Society Paper No. 25. Berkeley, Calif.: Kroeber Anthropology Society, 1961.

Stoffle, Richard W. *Caribbean Fisherman Farmers: A Social Assessment of Smith-*

sonian King Crab Mariculture. Ann Arbor: Institute for Social Research, University of Michigan, 1986.

Stoffle, Richard W., Diane E. Austin, Brian K. Fulfrost, Arthur M. Phillips III, and Tricia F. Drye. *Past, Present, Future: Managing Southern Paiute Resources in the Colorado River Corridor.* Pipe Spring, Ariz. and Tucson: Southern Paiute Consortium, Bureau of Applied Research in Anthropology, and the University of Arizona, 1995.

Stoffle, Richard W., Diane E. Austin, David B. Halmo, and Arthur M. Phillips III. *Ethnographic Overview and Assessment: Zion National Park, Utah and Pipe Spring National Monument, Arizona.* Tucson: Bureau of Applied Research in Anthropology, University of Arizona, 1997.

Stoffle, Richard W., Michael J. Evans, and Florence V. Jensen. *Native American Concerns and State of California Low-Level Waste Disposal Facility: Mohave, Navajo, Chemehuevi, and Nevada Paiute Responses.* Menlo Park, Calif.: Cultural Systems Research, 1987a.

Stoffle, Richard W., David B. Halmo, Michael J. Evans, and Diane E. Austin. *Big River Canyon.* Tucson: Bureau of Applied Research in Anthropology, University of Arizona, 1994.

Stoffle, Richard W., Florence V. Jensen, and Danny L. Rasch. *Coho Stocking and Salmon Stamps: Lake Michigan Anglers Assess Wisconsin's DNR Policies.* Kenosha: University of Wisconsin–Parkside, 1981.

Stoffle, Richard W., Michael W. Traugott, Florence V. Jensen, and Robert Copeland. *Social Assessment of High Technology: The Superconducting Super Collider in Southeast Michigan.* Ann Arbor: Institute for Social Research, University of Michigan, 1987b.

Straus, Robert. The Nature and Status of Medical Sociology. *American Sociological Review* 22:200–204, 1957.

Stuck, Kenneth E. and Charles M. Downing. A Phase I Archaeological Survey and Phase II Evaluation of Site 44HT44 Associated with the Proposed Pentran Bus Parking Lot, City of Hampton, Virginia, Project: U000–114–V19, PE101. Williamsburg, Va.: William & Mary Center for Archaeological Research for the Virginia Department of Transportation, 1995.

Stufflebeam, Daniel L. Excerpts from "Evaluation as Enlightenment for Decision-Making." In *Educational Evaluation: Theory and Practice.* Belmont, Calif.: Wadsworth Publishing, 1973.

Stull, Donald D. Action Anthropology among the Kansas Kickapoo. Paper presented at the Society for Applied Anthropology meetings in Philadelphia, 1979.

Stull, Donald D. and Jean J. Schensul, eds. *Collaborative Research and Social Change: Applied Anthropology in Action.* Boulder, Colo.: Westview Press, 1987.

Suchman, Lucy. *Plans and Situated Actions: The Problem of Human-Machine Communication.* Cambridge: Cambridge University Press, 1987.

Sussex, James N. and Hazel H. Weidman. Toward Responsiveness in Mental Health Care. *Psychiatric Annals* 5(8):306–311, 1975.

Tax, Sol. Anthropology and Administration. *American Indigena* 5(1):21–33, 1945.

Tax, Sol. The Fox Project. *Human Organization* 17:17–19, 1958.

Tax, Sol. Extracts from "Introduction" to A Reader in Action Anthropology. In

Documentary History of the Fox Project. F. Gearing et al., eds. Chicago: University of Chicago, Department of Anthropology, 1960a.

Tax, Sol. Action Anthropology. In *Documentary History of the Fox Project*. F. Gearing et al., eds. Chicago: University of Chicago, Department of Anthropology, 1960b.

Taylor, P. V. *The Texts of Paulo Freire*. Buckingham: Open University Press, 1993.

Textor, Robert B., ed. *Cultural Frontiers of the Peace Corps*. Cambridge, Mass.: M.I.T. Press, 1966.

Thompson, Laura. Action Research among American Indians. *Scientific Monthly* 70:34–40, 1950.

Thompson, Laura. U.S. Indian Reorganization Viewed as an Experiment in Social Action Research. In *Estudios Antropologicos Publicado en Homenaje a Doctor Manuel Gamio*. Mexico: Direccion General de Publicaciones, 1956.

Thompson, Laura and Alice Joseph. *The Hopi Way*. New York: Russell Sage Foundation, 1944.

Trend, M. G. The Anthropologist as Go-fer. Paper presented at the meetings of the Society for Applied Anthropology, St. Louis, 1976.

Trend, M. G. Anthropological Research Services: Some Observations. *Human Organization* 36(2):211–212, 1977.

Trend, M. G. On the Reconciliation of Qualitative and Quantitative Analyses: A Case Study. *Human Organization* 37:345–354, 1978a.

Trend, M. G. Research in Progress: The Minnesota Work Equity Project Evaluation. *Human Organization* 37(4):398–399, 1978b.

Tripp, Robert. *Including Dietary Concerns in On-Farm Research: An Example from Imbabura, Ecuador*. Mexico: Centro Internacional de Mejoramiento de Maiz y Trigo, 1982.

Tripp, Robert. Anthropology and On-Farm Research. *Human Organization* 44(2): 114–124, 1985.

Trotter, Robert T. II. A Case of Lead Poisoning from Folk Remedies in Mexican American Communities. In *Anthropological Praxis*. Robert M. Wulff and Shirley J. Fiske, eds. Pp. 146–159. Boulder, Colo.: Westview Press, 1987.

Trotter, Robert T. II, ed. *Anthropology for Tomorrow: Creating Practitioner-Oriented Applied Anthropology Programs*. Washington, D.C.: American Anthropological Association, 1988.

Turner, Allen C. *Southern Paiute Research and Development Program: A Pre-Proposal*. Cedar City: Southern Utah State College, 1974.

Uhlman, Julie M. The Delivery of Human Services in Wyoming Boomtowns. In *Socio-economic Impact of Western Energy Development*. Berry Crawford and Edward H. Allen, eds. Ann Arbor, Mich.: Science Publishers, 1977.

Uphoff, Norman. Fitting Projects to People. In *Putting People First: Sociological Variables in Rural Development*. 2nd ed. New York: Oxford University Press for the World Bank, 1991.

U.S. Administration on Aging. *Achieving Cultural Competence: A Guidebook for Providers of Services for Older Americans and Their Families*. http://www.aoa.gov/minorityaccess/guidbook2001/, 2001.

U.S. Agency for International Development. *Handbook 3, Project Assistance*. Washington, D.C.: U.S. Agency for International Development, 1975.

U.S. Congress. National Environmental Policy Act of 1969 (PL 91–190). *United States Statutes at Large* 83:852–856, 1971.

U.S. Congress. River and Harbor and Flood Control Acts of 1970 (PL 91–611). *United States Statutes at Large* 84:1818–1835, 1972.

U.S. Department of Health and Human Services, Office of Minority Health. *Assuring Cultural Competence in Health Care: Recommendation for National Standards and an Outcomes-Focused Research Agenda.* http://www.omhrc.gov/clas/cultural1a.htm, n.d.

U.S. Department of the Interior. *National Register Criteria for Evaluation of Cultural Resources.* Secretary of the Interior's Professional Qualifications Standards. *Code of Federal Regulations,* Title 36, Part 61, Appendix A, 1983.

U.S. Department of the Treasury, Internal Revenue Service. *Tax Exempt Status for Your Organization, Publication 557.* Washington, D.C.: Government Printing Office, 1988.

U.S. Public Health Service. *Healthy People 2000: National Health Promotion and Disease Prevention Objectives.* Publication (PHS)91–50212. Washington, DC: U.S. Public Health Service, 1991.

Useem, John. *Economic and Human Resources—Yap and Palau, Western Carolines.* Ponape: U.S. Commercial Company, 1947.

Van Tassell, Jon and Karen L. Michaelson. *Social Impact Assessment: Methods and Practice (Interstate 88 in New York). Final Report: National Science Foundation, Student-Originated Study Grant, Summer, 1976.* Binghamton: Department of Anthropology, State University of New York at Binghamton, 1977.

van Willigen, John. Abstract Goals and Concrete Means: Papago Experiences in the Application of Development Resources. *Human Organization* 32(1):1–8, 1973.

van Willigen, John. Applied Anthropology and Community Development Administration: A Critical Assessment. In *Do Applied Anthropologists Apply Anthropology?* M. Angrosino, ed. Athens: University of Georgia Press, 1976.

van Willigen, John. Recommendations for Training and Education for Careers in Applied Anthropology: A Literature Review. *Human Organization* 38(4):411–416, 1979.

van Willigen, John. *Anthropology in Use: A Bibliographic Chronology of the Development of Applied Anthropology.* Pleasantville, N.Y.: Redgrave Publishers, 1981a.

van Willigen, John. Applied Anthropology and Cultural Persistence. In *Persistent Peoples: Cultural Enclaves in Perspective.* George Pierre Castile and Gilbert Kushner, eds. Tucson: University of Arizona Press, 1981b.

van Willigen, John. The Great Transformation? Applied Training and Disciplinary Change. *Practicing Anthropology* 4(3 and 4):16–17, 1982.

van Willigen, John. *Guide to Training Programs in the Applications of Anthropology.* Washington, D.C.: Society for Applied Anthropology, 1985.

van Willigen, John. *Becoming a Practicing Anthropologist: A Guide to Careers and Training Programs in Applied Anthropology.* NAPA Bulletin 3. Washington, D.C.: American Anthropological Association, 1987.

van Willigen, John. Types of Programs. In *Anthropology for Tomorrow: Creating*

Practitioner-Oriented Applied Anthropology Programs. Robert T. Trotter II, ed. Washington, D.C.: American Anthropological Association, 1988.

van Willigen, John. *Anthropology in Use: A Source Book on Anthropological Practice.* Boulder, Colo.: Westview Press, 1991.

van Willigen, John and Billie R. DeWalt. *Training Manual in Policy Ethnography.* Washington, D.C.: American Anthropological Association, 1985.

van Willigen, John, Billie R. DeWalt, Timothy Frankenberger, and John Lichte. Rapid Rural Reconnaissance. In *Training Manual for Policy Ethnography.* Washington, D.C.: American Anthropological Association, 1985.

van Willigen, John and Timothy L. Finan, eds. *Soundings: Rapid and Reliable Research Methods for Practicing Anthropologists.* NAPA Bulletin 10. Washington, D.C.: American Anthropological Association, 1991.

van Willigen, John, Barbara Rylko-Bauer, and Ann McElroy, eds. *Making Our Research Useful: Case Studies in the Utilization of Anthropological Knowledge.* Boulder, Colo.: Westview Press, 1989.

Villa-Rojas, Alfonso. *Los Mazatecas y el Problema Indigena de la Cuenca del Papaloapan.* Mexico: I.N.I., 1955.

Vlachos, Evan, ed. *Social Impact Assessment: An Overview.* Fort Belvoir, Va.: Army Corps of Engineers, Institute for Water Resources, 1975.

Vlachos, Evan, Walter Buckley, William F. Filstead, Sue-Ellen Jacobs, Magoroh Maruyama, John H. Peterson, Jr., and Gene Willeke. *Procedural Guidelines for Social Impact Assessment.* Arlington, Va.: U.S. Army Corps of Engineers, Institute for Water Resources, 1975.

Voget, Fred W. *A History of Ethnology.* New York: Holt, Rinehart and Winston, 1975.

Walbran, Shannon. Tiao Rocha: Brazilian Prince of the Methodology of Fun. *Changemakers.net Journal* (November). http://www.changemakers.net/journal/99november/walbran.cfm, 1999.

Wallace, Anthony F. C. Some Reflections on the Contributions of Anthropologists to Public Policy. In *Anthropology and the Public Interest: Fieldwork and Theory.* Peggy Reeves Sanday, ed. New York: Academic Press, 1976.

Ward, G. W. The National High Blood Pressure Education Program: An Example of Social Marketing. In *Marketing Health Behavior: Principles, Techniques and Applications.* L. Frederickson, L. J. Solomon, and K. A. Brehony, eds. New York: Plenum, 1984.

Wasson, Christina. Ethnography in the Field of Design. *Human Organization* 59(4):377–388, 2000.

Wax, Rosemary H. *Doing Fieldwork: Warnings and Advice.* Chicago: University of Chicago Press, 1971.

Weaver, Thomas. *To See Ourselves: Anthropology and Modern Social Issues.* New York: Scott, Foresman, 1973.

Weaver, Thomas and Theodore Downing, eds. *The Douglas Report: The Community Context of Housing and Social Problems.* Tucson: Bureau of Ethnic Research, University of Arizona, 1975.

Weaver, Thomas et al. *Political Organization and Business Management in the Gila River Indian Community.* Tucson: Bureau of Ethnic Research, University of Arizona, 1971.

Weber, George H. and George J. McCall, eds. *Social Scientists as Advocates: Views from the Applied Disciplines*. Beverly Hills, Calif.: Sage, 1978.

Weidman, Dennis. Personal communication, 2001.

Weidman, Hazel H. Implications of the Culture-Broker Concept for the Delivery of Health Care. Paper presented at the meetings of the Southern Anthropological Society, Wrightsville Beach, N.C., 1973.

Weidman, Hazel H. Toward the Goal of Responsiveness in Mental Health Care. Paper presented at the Department of Psychiatry, University of Miami, 1974.

Weidman, Hazel H. *Concepts as Strategies for Change*. A Psychiatric Annals Reprint. New York: Insight Communications, 1975.

Weidman, Hazel H. In Praise of the Double-Bind Inherent in Anthropological Application. In *Do Applied Anthropologists Apply Anthropology?* M. V. Angrosino, ed. Southern Anthropological Society Proceedings No. 10. Athens: University of Georgia Press, 1976.

Weidman, Hazel H. The Transcultural View: Prerequisite to Interethnic (Intercultural) Communication in Medicine. *Social Science and Medicine* 13B:85–87, 1979.

Weidman, Hazel H. Research Strategies, Structural Alterations and Clinically Applied Anthropology. In *Clinically Applied Anthropology*. N. J. Chrisman and T. W. Maretzki, eds. Dordrecht: Reidel Publishing Company, 1982.

Weidman, Hazel H. Personal correspondence, 1985.

Weiss, Carol H. *Evaluating Action Programs: Readings in Social Action and Education*. Boston: Allyn and Bacon, 1972.

Weiss, Carol H. Introduction. In *Using Social Research in Public Policy Making*. Carol H. Weiss, ed. Pp. 1–22. Lexington, Mass.: D.C. Heath, 1977.

Weiss, Carol H. Measuring the Use of Evaluations. In *Utilizing Evaluation*. James A. Ciarlo, ed. Pp. 17–33. Beverly Hills, Calif.: Sage, 1981.

Weiss, Carol H. and Michael Bucuvalas. Truth Test and Utility Test: Decision Makers' Frame of Reference for Social Science Research. *American Sociological Review* 45:302–313, 1980.

Wellhausen, Edwin J. The Agriculture of Mexico. *Scientific American* 235:128–150, 1976.

Werge, Robert W. *Anthropology and Agricultural Research: The Case of Potato Anthropology*. Lima, Peru: International Potato Center, 1977.

Werner, David and Bill Bower. *Helping Health Workers Learn*. Palo Alto, Calif.: Hesperian Foundation, 1982.

Whiteford, Linda M. Staying Out of the Bottom Drawer. *Practicing Anthropology* 9(1):9–11, 1987.

Whyte, William Foote, Davydd J. Greenwood, and Peter Lazes. Participatory Action Research: Through Practice to Science in Social Research. In *Participatory Action Research*. William Foote Whyte, ed. Pp. 19–55. Newbury Park, Calif.: Sage, 1991.

Whyte, William Foote and Kathleen King Whyte. *Making Mondragon: The Growth and Dynamics of the Worker Cooperative Complex*. Ithaca, N.Y.: ILR Press, 1988.

Willard, William. The Agency Camp Project. *Human Organization* 36(4):352–362, 1977.

Williams, Bruce T. *Integrated Basic Services Project: A Baseline Survey*. UNICEF/ Malawi: Centre for Social Research, University of Malawi, 1980.

Williams, Bruce T. *UNICEF-Assisted Women's Programs in Malawi: An Evaluation and Summary of Findings on the Homecraft Workers' Program and the Female Community Development Assistant's Program*. UNICEF/Malawi: Centre for Social Research, University of Malawi, 1981.

Wolf, C. P. Social Impact Assessment: A Methodological Overview. In *Social Impact Assessment Methods*. Kurt Finsterbusch, Lynn G. Llewellyn, and C. P. Wolf, eds. Beverly Hills, Calif.: Sage, 1983.

Wolf, Eric R. Aspects of Group Relations in a Complex Society: Mexico. *American Anthropologist* 58:1065–1078, 1956.

Wolfe, Alvin W., Erve Chambers, and J. Jerome Smith. *Internship Training in Applied Anthropology: A Five-Year Review*. Tampa: Human Resources Institute, University of South Florida, 1981.

Worthen, Blaine R. and James R. Sanders. *Educational Evaluation: Theory and Practice*. Belmont, Calif.: Wadsworth Publishing, 1973.

Wulff, Robert N. *Housing the Papago: An Analytical Critique of a Housing Delivery System*. Los Angeles: International Housing Productivity Project, University of California, Los Angeles, 1972.

Wulff, Robert N. Anthropology in the Urban Planning Process: A Review and an Agenda. In *Do Applied Anthropologists Apply Anthropology?* M. Angrosino, ed. Athens: University of Georgia Press, 1976a.

Wulff, Robert N. *Tampa's Community Centers: An Analysis of Recreation Programming and Policy*. Tampa: Human Resources Institute and Center of Applied Anthropology, University of South Florida, 1976b.

Wulff, Robert N. *Vicos in Watts: Testing Anthropological Change Strategies in Urban America*. ERIC Microfiche. Princeton, NJ: Educational Testing Service, 1977.

Young, Douglas W. Nonviolent Alternatives among the Enga of Papua New Guinea Highlands. *Social Alternatives* 16(2):42–45, 1997.

Zilverberg, Grace M. and Anita Courtney. *The Status and Potential of the Fruit and Vegetable Market in the Kentucky Bluegrass Region*. Frankfort: Kentucky Department of Agriculture, 1984.

Index

About the Author

JOHN VAN WILLIGEN is Professor of Anthropology at the University of Kentucky.